Discrimination Stories

Discrimination Stories

EXCLUSION,
LAW, AND
EVERYDAY LIFE

Colleen Sheppard

DELVE
BOOKS | TORONTO

Published in 2021 by

Irwin Law Inc
Suite 206, 14 Duncan Street
Toronto, ON   M5H 3G8
www.irwinlaw.com

ISBN 978-1-55221-537-1 (print) | 978-1-55221-538-8 (PDF) | 978-1-55221-644-6 (epub)

Library and Archives Canada Cataloguing in Publication

Title: Discrimination stories: exclusion, law, and everyday life / Colleen Sheppard.
Names: Sheppard, Colleen, author.
Description: Includes bibliographical references and index.
Identifiers: Canadiana (print) 20210319771 | Canadiana (ebook) 20210319844 |
    ISBN 9781552215371 (softcover) | ISBN 9781552215388 (PDF) |
    ISBN 9781552216446 (HTML)
Subjects: LCSH: Discrimination — Law and legislation — Canada.
Classification: LCC KE4395 .S54 2021 | LCC KF4483.C5 .S54 2021 kfmod |
    DDC 347.1028/7—dc23

Canadä

Ontario
Ontario Media Development
Corporation
Société de développement
de l'industrie des médias
de l'Ontario

Printed and bound in Canada.

1 2 3 4 5   24 23 22 21 20

For Kara & Nico

Contents

Preface

THE IDEA FOR this book project came to me when my daughter encouraged me to write a book that was accessible and nontraditional. I thought about some of the case studies I was reading in my research on discrimination — cases that touched me because of the strength of the individuals involved, the commitment of family members to each other, the harshness of exclusion and discrimination, the everyday situations that suddenly become moments of injustice, and the insights they provide into the strengths and limits of anti-discrimination law. And I decided to highlight these cases, and the people involved in them, as a way of illustrating important themes in equality law. The stories of discrimination included in this book teach us about law, legal concepts, and norms; beyond that, they teach us about human relations and resilience.

I was greatly assisted by inspiring and energetic research assistants, whose interest and engagement in the project were invaluable. I wish to extend my sincere thanks to Emma Brown, Aliah El Hounia, Dominique Grégoire, Maya Gunnarsson, Gabriella Jamieson, Rebecca Jones, Natalia Paunic, Genny Plumptre, Nathaniel Reilly, Rachelle Rose, Diana Stepner, and Angela Yang for their research and editorial assistance. I love working with students and find their intelligence, creativity, and hope for the future rejuvenating. I am also indebted to Sarah Bardaxoglou, for her thoughtful comments on the draft manuscript.

I am privileged to work at the McGill Faculty of Law and to be affiliated with the McGill Centre for Human Rights and Legal Pluralism, where I have supportive colleagues and excellent resources. Special thanks to Adelle Blackett, whose knowledge and insights about equality and inequality continue to enrich my learning in our everyday working lives. I am so glad that we work and laugh together in the old mansion that was once the exclusive domain of the white male law professor.[1]

This book is part of a larger project on *Systemic Discrimination: Challenges and Complexities*, funded by the Social Sciences and Humanities Research Council. Its inclusion in the larger project attests to the support for projects that include the sharing of legal knowledge in accessible ways to the broader Canadian public. I also wish to thank Lesley Steeve, vice-president and editor-in-chief at Irwin Law. She has been an enthusiastic and patient supporter of the project since the very first day I proposed it to her and provided invaluable editorial insights as the book evolved.

Finally, I wish to thank my family. I was reassured when my ninety-two-year-old mother, Norah Sheppard, liked listening to me read the opening sections of the chapters and the conclusion. She would give me good advice and then delve into a discussion of politics and climate change. My sister, Dale Sheppard, provided the original artwork for the cover from a painting entitled "Connections." My daughter, Kara, was an incredible source of support whenever my energy started to wane, propelling me forward with some invincible force. My son, Nico, is always pushing the boundaries of disciplinary knowledge, asking critical and pragmatic questions about law and social justice. And my husband, Derek, shared ideas and insights into the historical and systemic realities of racism and provided editorial and wordsmithing suggestions, while ensuring a constant flow of beautiful music from around the world. Words cannot express how much you all mean to me.

Introduction

She told me that our stories are the ladders that make it easier for us to touch the stars.

— DONOVAN LIVINGSTON, 2016[1]

A NUMBER OF years ago, I was asked to give a speech at a conference organized by high-school girls about the role of law in young women's lives. I focused on the law, coercion, and young women and discussed various ways in which the law played a coercive role, using examples from actual legal cases. At the end of my talk, the first question I was asked was, "What is coercion?" Needless to say, I hadn't defined the meaning of coercion — "the action or practice of persuading someone to do something by using force or threats"[2] — at the outset and had simply assumed that everyone knew what it meant. I was taken aback and realized the mistake that I had made. I explained it as clearly as I could but was left humbled by the experience. It raised an important question: How can we ensure that we communicate the meaning of legal concepts in ways that make sense to broad and diverse audiences? If we want scholarly work to be accessible, we need to think carefully about how we communicate the things we learn in our research.

In my work, I have focused a lot of my teaching and research on discrimination and equality rights. While the organizing theme throughout the chapters is discrimination, the underlying animating principle is equality. The two concepts are closely related — equality

1

flourishes when discrimination is eradicated. One speaks to the positive; the other to the negative. There are two key sources of legal protection for equality and non-discrimination in Canada.

First, there are human rights statutes or codes that prohibit discrimination in specific contexts, such as employment, housing, and access to services. Provinces, territories, and the federal government have all enacted statutes setting out protections against discrimination. Most of these human rights laws emerged in the 1960s and 1970s.[3] They provide protection against discrimination linked to race, colour, national or ethnic origin, sex, religion, age, mental and physical disabilities, and sexual orientation. Additional kinds of discrimination are also sometimes protected, such as discrimination related to language, political opinions or beliefs, family status, pregnancy, and gender identity and expression, as well as discrimination against those who have been incarcerated. These grounds were included in human rights laws to remedy the recognized problems of discrimination facing certain groups and communities.

Second, the *Canadian Charter of Rights and Freedoms* recognized equality and non-discrimination as an important part of Canada's constitutional law.[4] The equality rights provisions, which came into effect in 1985, secured equality before and under the law, equal protection, and equal benefit of laws without discrimination. The constitutional equality guarantees also included explicit protection for ameliorative programs or affirmative action to redress historical and ongoing group-based disadvantages. The *Charter* provides protection against governmental and legislative sources of discrimination.

One of the most important legal developments in relation to the meaning of equality and non-discrimination is the recognition that simply treating everyone the same does not result in equal outcomes. Depending on the circumstances, realities, and needs of different groups, equal treatment may be a recipe for inequality or discrimination. Similarly, sometimes it is necessary to treat individuals differently to achieve equal results. Accordingly, Canadian equality law rejects formal equality (treating everyone the same regardless of actual needs and circumstances) and instead endorses substantive equality (ensuring equitable outcomes).[5] As we will see, an expansive

2

interpretation of *Charter* equality rights was built upon earlier developments in the interpretation of human rights legislation, specifically an extensive effects-based definition of discrimination.

In this book, I focus on discrimination stories arising in the context of human rights complaints made pursuant to human rights statutes rather than constitutional cases. These cases often arise in everyday situations when individuals experience what they believe to be discriminatory exclusion, unfairness, or inequities. Human rights complaints are much easier to initiate than constitutional equality rights claims; they are also adjudicated in specialized human rights tribunals, which are less formal than courts. As the frontline decision makers who hear the full factual details of the case, human rights tribunal adjudicators are often at the forefront of innovative new legal ideas and concepts. In some cases, the tribunal decisions are appealed or reviewed by courts, which can lengthen the process and complicate receiving a remedy for discrimination, as demonstrated in some of the stories in this book. It is important to note that courts are also a first resort in some cases, although the forum is less friendly to claimants without a lawyer. Ultimately, no matter the venue, the individuals behind these proceedings have powerful stories to tell.

The stories of those pursuing legal remedies reveal moments of real contestation by individuals and groups who feel wronged by discriminatory practices and laws. Their legal cases teach us about the importance of individuals seeking and obtaining recognition for the discrimination they have faced and accountability for such harm from others. We remember the lessons embedded in stories, appreciating the complexities and nuances of diverse experiences of inequality. And the concrete circumstances and factual contexts help to provide insights into the meaning of equality and non-discrimination. Despite growing media attention to discrimination cases, however, core legal concepts in equality and anti-discrimination law are not widely understood. Therefore, each chapter of this book focuses on a specific aspect of discrimination law and tries to make it understandable. These aspects of discrimination law include the different types of discrimination and some of the complexities that arise in interpreting, applying, and enforcing anti-discrimination protections.

Chapter 1 begins with a case involving racial profiling in a large department store.[6] It occurred when Jacqueline Nassiah, who had gone after work to pick up a few things to send to her sister in Trinidad and Tobago, was stopped by a store security guard, aggressively questioned by a police officer, and accused of shoplifting. She was detained for over an hour and a half, and then released when the security guard and police officer realized that they were mistaken. Nassiah's case was found to involve racial profiling — in this case, in a consumer context. Racial profiling involves race-based differential treatment, and to fully comprehend why it happens, we need to situate it in a larger context of systemic racism in society and in security and policing practices that are linked to both conscious and unconscious biases. Jacqueline Nassiah's human rights case, therefore, provides important insights into the meaning and impact of racial profiling and provides a starting point for understanding why racial profiling constitutes discrimination.

In Chapter 2, I turn to a human rights case that took place over two decades ago involving a young girl with cerebral palsy, Tammy McLeod.[7] Using a wooden ramp to assist her in bowling, she qualified to compete in a regional bowling competition. The rules of bowling, however, were not written with the circumstances of a young girl with cerebral palsy in mind. She was disqualified because the use of the ramp was not allowed at the regional level. McLeod and her parents filed a human rights complaint and were ultimately vindicated in their struggle for inclusion. It was too late for the regional bowling competition, but McLeod's case provides us with a poignant example of *adverse impact discrimination*, a critically important concept in anti-discrimination law. It occurs when apparently neutral rules have disproportionate effects on different groups in society — in this case, persons with disabilities.

Chapter 3 deals with a pathbreaking case in Canadian anti-discrimination law.[8] The case was launched by a small women's advocacy organization in Quebec called Action travail des femmes, which works to ensure equitable working conditions for women and greater access to jobs traditionally occupied by men. The organization brought a human rights complaint involving over 150 women against Canadian National Railway (CN) for sex-based employment discrimination in the railyards. Action travail des femmes won before the Canadian Human Rights Tribunal,[9] but CN appealed the case all the way up to the Supreme Court of Canada, where the Court affirmed that women at CN had experienced what was called *systemic discrimination*. The Supreme Court explained that a systemic approach is based on the recognition that discrimination goes beyond individual misconduct, quoting the following passage from an important Royal Commission Report on workplace equality:

> Rather than approaching discrimination from the perspective of the single perpetrator and the single victim, the systemic approach acknowledges that by and large the systems and practices we customarily and often unwittingly adopt may have an unjustifiably negative effect on certain groups in society.[10]

This chapter, therefore, examines systemic discrimination. It is a challenging concept that involves an interconnected web of individual (micro), institutional (meso), and structural (macro) discrimination. Systemic discrimination implicates individual misconduct when it becomes widespread in an organization or implicates abuses of institutionalized power. It also occurs at the institutional level in relation to policies, rules, and practices, some of which appear neutral but have discriminatory effects. Finally, deeper structural patterns of systemic inequality (such as poverty and racism) impact individuals and communities across life cycles and generations.

Recognition of systemic discrimination prompted the emergence of proactive equity programs (e.g., affirmative action) aimed at breaking the cycles of historic and ongoing discrimination within institutions. Chapter 4, therefore, examines debates around affirmative action and proactive equity measures, beginning with a short historical overview of these measures in Canada. One important example is the education equity initiative at the Schulich School of Law at Dalhousie University. It was established to redress the underrepresentation of individuals from the Black and Mi'kmaq communities in the legal profession in Nova Scotia. It demonstrates the importance of an expansive approach to equity initiatives. They should not be limited to preferential treatment policies that are tacked onto an unquestioned institutional status quo. Instead, they should be designed to question and revise the institutional practices, policies, and traditions that result in underrepresentation and exclusion in the first place. Therefore, before reviewing the legal justifications for such initiatives, I outline a broad definition of equity programs.

In this chapter, I also outline some of the underlying rationales for equity initiatives. In this regard, I maintain that the most compelling argument supporting proactive equity initiatives is the need to remedy ongoing denials of equal opportunity in societal and institutional contexts. For example, social and economic inequities in Indigenous and Black communities in Nova Scotia create obstacles for students from those communities in accessing legal education and the legal profession. More generally, deeply embedded stereotypes continue to influence hiring and promotion decisions. Not implementing proactive equity measures therefore means that discriminatory exclusions persist and reproduce themselves through the adverse effects of institutional policies and practices, as well as the consequences of conscious and unconscious biases in the minds of institutional gatekeepers and decision makers. In other words, there is no neutral, equitable starting point *without* equity initiatives — to do nothing is to leave systemic inequalities unchecked and unremedied. Other important justifications for equity initiatives include promoting diversity, providing role models, enhancing sensitive community-based professional and public services, and securing equitable representation in societal positions of power and prestige.

Having outlined the key dimensions of anti-discrimination law — direct, adverse effects and systemic discrimination (as well as proactive equity initiatives), I turn in chapters 5 and 6 to two specific societal contexts to illustrate how complex problems of direct, adverse impact, and systemic discrimination occur. There are numerous societal and institutional contexts that I could have analyzed through the lens of discrimination law, such as institutions providing elder care, migrant worker programs, public housing, the healthcare system, schools, and workplaces. Despite the vast array of possible contexts where issues of discrimination arise, I have chosen two areas in which I have been doing research over the past couple of years.[11] Chapter 5 focuses on sexual violence and inequality in Canadian universities and colleges. I explain how sexual violence is integrally connected to discrimination. I also introduce the idea of *equitable freedom*, which is equality in the exercise of freedom in our everyday lives. Although equality is usually associated with rights, here I highlight the importance of equality in relation to freedom. Being equally free to live and enjoy life without the fear, risk, or threat of sexual violence is critical to a sense of belonging and well-being.

In Chapter 6, I turn to inequality in the lives of Indigenous children, families, and communities. I begin with the story of Maurina Beadle and her son Jeremy. Their story is about the need to respond appropriately to the healthcare needs of Indigenous children to ensure that they are not institutionalized. Maurina Beadle was forced to go to court for the financial support she needed to continue caring for her son at home.[12] Her strength and determination, combined with the support of her community and the Pictou Landing First Nations Band Council, kept Jeremy in his community. The case was heard by one of the few Indigenous judges in Canada, Justice Leonard Mandamin, who had the capacity to hear, to understand, and to respond to her claims. Chapter 6 also tells the story of the incredible tenacity and struggle of social worker, activist, and legal scholar, Cindy Blackstock, to challenge the underfunding of child protection services on reserves and in the Yukon.[13] After nine years of fighting the case, the First Nations Child and Family Caring Society and Assembly of First Nations were successful; the underfunding of Indigenous child protection services was found to be discriminatory. Yet, First Nations children are still waiting for equitable funding and services.

Beyond the complexity of the institutional contexts of discrimination, chapters 7 and 8 explore two areas where there is considerable debate and uncertainty in anti-discrimination law. Chapter 7 assesses the complexities of human identity — complexities that challenge the very group-based categories that are so central to anti-discrimination law. One challenge arises when individuals face discrimination on multiple grounds. For example, in an important human rights case highlighted in Chapter 7, Levan Turner maintained that he experienced employment discrimination due to the combined and intersecting effects of his race, age, and disability.[14] His case provides us with a starting point for looking the complexities of intersectionality in anti-discrimination law.[15] A second complexity arises when individuals with similar identities "perform" their identities differently.[16] Individuals may face different forms of discrimination based on how they live their identities. Finally, when individuals do not fit into any of the traditional group-based categories, a further layer of complexity emerges. Individuals may be biracial; have nonbinary gender identities; or have parents from different religious, linguistic, or national origins. How does anti-discrimination law deal with situations where individual identities do not fit neatly into one or more recognized group-based categories? As a result of these complexities, the group-based categories at the heart of anti-discrimination law are being deeply challenged.

Chapter 8 addresses the potential for conflict between the protection of equality and respect for fundamental freedoms, such as freedom of expression or religion. While this is a necessarily complex area of human rights law, I focus on controversies relating to freedom of expression and equality in relation to hate speech. In doing so, I suggest that it is important to be attentive to how we frame debates about "conflicting" rights and freedoms. In many instances, it is not a question of rights versus freedoms; rather, it is a question of freedoms versus freedoms. Reframing the question in this way underscores the fact that there is no response that fully protects freedom. Somebody's freedom is going to be violated — either one's freedom of speech or one's freedom to live without the fear or threat of violence. In addressing these issues, therefore, it is important to understand why people use hateful speech and to identify questions of power and privilege that impact the contexts in which conflicting freedoms arise. Despite recognition of the need to mediate and regulate conflicting freedoms, legal intervention may not always provide an effective response. It is hard to regulate expression, and there are risks in attempting to do so. Recognizing these challenges, I conclude by considering some alternative approaches that may secure more effective protection against hateful speech.

This book is designed to expand our collective knowledge of both the strengths and weaknesses of law. I hope to convey some of the important ways in which anti-discrimination law in Canada has evolved to provide more expansive protection against discrimination, evolving beyond an individual differential treatment definition to include effects-based discrimination and larger systemic inequalities. However, in many of the cases discussed in this book, the remedy provided after lengthy legal proceedings was too little, too late. Equality in our human relations cannot be crafted exclusively by courts or tribunals, despite their significance and importance: it is a much broader project. Anti-discrimination cases alone are incapable of remedying deeply embedded structural and systemic problems of inequality in society.[17] Thus, while I hope this book will empower and encourage individuals and groups to claim their legal entitlements to equality and non-discrimination, I recognize the need for political, social, legal, and institutional change beyond courts and tribunals. To secure equality and inclusion in the human relationships and decision-making processes of our everyday lives, we will require creative and innovative institutional initiatives, legal strategies, and social mobilization.

Be Careful Going Shopping:
Racial Profiling in Everyday Life

WHEN JACQUELINE NASSIAH went to the mall to buy clothes, she was unaware that before the day was over, she would be accused of shoplifting, detained by a store security guard, told that she couldn't call her babysitter, aggressively questioned by a police officer, and then finally let go when those involved realized that she had done nothing wrong.[1] How did this happen? Shopping at a department store is not an exceptional or suspicious activity. Neither is taking a walk or a drive mid-day along a busy city street;[2] working as a replacement letter carrier in a wealthy neighbourhood;[3] walking through a mall with a friend to a coffee shop;[4] or taking a taxi.[5] But while engaged in these everyday activities, individuals from Black and other racialized communities have been stopped by security guards or police officers and mistreated as potential suspects.[6] Unwarranted suspicion that these individuals are engaged in some form of wrongdoing, despite the fact that they are doing nothing out of the ordinary, is the starting point of racial profiling. Moreover, in situations where Black, Indigenous, or other racialized individuals are stopped or detained, challenging the authority of the police officer or the security guard often escalates the risk of additional harm to the individual targeted by the racial profiling. So let's begin with Jacqueline Nassiah's story as a starting point for thinking about racial profiling.

Jacqueline Nassiah's Case

The Incident: Being Detained and Falsely Accused of Shoplifting

On February 18, 2003, Jacqueline Nassiah went to a large department store to buy some bras to send to her sister in Trinidad. She had been planning a quick stop at the store after work since she needed to pick up her son from his babysitter. She wore pants with no pockets, a pullover sweater, boots, and a winter coat. After looking around the store, she tried on two bras in the change room, and ended up buying four bras in total. As she was leaving the store, however, she was stopped by a security guard, who accused her of stealing store merchandise. Based on camera surveillance, the security guard believed that Nassiah had entered the change room with two bras and left holding only one. In spite of numerous obstructions and interruptions in the camera surveillance, the security guard nevertheless became suspicious that she had crafted a plan to steal a bra. After contacting a sales associate to confirm that she had not left a bra in the change room, he double-checked the room himself, then followed Nassiah around the store until she had paid and was leaving the store. It was at this point that he stopped her and confronted her with the accusation of theft.

Nassiah was shocked by the accusation. She offered to show the security guard her purchases and receipt. He refused to look at the receipts of merchandise, and instead insisted that she accompany him back to the security office. A female attendant was brought into the security office and escorted Nassiah to the bathroom to be searched. Nassiah testified that she was asked to take off her boots and lift her sweater to show that she was not wearing the "missing" bra. Despite no evidence of any additional bra, the security guard persisted in his accusation, calling the police to report that a "Black female" had been caught stealing. Already late to pick up her son from his babysitter, she asked if she could call to explain her delay, but was told that the only call she could make was to her lawyer.

About an hour after the security guard detained Nassiah, a police officer arrived at the store. Both the security guard and the police officer were white men. Upon hearing the security guard's account and seeing Nassiah, the police officer asked, "Does she speak English?"[7] He then entered the security room and began to question her. "Where's the bra?" was the first question he asked her, and the question he would continue to put to her despite her denial of any theft, her insistence upon her innocence. He persisted even after checking that she had no criminal record and nothing indicating that she had been involved in any "suspicious activity."[8] When Nassiah maintained her innocence, he became aggressive, and said, "fucking foreigner ... if you don't tell me where the bra is, I'm going to take you downtown."[9] Nassiah was deeply humiliated and frightened by the police officer's treatment; nevertheless, she withstood this abusive language, a second search, and an additional forty-five minutes of detention as the police officer attempted to eliminate the various places the bra could be. Ultimately it was Jacqueline Nassiah herself who suggested that she might have appeared to have only one bra as she left the fitting room because she was holding both of them in her left hand. Viewing the tape with this suggestion in mind, the police officer and security guard realized that this was indeed the case, and their demeanour changed immediately. The police officer apologized and offered to walk Nassiah to her car, an offer that frightened her and that she declined.

Despite having been released from her forced store detention, for Nassiah, the event and its after-effects were far from over. She was extremely upset by the incident and shared the distressing experience with her brother when she got home, and with her work supervisor the next day. They encouraged her to file a human rights complaint. She decided to make her complaint against the police officer, Richard Elkington, and the Peel Police Department. As she explained:

> I was shocked, frightened and humiliated by this officer's verbal aggression towards me. I'm not a person who speaks to people in this manner, and neither do I expect to be treated in this manner, especially by a police officer....
>
> This is not the Canada I came to, to make a good life for my family; this is not what my understanding of what the police service was.[10]

Findings of Discrimination

The Ontario Human Rights Tribunal concluded that the police officer's investigation of the alleged theft was discriminatory. The Human Rights Tribunal adjudicator, Kaye Joachim, held that the officer's question, "Does she speak English?" and his "fucking foreigner" comment amounted to overt discrimination. She also found that the heightened suspicion and hostility Nassiah experienced was a form of racial profiling, linked to conscious and unconscious racial biases.[11] Drawing on expert social science evidence and research, the adjudicator explained that racial profiling can impact not only the initial decision regarding who is stopped or searched, but also *how individuals are investigated*:

> I find the racial profiling social science evidence is relevant because it speaks to, not just the initial decision to stop, detain, pursue an investigation, but also supports the general phenomenon that the *scrutiny applied to the subsequent investigation* is different, more heightened, more suspicious, if the suspect is Black. The stereotyping phenomenon is the same, whether it manifests itself in the discretion to stop/arrest/detain a person in part because they are Black, or whether it manifests itself in the form of greater suspicion, scrutiny, investigation in whole or part because a suspect is Black.[12]

The adjudicator found that Nassiah was subjected to greater suspicion during the police investigation because of her race, as evidenced by a number of the police officer's actions and assumptions, including the following:

- He stereotypically assumed that a Black suspect may not speak English well.
- He accepted the security guard's assertion that he had video tape evidence of theft without even looking at the video; he proceeded to investigate assuming that Mr. Nevers [the security guard] was telling the truth, although he had no basis for determining the relative credibility of Mr. Nevers versus Ms. Nassiah.

- He adopted an assumption of guilt approach to the investigation by asking, "where's the bra" as his first question, which was not the "textbook" or the "preferred" approach.
- The video tape provided very weak evidence of theft; it did not clearly indicate whether Ms. Nassiah had even entered the fitting room with two bras; it was equally unclear how many bras she held immediately upon exiting the fitting room; the willingness to infer theft from the video was unreasonable; to persist in asking, "where's the bra" after viewing the weak video evidence demonstrates a high degree of suspicion[.]
- He arranged for a second search of Ms. Nassiah's person, although he had no reason to believe that the first search was inadequate.
- After the second physical search, he was still not satisfied that the evidence was insufficient to lay a charge of theft, but he continued to investigate rather than releasing her.
- [The Peel Police Department's] own expert testified that ... Officer Elkington pursued Ms. Nassiah more diligently than ordinarily because she was Black. He spent a minimum of 45 minutes ... diligently pursuing an allegation of theft of a bra worth less than $10, in the face of fragile video evidence.[13]

In light of these findings, Nassiah won her case. Four years after experiencing the humiliation, fear, and shock of being wrongfully detained and accused, the discriminatory treatment she received was condemned. She received $20,000 in damages for the violation of her rights. The Peel Police Department was also ordered to take a number of steps to prevent racial profiling by its officers.[14] Yet, as she said at a press conference following the decision:

> With the outcome, I see that justice has been served and I'm glad for that ... But the fear — it has changed my life.[15]

Understanding Racial Profiling as Discrimination

IN A GROWING number of cases, individuals are challenging police officers, security guards, and others in positions of authority who stop and question them without reasonable cause. Individuals are also questioning the way they are treated after being stopped, often being made to feel like they are presumed guilty, at fault, or not entitled to be in public spaces. According to human rights laws, it is illegal for a police officer, security guard, or other person with authority to treat an individual differently on the basis of their race, or their national or ethnic origin. Treating individuals differently in ways that are harmful and unfair based on their national or ethnic origin, race, or the colour of their skin is one of the oldest and most widely recognized types of discrimination. As the *Nassiah* case teaches us, racial profiling is a form of discrimination. It occurs when individuals are treated differently by *persons in authority*, not because of what they have done, but because of how they look. As the adjudicator in Nassiah's case explains,

> Racial profiling is a form of racial discrimination. There is nothing novel in finding that racial profiling is contrary to the *Human Rights Code* ... It is and always has been contrary to the *Code* for the police to treat persons differently in any aspect of the police process, because of their race, even if race is only one factor in the differential treatment.[16]

A growing body of research has documented the phenomenon of racial profiling.[17] Individuals from racialized communities are disproportionately stopped by the police, excluded, questioned, or searched in situations when they have not done anything to appear suspicious; if they were white, they would not experience such a pattern. The Quebec Human Rights Commission defines racial profiling as follows:

> Racial profiling is any action taken by one or more people in authority with respect to a person or group of persons, for reasons of safety, security or public order, that is based on actual or presumed membership in a group defined by race, colour, ethnic or national origin or religion, without factual grounds or reasonable suspicion, that results in the person or group being exposed to differential treatment or scrutiny.
>
> Racial profiling includes any action by a person in a situation of authority who applies a measure in a disproportionate way to

certain segments of the population on the basis, in particular, of their racial, ethnic, national or religious background, whether actual or presumed.[18]

While most definitions and discussions of racial profiling focus on the actions and practices of police officers, security guards, border guards, and customs officials, there is growing recognition of racial profiling in other contexts. For example, the Nova Scotia Human Rights Commission published an important report on what it calls "consumer racial profiling" which "is the practice of targeting a consumer for discriminatory treatment based on the consumer's race, or ethnicity, or both."[19] As explained in the report:

> Consumer racial profiling can take many forms, including avoidance (ignoring); rejection (refusing service); discouragement (providing slow service); verbal actions (using degrading racial epithets); and physical actions (subjecting to detentions, interrogations, or arrests).[20]

After surveying over 1,000 consumers and conducting focus groups in Nova Scotia, the researchers concluded that consumer racial profiling impacts a number of racialized communities, particularly Black, Indigenous, and Middle Eastern communities.[21] Jacqueline Nassiah is not alone in having experienced racial profiling while shopping — a necessary and often mundane part of our everyday lives. In Nassiah's case, the incident was serious and involved being detained and questioned by the security guard and the police. In many instances, however, an incident will involve small acts of humiliation and mistreatment that undermine one's sense of belonging and well-being. Such small incidents of differential discriminatory treatment have been called "everyday discrimination" and "microaggressions" — casual, subtle, degrading comments, insults, or actions against racialized or other marginalized social groups.[22]

While some cases of racial profiling are the result of conscious and overt racism, in other cases, the racism may actually result from unconscious biases and stereotypes. Social cognition researchers are increasingly documenting a phenomenon known as unconscious or implicit bias, which results in racial profiling and other forms of discrimination that are not always intentional. It occurs when deeply embedded unconscious stereotypes and prejudices affect individual preferences, as well as the decisions and choices individuals make. As explained in the *Nassiah* case:

> [P]olice officers, like all members of society, develop unconscious stereotypes about racial groups and subconsciously act on those stereotypes during routine police investigations. When, for example, a police officer concludes that a young Black male driving an expensive car in a certain neighbour [*sic*] fits the profile of a potential drug dealer, an unconscious stereotype about Black people may be operating.[23]

Even individuals who believe in equality and non-discrimination may still make choices and decisions that are infused with implicit bias and result in unconscious discrimination.[24] Beyond overt racism, implicit biases and stereotypes often prompt police officers to disproportionately and unconsciously target racial minorities — a pattern confirmed in policing data.[25]

But where do these "unconscious or implicit" biases come from? They impact individual choices and decision making, but they also reveal a broader cultural or societal problem of racism and inequality. Children learn the biases that affect their decision making as adults. Race-based stereotypes are embedded in social and cultural norms — in the deep divisions that keep communities apart and instill fear of difference. Indeed, in one study about how to change implicit or unconscious biases, it was found that being aware of the risk of such biases helps to reduce bias; having direct personal contact with individuals different from oneself was also effective in countering implicit bias.[26] Still, the phenomenon of racial profiling borne of both conscious and unconscious negative stereotypes about racialized communities teaches us that the problem is both individual and societal. In discrimination law, we often say that the discrimination has both individual and broader systemic dimensions. As the adjudicator noted in the *Nassiah* case, the phenomenon of racial profiling is not just an isolated individual problem:

What is new (in the last two decades) is the mounting evidence that this form of racial discrimination is not the result of isolated acts of individual "bad apples" but part of a systemic bias in many police forces. What is also new is the increasing acceptance by the Courts in Canada that racial profiling by police occurs in Canada and the willingness to scrutinize seemingly "neutral" police behaviour to assess whether it falls within the phenomenon of racial profiling. [27]

Racial profiling, therefore, is a form of race discrimination that may be overt, unconscious, or institutionalized. Indeed, the highest Court in Ontario has recognized that racism often occurs in three interrelated ways, including (1) express and overt racism; (2) unconscious stereotypes that prompt discrimination; and (3) institutional bias:

> [R]acism is manifested in three ways. There are those who expressly espouse racist views as part of a personal credo. There are others who subconsciously hold negative attitudes towards black persons based on stereotypical assumptions concerning persons of colour. Finally, and perhaps most pervasively, racism exists within the interstices of our institutions. [28]

To prevent it, we need to respond to it at all levels — urging individuals not to make decisions rooted in stereotypes and biases, increasing awareness of unconscious bias, and addressing the ways in which society and institutional structures and practices reinforce and perpetuate such biases. [29]

Proving Racial Profiling

IN ITS BACKGROUND paper and guidelines on data collection, *Count Me In! Collecting Human Rights-Based Data*,[30] the Ontario Human Rights Commission underscores the importance of collecting grounds-based data to identify patterns of discrimination. Even if we have general data about racial profiling in policing, however, it is still hard to prove that a specific incident involving the police was discriminatory. The basis for a search or stop must be related to reasonable and legitimate suspicions of wrongdoing and not to an individual's race or ethnic or national origin. But in reality, it is difficult in many instances to know whether there really was a reasonable or legitimate reason for the treatment accorded to an individual from a racial minority community. The assessment of what constitutes suspicious behaviour is often deeply permeated by unfair stereotypes and racial bias.

Think about the *Nassiah* case. Jacqueline Nassiah was videotaped while in the lingerie section of the store. Why was she targeted for video surveillance? The security guard said that he first started his surveillance of Nassiah because she seemed to be "looking around" suspiciously. It would seem quite normal to look around while shopping — indeed, that is what one does. She was then videotaped going into the change room carrying two bras. Although there are breaks in the video coverage, the security guard incorrectly believed she had stolen a bra, confronting her as she left the store and accusing her of theft. Moreover, he refused to believe her denials and continued to detain her despite finding no evidence of any stolen bra. The police were summoned and she was treated rudely and with heightened suspicion by the police officer, searched a second time, and finally let go once the video was re-examined and the error discovered, an error that Nassiah herself had to point out. Would this have happened if she were white? After assessing all of the evidence, the adjudicator concluded, "I find that Ms. Nassiah was discriminated against when she was subjected to a more intensive, suspicious and prolonged investigation because she is Black."[31]

In reaching this conclusion, the human rights adjudicator reviewed not only the specific details and events that occurred at the store that day, but also considered the extensive social science evidence about racial profiling, noting that "the social science evidence establishes that statistically, racial minorities, particularly Black persons, are subject to a higher level of suspicion by police because of race, often coupled with other factors."[32] While acknowledging that the social science studies of racial profiling by police were done in the Toronto area rather than in the Peel Region where Jacqueline Nassiah's ordeal occurred, Adjudicator Joachim concluded:

The multi-ethnic character of Peel is sufficiently similar to Toronto that ... studies in the Toronto area can be reliably applied to the Peel region. The fact that racial profiling occurs in policing in the Toronto Region and likely occurs in the Peel Region does not answer the question of whether Ms. Nassiah was discriminated against in this particular case. However, the evidence is useful in identifying factors or clues which point toward racial profiling/ discrimination which might otherwise appear neutral if taken in isolation and without an awareness of the phenomenon of racial profiling.[33]

While adjudicators must be careful not to presume that general studies about the realities of racial profiling prove its occurrence in a specific case, knowledge about the broader patterns of discrimination in society often assist them in understanding the dynamics of particular events and in accurately assessing what most likely happened in a specific case.[34] In *Nassiah*, it was also noted that racial profiling may be caused either by overt racism or by unconscious bias.[35] For all of these reasons, the Ontario Human Rights Tribunal was convinced that racial profiling had occurred in violation of the Ontario *Human Rights Code*.

Many Cases, Even More Stories: The Prevalence of Racial and Other Types of Profiling

JACQUELINE NASSIAH'S CASE tells us one specific story of racial profiling. But the challenges of proving racial profiling have arisen in numerous human rights cases. In some cases, individuals have succeeded in convincing adjudicators and judges that they have experienced racially discriminatory treatment; in other cases, they have not.[36] What is significant with respect to these cases (even in cases where the claimants have lost) is that we have a public record of the racial profiling allegations because the incidents resulted in some kind of legal claim or action.[37] In Nassiah's case, she filed a human rights complaint and the case was adjudicated with the reasoning and conclusions available for the public to read. The important support of her brother and her work supervisor reinforced her decision to assert her right to equality and non-discrimination.

Yet, in many — perhaps most — instances of racial profiling, no human rights complaint is ever filed. No adjudicator combs through the facts and circumstances to identify potential racial discrimination. Take Mica, a Black youth walking home from school in Toronto:

> I was walking home from school and they [the police] pulled up and started harassing me for no reason ... said I fit the description of someone they were looking for. After that they fling me in the car, banged my head into the car trunk. One of them searched me and one used his thing [nightstick] and hit me in my head. I told [a community worker] and she told me to file a complaint but I never did. I don't like causing problems so I just left it alone.[38]

This story emerged from a research study into racial profiling, which included stories outside of the formal parameters of legal cases and judgments. The study, *In Their Own Voices*, was conducted by Maureen Brown and commissioned by the African Canadian Community Coalition on Racial Profiling.[39] It documented African Canadian experiences of racial profiling by police officers in the Greater Toronto Area. Few of these incidents of profiling were ever brought before a court or tribunal. In Mica's story, following the police mistreatment, there were no further legal proceedings. If Nassiah had not filed a human rights complaint, we might never have heard about the discrimination she experienced.

In thinking about racial profiling, it is important to recognize diversity between racialized groups and overlapping forms of racism. The recent Ontario *Anti-Racism Act* acknowledges at the outset that "histories of systemic exclusion, displacement and marginalization" are "experienced in different ways by different racialized groups," including "anti-Indigenous racism, anti-Black racism, antisemitism and Islamophobia."[40] It is increasingly the case that racial profiling targets individuals based on racialized religious differences,[41] while Indigenous peoples have also long been the targets of racist policies and practices.[42]

Moreover, racial profiling may occur simultaneously with other types of profiling. In a British Columbia Human Rights Tribunal case, for example, when a private mall security guard asked an Indigenous woman with a disability, Gladys Radek, to leave the mall premises, the adjudicator found that she had been subjected to both *racial and disability-based profiling*.[43] When homeless or economically marginalized individuals are targeted for differential treatment by police or security guards, they experience what has been called *social profiling*.[44] Profiling individuals based on their political beliefs and involvement in political activism has been called *political profiling*.[45] This type of political profiling occurred in confrontations with the police during the widespread student protests in Quebec over proposed tuition increases in 2012. The underlying commonality with respect to all of these often-overlapping types of profiling is the unfair and inequitable reliance on an individual's group identity or identities by persons with power and authority to target them for harmful differential treatment.

Remedying and Preventing Racial Profiling

IN ADDITION TO the challenges courts and tribunals face in identifying racial and other forms of profiling, it is often difficult to remedy and to prevent. Depending on the nature of the case, different types of remedies may be ordered. Remedies are supposed to address the harms caused by the discriminatory treatment. When individuals file human rights complaints regarding racial profiling, they seek some compensation for the harms of racial profiling. Think of Jacqueline Nassiah. What remedy did she deserve for the wrongs she experienced? She was clearly traumatized, humiliated, and frightened by the events in the store. To compensate her for the mistreatment, the Ontario Human Rights Tribunal ordered the Peel Police Department and Officer Elkington jointly to pay her damages of $20,000. In particularly egregious cases, additional punitive damages may also be ordered. These individual monetary remedies are important and should be sufficiently high, both to provide some real compensation and to deter racial profiling in the future. Is $20,000 sufficiently high? Would $200,000 have been more effective in eradicating racial profiling?

While individual monetary compensation is important, there has been a growing emphasis on the need for more institutional remedies. These remedies are aimed at preventing future occurences of racial profiling through directives and training programs. While an individual police officer is responsible for a specific decision to engage in racial profiling, there are many ways in which police departments may take measures to prevent profiling by individual police officers. In the *Nassiah* case, the Peel Police Department was ordered to hire an external expert consultant to develop a specific directive prohibiting racial profiling in its policing practices and "to prepare training materials on racial profiling for new recruits, current officers and supervisors."[46] Sometimes referred to as public interest remedies or systemic remedies, these remedies require that the police department take some proactive initiatives to prevent racial profiling in the future. The focus of this second type of remedy is institutional reform.

One concern with respect to *individual* human rights remedies is that they provide relief to only a few individuals who actually file human rights complaints, persist in seeking to vindicate their rights, and successfully prove their cases in court or before human rights tribunals. Such cases are quite exceptional, time-consuming, and difficult to prove. In the face of this concern, one significant legal development is the emergence of class action lawsuits — alleging a pattern and practice of racial profiling affecting numerous individuals. In such cases, the amount of damages claimed for each individual affected is small, but in the aggregate, the amounts are very significant. For example, in 2013, a class action lawsuit was filed against the Peel Police Department claiming $125 million for systemic racism and profiling — a much greater sum than the $20,000 paid in the *Nassiah* case.[47] These class action lawsuits may therefore have greater potential to prompt significant institutional and systemic change on the part of the organization against whom the claim is made.[48]

In an interesting case in Nova Scotia — *Johnson v Sanford and Halifax Regional Police Service*[49] — human rights adjudicator Philip

Girard concluded that a police officer had engaged in racial profiling when he stopped a car (with Texas license plates) being driven by Earl Fraser, with Kirk Johnson in the passenger seat. Both men are Black. The car was owned by Kirk Johnson, who is originally from Nova Scotia and is well known as a heavyweight boxing athlete. He was visiting Halifax. The police officer refused to accept the validity of the car registration and insurance documentation, and ordered that the car be impounded. The next day, it was determined that the documents were valid and that the car should not have been seized. Kirk Johnson filed a human rights complaint for racial profiling. The adjudicator ordered both individual and institutional remedies.

The individual remedies included monies for travel back to Nova Scotia on numerous occasions to attend legal proceedings and associated meetings, as well as compensation for the harms of the discrimination itself. Adjudicator Girard explained that there had been harm to Johnson's self-esteem and to his reputation. He had been humiliated and felt betrayed by the police:

> He had followed his parents' teachings that he was to cooperate with the police and was not to blame racism for any problems he might have. Mr. Johnson often spoke in schools where he tried to pass on the same message, which is not always a popular one in the black community. It required some courage to do this. Yet this incident seemed to reveal that his message was flawed, that a law-abiding black citizen could still get in trouble with the police even though minding his own business.[50]

At an institutional level, Girard ordered "the Halifax Regional Police Service [to] ... engage the services of two consultants to conduct a needs assessment of its current policies and practices on anti-racism education and diversity training."[51] He also ordered the police service "to begin collecting and maintaining statistics on the race of all drivers of motor vehicles which are stopped by police officers, the mechanics to be determined following a proposal to be prepared by the police and submitted to the board of inquiry, for which purpose I would retain jurisdiction."[52]

One innovative dimension of his decision was his discussion of what has been called "restorative justice," an approach that seeks to restore relationships in the aftermath of wrongful action:

> There is no reason that the police complaints process could not be infused with restorative justice principles, which would focus in a much more responsive and empowering way on the complainant's real concerns.[53]

He explained that one way of doing so would be for police officers to apologize to citizens in the wake of wrongful discriminatory conduct. Despite a request for an apology in the *Johnson* case, the Halifax police officer involved in the racial profiling refused to apologize. Noting that a "forced apology" could be worse than no apology, the adjudicator refused to order the police officer to apologize. Nonetheless, he noted in his decision,

> I suggest that a sincere apology acknowledging the discriminatory aspects of this incident, in a form acceptable to the complainant, might go some way towards putting relations between the police as a whole and the black community on a better footing.[54]

Conclusion

RACIAL PROFILING IS a form of discrimination that is prohibited in Canada's human rights laws. It is particularly troubling because it involves interactions between individuals and persons who have power and authority over others. The reality of profiling has increasingly been documented by social scientists and identified through the collection of race-based data by police and other government officials. It results from both overt negative racial biases and stereotypes, and unconscious racial biases that prejudice official decision making. It is sometimes embedded in seemingly neutral policies and practices. Jacqueline Nassiah's story contains important lessons about the inequitable risks of racial profiling in everyday life. While she was ultimately vindicated, her story teaches us that preventing discrimination must be our first priority. Once the damage is done, no amount of money can redress the enduring fear, trauma, and harm. Still, Nassiah's strength and stamina in pursuing a human rights complaint provide us with an important historical record of the discrimination she experienced. She helped to advance our understanding of the phenomenon of racial profiling and made it easier for others to seek redress. For all of that, we owe her our utmost respect and gratitude.

When Rules Exclude:
On Bowling and Equality

My name is Tammy Lee McLeod. I am 11 years old. I love bowling so much I want to be a star! Bowling is the only sport that I am able to play right along with my friends. I am a pretty good bowler and have qualified for several tournaments. When they told me I was not allowed to bowl in them I was very mad. All I want to do is go out and bowl and have fun and be able to compete just like my friends!

— TESTIMONY OF TAMMY MCLEOD, CITED IN *MCLEOD V YOUTH BOWLING COUNCIL OF ONTARIO*, ONTARIO BOARD OF INQUIRY, 1988[1]

WE OFTEN DO not stop to consider the implications of the myriad rules and regulations that we confront every day: we simply follow them. But the rules that shape our lives are not completely neutral — they have generally been developed and applied by those who belong to the dominant group in any given social structure. This means that rules that appear neutral can have very unequal effects on individuals and groups, even to the point of excluding people from opportunities or activities and undermining the possibility for participating in the surrounding community. Anti-discrimination law is concerned with rules that unfairly exclude particular individuals, such as children and adults with disabilities. The rules and regulations of society — the standard norms — often do not take into account the different needs and realities facing persons with disabilities. Increasingly, individuals with disabilities have challenged apparently neutral rules and revealed their exclusionary effects. Tammy McLeod and her parents, in challenging Tammy's exclusion from a regional bowling tournament, were at the forefront of raising awareness about the discriminatory effects of society's rules. Her human rights case is the focus of this chapter.

Tammy McLeod's Case
Excluded from the Tournament

This is a story about Tammy McLeod when she was a young girl.[2] She has cerebral palsy, a medical condition that affects her motor coordination and speech, and requires her to use a wheelchair for mobility, but does not affect her mental capacities. When Tammy was six years old, she began bowling with the help of her parents. Tammy's father built her a simple wooden ramp — a "ramp assist." Her mother would carry her up to the bowling lane, put the wooden ramp on Tammy's lap, and place a bowling ball at the top of the ramp. Tammy would take hold of the ball, move the ramp into the best position to guide the ball's direction, and then release it. The incline of the ramp gave the ball the speed necessary to reach the end of the bowling lane.

This process allowed Tammy to bowl with her brother and school friends every Saturday morning at the local bowling alley, and brought Tammy and her family a great deal of joy. Tammy became more and more skilled with the ramp as she grew older, and she competed in a Bantam league with sixty other children. When she was eleven years old, she entered the annual "4 Steps to Stardom" tournament, which involved local, regional, provincial, and national competitions. At the first of the four levels of competition, Tammy qualified to progress to the next level of competition. Shortly thereafter, however, she was informed by the local administrator of the Youth Bowling Council that she was disqualified from further participation in the tournament because of her use of the ramp. The Youth Bowling Council administrator considered the use of the ramp to violate the Canadian 5 Pin Bowlers' Association Official Rules and Regulations (1978), specifically, rule 1(b) that stated, "A bowling ball must be delivered entirely by manual means and shall not incorporate any device either in the ball or affixed to it."

Tammy was deeply upset by her exclusion from the tournament and stopped bowling completely for a year following her disqualification. Still, she did not give up on her right to be included in the competition. She and her parents filed a complaint with the Ontario Human Rights Commission. They claimed that her exclusion from the competition was a discriminatory denial of recreational services based on Tammy's disability. Tammy spoke for herself through the written statement quoted above. Little did she know that her complaint and statement were just the beginning of a legal journey that would last for nearly a decade. By the time she won her case, the possibility of participating in the initial bowling tournament was a distant dream; however, the principle of equality and the rights of persons with disabilities were affirmed.

Findings of Discrimination

Tammy's case was first heard by Professor Constance Backhouse, who chaired the Human Rights Board of Inquiry hearing on July 18, 1988 — close to three years after Tammy's exclusion from the competition. Professor Backhouse had to determine whether the Youth Bowling Council's exclusion of Tammy from the regional bowling tournament constituted unreasonable discrimination on the basis of disability in violation of the Ontario *Human Rights Code*.

Testifying on Tammy's behalf, the local bowling program director, May Calcutt, supported Tammy's right to play in the tournament. She also explained that none of the other children had ever complained about Tammy's inclusion in the competition. Expert witness Conn Casey, who had extensive professional bowling and coaching experience, did a series of tests on the ramp assist that Tammy used and concluded that "in [his] opinion, Tammy [had] no advantage at all." Professor Backhouse summarized Casey's assessment in her decision:

> The inability to vary the speed significantly, and the low speeds involved were disadvantageous to Tammy's game. Casey testified that the ramp was too small to create great velocity, and that Tammy could not develop enough ball speed to create the pin carry the other children had. Considering both accuracy and speed, Casey concluded that "overall, Tammy is at a disadvantage with the other children."[3]

When he was cross-examined by the lawyer for the Ontario Youth Bowling Council, Casey "admitted that with children, the key to their competitive success was control of the ball" and that "Tammy used no skill in releasing the ball, since the ramp controlled its release."[4]

Eric Whittaker, the chief executive officer of the Ontario 5 Pin Bowlers' Association, testified as an expert witness on behalf of the Ontario Bowling Association. Although he had not tested Tammy's wooden ramp, his main objection was that "it allowed a consistent release of the ball." Since Tammy could not control the hand movements most bowlers used to control the release of the ball, her participation would, in Whittaker's view, "compromise competition." Thus, as the lawyer for the Ontario Youth Bowling Council argued, Tammy was not really bowling: "'Ramp bowling' [is] a form of bowling, but one which was entirely different in skill level from the ordinary game of bowling. The ordinary bowler [has] to involve his/her anatomy in stance, approach to the fault line, arm swing, follow through and release."[5] The Bowling Council's lawyer argued that Tammy's exclusion should be exempt from protection under the Ontario *Human Rights Code* since it was reasonable and justified by the very definition of the sport of bowling itself. Moreover, it was suggested that "[c]ompetitions would no longer measure equal skills, the skills of ordinary bowlers would be compromised, and the nature of artificial aids would require constant scrutiny."[6] Finally, there was a concern that if Tammy won her case, it would open the "floodgates" for children with disabilities seeking access to competitive bowling.

Faced with this evidence and these arguments, Backhouse concluded that Tammy had been discriminated against by the Ontario Youth Bowling Council and that she should be allowed to participate, using her ramp assist, in competitive bowling tournaments. How did Backhouse reach this decision? First, she concluded that the rule requiring the bowling ball to be delivered without the assistance of a ramp had an adverse and negative exclusionary effect on individuals like Tammy. As Backhouse explains, the rule "appears on the face of it to be a neutral rule, applicable to all individuals equally. However, its impact is disproportionately damaging to some physically disabled people."[7] Specifically, she ruled that "[h]olding all devices

32

ineligible bars individuals with cerebral palsy from the opportunity to bowl."[8]

Having found that the application of the rule in this case resulted in exclusion based on disability, Backhouse then went on to consider whether it could be justified. The Ontario *Human Rights Code* allows some exceptions when exclusionary rules are "reasonable" and based on good faith. The key argument advanced by the Ontario Bowling Association was that the principle of fair competition would be compromised if Tammy were allowed to use a ramp. In examining this concern, Backhouse explained:

> The concept of competition, while essential to much sport, should not be used to bar access to "differently-abled" individuals. In competitive sport, outcome, not process is the critical variable. Competition is designed to rank individuals in order of athletic merit. Rules are designed to ensure the process is not unfair, so that no one will have an unfair advantage and the best will win.[9]

As she went on to clarify,

> Rules should be designed to accommodate variation insofar as this does not prejudice the outcome. Disabled persons who need to alter the process of a sport should be given competitive opportunities where this does not result in an unfair advantage with respect to the outcome.[10]

Since the expert evidence had revealed that Tammy did not have a competitive advantage using the wooden ramp assist, Backhouse concluded that there was no reasonable justification to exclude her. Indeed, she noted that the rules in adult bowling had changed to allow "artificial or medical aids":

> Rule 5(a) Where an artificial or medical aid is necessary for grasping and/or delivering the bowling ball because of any ... disability of the hand or arm ... permission to use such aid in sanctioned league or tournament competition, may be granted by the Board of Directors of the Provincial 5 Pin Bowlers' Association under the following conditions:

1) The aid does not incorporate a mechanical device with moving parts which would impart a force or impetus to the ball.

2) A description or drawing and/or model of the aid is furnished to the Provincial 5 Pin Bowlers' Association for examination.

3) A doctor's certificate, describing the disability, together with his/her recommendation that the aid should be used, is furnished to the Provincial 5 Pin Bowlers' Association.[11]

Thus, Professor Backhouse found in favour of Tammy, ordered the Youth Bowling Council to allow her to compete in competitive bowling tournaments, and awarded her damages for the mental anguish she experienced. She further ordered the Youth Bowling Council to "develop and enact a rule setting forth a fair procedure for young bowlers with hand or arm disabilities to seek exemption from the general provisions prohibiting mechanical devices," suggesting that the revised rules developed for adults provided a ready model.[12]

The decision of the Ontario Human Rights Board of Inquiry was not the end of the legal process, however. The Ontario Youth Bowling Council challenged Backhouse's decision in the courts, but Ontario Divisional Court Justice Dennis Lane agreed with Backhouse in terms of the results and upheld the decision to allow Tammy to compete.[13] His reasons for doing so, however, differed. Justice Lane concluded that the essence of bowling is "manual propulsion and release" of the ball.[14] He went on, therefore, to conclude that Tammy's disability made it impossible for her "to perform the essential act of bowling — manual control and release of the ball."[15] Here we see how even the very definition of bowling is expressed in terms that correspond to the reality of the majority.

Nevertheless, Justice Lane agreed with Professor Backhouse that the apparently neutral rule prohibiting the ramp did give rise to adverse effect discrimination. Furthermore, he explained,

such a rule is not to be struck down in its entirety if it is rationally related to the needs of the council, but rather is to be upheld in its general application and the facts examined closely to determine if the provider of the service — the council — could have accommodated the applicant without undue hardship.[16]

Therefore, his judgment focused on the concept of the *duty to accommodate* in human rights law. He thought it was critical to decide whether Tammy's disability could be accommodated to allow her to participate in competitive bowling without imposing any undue hardship on the council or other competitors. In this regard, he concluded:

> There is no evidence of hardship to the competitors. They are not required to alter the manner in which they bowl in any way. The evidence is clear that Tammy's device gives her no competitive advantage over others. . . . No evidence was given by any competitor complaining of Tammy's device. The children appear to be completely accepting of her.[17]

Accordingly, the Divisional Court concluded that Tammy should be accommodated by allowing her to use the wooden ramp to participate in competitive bowling. However, following this decision in Tammy's favour, the Ontario Bowling Council appealed to the Ontario Court of Appeal. Four years later, in 1994, the Ontario Court of Appeal (in a very short judgment) affirmed the Ontario Divisional Court's ruling.[18]

Despite the long delays in obtaining human rights justice in her case, and her exclusion from the regional tournaments at the heart of her initial complaint, Tammy returned to competitive bowling. Clearly a skilled athlete, Tammy became an Olympian, representing Canada at the Paralympics. She competed in swimming and then in boccia, a precision ball sport not dissimilar from bowling that was designed for athletes with cerebral palsy, and that has since come to be played by people with other motor disabilities.[19]

Dominant Norms and Definitions

TAMMY WAS PROHIBITED from bowling because of a rule constructed in a world where most people do not have cerebral palsy. Her needs and daily realities were not taken into account when the bowling rules were written. But who gets to define what bowling really is? And why shouldn't definitions change when their exclusionary effects are revealed? There is nothing cast in stone about the meaning of bowling. It is a social construct in that its meaning depends on how society defines "bowling." The definition of "bowling" depends on the rules of the Canadian 5 Pin Bowling Association, and indeed, they have changed over the years. Tammy's experience of exclusion reminds us that what appear to be neutral and widely accepted norms in society reflect a particular worldview — a view that may have intended or unintended exclusionary consequences.

What is troubling with respect to the Ontario Divisional Court decision is its failure to challenge the traditional definition of bowling in any way. Justice Lane wrote that the "essence" of bowling was to release the ball manually without any assistance. Accordingly, Tammy was told that she was not "really" bowling if she used the wooden ramp, but that she could be accommodated to allow for her participation.[20] How could she participate in a bowling competition and not really be bowling? Indeed, even before Justice Lane's decision, the adult rules in bowling had been revised to allow "for an artificial or medical aid ... for grasping and/or delivering the bowling ball." Why couldn't the court have simply concluded that the wooden ramp accommodated Tammy's needs, which made it possible for her to bowl differently than the norm? Such a conclusion would recognize that different people do things differently, and that we need to accept the possibility that there is more than one way to exist in this world. Think of all the other definitions and rules in society that appear neutral and yet may have exclusionary effects.

Too often, the definitions, norms, and practices that result in exclusion are not challenged or revised. As discussed further below, while it is not always possible to change the traditional rules and practices in society, it is always important to ask the question of whether such change *should* occur. If we are to be a welcoming and equitable society, we need to continue to question the rules and norms of society — always. And the direction of that change will often be led by those whose lives do not fit readily into the traditional rules and norms: the Tammys of this world and their parents, who teach us that there are different ways to bowl — different ways to succeed — and different ways to participate in common social endeavours.

When Rules Exclude: Understanding Adverse Impact Discrimination

MANY OF THE rules and regulations that govern our everyday lives do not take into account the needs or circumstances of minority groups or communities; the rules are designed by and for the majority. The exclusionary and harmful effects of such rules are often not intended, nor even imagined, when they are being written. Nonetheless, since the 1980s, Canadian anti-discrimination law has recognized that even apparently neutral rules and policies may be discriminatory if they have disproportionately negative and exclusionary effects on groups protected by human rights laws. In Canada, this type of discrimination is referred to as "adverse impact discrimination" or "indirect discrimination."[21]

The first case where the Supreme Court of Canada acknowledged adverse impact discrimination involved allegations of religious-based discrimination linked to a Saturday work rule for department store employees.[22] At the time of the case, stores were generally closed on Sundays, and employees were expected to be available to work for the rest of the week. After converting to the Seventh Day Adventist religion, which has a Saturday Sabbath, Theresa O'Malley claimed that requiring her to work on Saturdays was discriminatory. The Supreme Court of Canada agreed. Although the work schedule was not designed to discriminate against religious minorities whose Sabbath is Saturday, such was its effect. In the face of such effects, the employer was required to accommodate the employee by reorganizing the work schedule if it were feasible to do so. The Supreme Court emphasized that human rights laws are concerned with the effects of rules, not the intent of the alleged discriminator. The purpose of human rights laws is to compensate the victim of discrimination rather than to punish the perpetrator. In this way, anti-discrimination law fundamentally differs from criminal law, since the latter focuses on punishing the wrongdoer in situations where the perpetrator intended to harm the victim.

Many cases involving adverse impact discrimination have involved allegations of effects-based discrimination linked to disability and religion. For individuals with disabilities and for individuals from religious and racialized communities, many seemingly neutral rules and customs clearly have disproportionately negative effects on their inclusion in everyday institutions and activities. If there is no ramp for wheelchair access to a building, no braille in elevators, or no day off work for a religious holiday not celebrated by the majority population, society's general rules and norms have negative discriminatory effects. However, in some cases, these rules and customs can be justified despite their discriminatory effects, and this is discussed in more detail below.

Adverse impact discrimination cases have also arisen in contexts other than disability and religion. In one case, for example, the Supreme Court of Canada concluded that an aerobics fitness test for forest firefighters resulted in sex discrimination.[23] Though some men did not pass the test and some women passed it, a significantly higher percentage of women failed. The adverse effects did not result in the total exclusion of the group, but did exclude a disproportionately high number of women. Since the aerobics standard had not been formulated to take into account sex-based differences, and had not been shown to be necessary for health or safety reasons, it was found to be discriminatory. Similarly, standardized tests and high school diploma requirements have been found to have discriminatory race-based effects, which are linked to the historical impact of racism on access to education.[24]

In a recent decision, *Fraser v Canada (Attorney General)*,[25] the Supreme Court of Canada again concluded that an apparently neutral legal rule, included in a federal law regulating pension and retirement plans in the federal Royal Canadian Mounted Police, resulted in adverse impact discrimination on the basis of sex. Women who had participated in job-sharing to accommodate their work and childrearing obligations were disproportionately disadvantaged by the pension rule. The case involved a question of non-discrimination and equality rights pursuant to the Canadian *Charter* because the pension plan rules were part of a federal law. In her majority opinion, Justice Rosalie Abella clarified the key question in adverse impact discrimination cases as follows:

Instead of asking whether a law explicitly targets a protected group for differential treatment, a court must explore whether it does so indirectly through its impact on members of that group. . . . A law, for example, may include seemingly neutral rules, restrictions or criteria that operate in practice as "built-in headwinds" for members of protected groups.[26]

She further explained that to determine whether the effects of a law or policy have negative effects on specific groups, "evidence of statistical disparity and of broader group disadvantage may demonstrate disproportionate impact; but neither is mandatory, and their significance will vary depending on the case."[27]

What has emerged very clearly with respect to anti-discrimination law is that the focus should be on the effects of discrimination or exclusion on the victim rather than the intent of the discriminator. Often it is very difficult to discern whether there is an intent to discriminate — sometimes intentional discrimination is masked in seemingly neutral rules and practices. As Justice Gérard La Forest wrote in an important sexual harassment decision, since anti-discrimination law is "essentially concerned with the removal of discrimination, as opposed to punishing anti-social behaviour, it follows that the motives or intention of those who discriminate are not central to its concerns."[28] In short, rules that appear neutral and that are not intended to be a source of discrimination or exclusion may nevertheless be found to be discriminatory and in violation of human rights laws as a result of their effects. It is critical, therefore, to challenge even seemingly neutral rules and practices when they operate to exclude groups protected by human rights legislation.

Substantive Equality: Ensuring Equitable Outcomes

WHILE THE CONCEPT of discrimination has evolved to recognize adverse impact discrimination, a similar trend is apparent in relation to the legal meaning of equality. Legal equality was historically understood to mean treating everyone the same, regardless of group status. However, since the late 1980s, the concept of substantive equality has emerged. Substantive equality is measured in relation to equitable outcomes. Sometimes equitable outcomes are achieved by treating everyone the same, but in other situations, equitable outcomes can only be secured by treating people differently. For example, in Tammy's case, permitting her to use a ramp in bowling allowed her to enjoy substantive equality and compete with others. As Justice William McIntyre stated in the first Supreme Court of Canada decision interpreting the meaning of equality in the *Canadian Charter of Rights and Freedoms*, "for the accommodation of differences, which is the essence of true equality, it will frequently be necessary to make distinctions."[29] The concept of substantive equality is integral to the stories told in many chapters of this book.

Recognition of how identical treatment may generate inequitable results is illustrated in this popular image illustrating equality and equity.[30]

PERMISSION TO USE IMAGE GIVEN BY CRAIG FROEHLE.

Giving those who are different heights — and therefore have different needs — boxes of the same height to watch the game is clearly unfair. Although the left half of the image is sometimes labelled "equality" and the right side, "equity," from a legal perspective, the left side refers to "formal equality." Formal equality is based on a much more restrictive and narrow understanding of equality than the substantive equality concept widely accepted in our human rights laws. The right side, or "equity" image, therefore, could be labelled "substantive equality." In other words, equality cannot simply be equated with "formal equality" or treating all individuals the same in a world where different individuals and groups have diverse needs and divergent life circumstances. Equality is a much more expansive concept that focuses on equitable outcomes. Sometimes treating everyone the same will result in equality, but not always. Clearly, treating everyone the same in this image generates inequitable results: the image on the left depicts a situation which is discriminatory even though each person is being treated the same. The right side is non-discriminatory and speaks to the importance of accommodating differences to ensure equal outcomes. There are also larger structural issues that this diagram prompts us to think about — like who has access to seats inside the sports arena and who gets to play baseball out on the field? Too often, we fail to challenge those larger sources of inequality.

From Exclusion to Inclusion: Changing Norms and Accommodating Difference

IN SITUATIONS WHERE apparently neutral rules and practices operate to disproportionately exclude individuals, there are two pathways to inclusion. One option is to eliminate or revise the rule in question to alleviate its discriminatory effects; the other is to leave the rule in place but to accommodate the individuals impacted by the rule. In Tammy's case, the rule was not changed for everyone; instead, she was accommodated to allow her to use the ramp.

Changing the Rule for Everyone

It is always important to consider whether or not a rule, policy, or practice could be changed for everyone. For example, if we are building an entrance way to a building and we have a choice about whether to include steps or a ramp, we know that a ramp would allow more people to access a building easily without special accommodation. If a bus driver calls out the name of the next stop, it assists not only sight-impaired passengers, but also those who may not be familiar with the neighbourhood.[31] In the equity image above, we could replace the wooden fence with a chain-link fence. These examples reflect a "universal design" approach. As stated in the *United Nations Convention on the Rights of Persons with Disabilities,*

> "Universal design" means the design of products, environments, programmes and services to be usable by all people, to the greatest extent possible, without the need for adaptation or specialized design. "Universal design" shall not exclude assistive devices for particular groups of persons with disabilities where this is needed.[32]

Note that universal design does not always mean that the rule is changed for everyone. In Tammy's case, for example, it made sense for most of the children to continue to bowl without an assistive device while allowing Tammy to use one. Indeed, the UN Convention definition recognizes that special assistive devices are sometimes needed, even in a world where universal design is more widely embraced.[33]

Nevertheless, taking universal design seriously means thinking about how to construct our world so as to make it as welcoming as possible for as many people as possible. To do this effectively requires knowledge about the needs and concerns of diverse groups in society. If a small minority of people without disabilities devises the rules and policies, and designs institutional spaces, it is not surprising that such rules and spaces will have adverse effects on those excluded from the rulemaking and institution-building processes. For this reason, universal design principles have democratic and participatory implications: more — and more diverse — people have to be involved in creating the rules. To make our society more inclusive requires more participatory input from those who have historically been excluded in society.

Individual Accommodation

When it is not feasible to change the rules to alleviate disparate effects, individual accommodation is critically important to inclusion. The

UN *Convention on the Rights of Persons with Disabilities* also recognizes accommodation as an integral dimension of equitable inclusion.

> "Reasonable accommodation" means necessary and appropriate modification and adjustments not imposing a disproportionate or undue burden, where needed in a particular case, to ensure to persons with disabilities the enjoyment or exercise on an equal basis with others of all human rights and fundamental freedoms.[34]

David Lepofsky, a disability rights advocate, lawyer, and scholar, has clarified that the duty to accommodate has both procedural and substantive dimensions.[35] Employers, educational institutions, and service providers have a procedural duty to try to accommodate individuals — to consult, research options, and investigate what might be feasible and possible. They also have substantive duties to make changes to accommodate those who would otherwise be excluded.

While the duty to accommodate is an important pathway to inclusion, it has limits. Human rights laws only require reasonable accommodation that does not cause "undue hardship" (or an undue and disproportionate burden) to the employer, educational institution, or service provider.[36] What this means is that if public or individual safety would be undermined, or if accommodation costs too much, or if there are detrimental effects on others, then accommodation does not have to occur. For example, in Tammy's case, the adjudicators were careful to note that allowing Tammy to use the wooden ramp would not undermine the fairness of the competition. Genuine efforts to find feasible and fair accommodation must also be made before undue hardship can be raised as a justification for non-accommodation.

And, as noted above, it is important to consider whether a universal design approach is possible before assessing reasonable accommodation. Why is this so important? Simply because a universal design approach is more transformative — it changes the rules and norms for everyone rather than focusing on individual special treatment. Reasonable accommodation is absolutely necessary in some situations and we still need to rely on it. The reasonable accommodation model, however, leaves exclusionary rules and practices in place, while providing special accommodation to secure access to individuals who would otherwise be excluded for reasons such as disability, gender, and religion.

Conclusion

TAMMY MCLEOD'S CASE tells a powerful story about youth, social exclusion, family, and community, borne of a decision to prohibit a young girl with cerebral palsy from participating in a regional bowling competition. One of the key lessons from the case is how apparently neutral rules in society and organizations may have negative and inequitable effects on people who are different from dominant or majoritarian groups in society. Tammy was confronted with a rule that prevented her from participating in bowling competitions. The only way she could participate in bowling was to use the wooden ramp that her father had made her. Yet the rules of bowling were written by those who do not need to use a ramp assist to bowl.[37]

Her story reminds us that human rights law is not about what happens in official or distant governmental contexts; it is about the everyday lives of individuals and their families. It teaches us about how the heartbreak of a young girl prompted the girl and her parents to fight to secure respect for her human right to participate and be included in her community — a struggle she ultimately won, not only for herself, but also for others.

3

Excluded, Harassed, and Undervalued: The Struggle to Break Systemic Barriers

They told me they did not want me there.
How did they behave?
Well, they tried to confuse me.

Instead of telling me things like two or three moves at a time, which is all you have to do, they would tell me about 15 moves in a row, like talking really quickly, using the numbers, like this "take a locomotive, put it there, go here, go there," you know, like really — so that I would get confused, or they would tell me to jump off the train at a switch, I would get off at the switch, and they would leave me at the switch, and they would not tell me what they were doing, they would leave me there, or they would just go off on break, and they would not tell me they were going on break.

Sometimes they would leave me at a switch, or at an engine. They would say, "go release the brakes on that engine and wait for my signal"; I would never hear the signal, they would go off and eat lunch and leave me there. They used to do that all the time.

—— TESTIMONY OF CARLA NEMEROFF, CITED BY THE SUPREME COURT OF CANADA
IN *CN V CANADA (CANADIAN HUMAN RIGHTS COMMISSION)* 1987[1]

WHY IS IT that some people feel welcomed into an organization or workplace while others do not? Why is it that some people can work in an organization for many years and never really feel as though they belong? The subtle and not-so-subtle dynamics of inclusion and exclusion are the focus of this chapter. While many people tend to blame themselves for not being promoted or for not obtaining a leadership position, there are often very real obstacles that need to be recognized and named. For some, the pathway to inclusion is assimilation; they submerge their authentic selves in an effort to fit in.[2] For others, the refusal or inability to assimilate results in increasing marginalization and exclusion from organizational opportunities and belonging.

Despite the various ways exclusion and lost opportunities can occur, it is critical to examine the organizational and institutional dimensions of being left out — or of not fitting in. Individuals in leadership positions can make an enormous difference in organizations by lighting pathways forward as mentors and eliminating barriers to advancement. Too often, however, institutional leaders do not champion inclusion and instead reinforce and justify continued exclusion. Individuals from under-represented groups can work to buttress their own self-confidence, agency, and inclusion, but institutional contexts and cultures often create barriers that are difficult to overcome, making discriminatory exclusions look normal, fair, and acceptable, and individual advancement appear entirely merit-based.

This organizational or institutional perspective is an important focus of what has been called "systemic discrimination" — that is, widespread discrimination within institutions and society. Though systemic discrimination is also related to individual behaviour and larger societal structures of exclusion, institutional policies remain critical to understanding the legal concept. In her 1984 *Equality in Employment: A Royal Commission Report*, Justice Rosalie Silberman Abella emphasized the importance of examining discrimination through a systemic lens:

> The impact of behaviour is the essence of "systemic discrimination." It suggests that the inexorable, cumulative effect on individuals or groups of behaviour that has an arbitrarily negative impact on them is more significant than whether the behaviour flows from insensitivity or intentional discrimination.[3]

Justice Abella's report was deeply influential in subsequent court decisions and legislative developments, particularly her insight that "[s]ystemic discrimination requires systemic remedies."[4]

We begin this chapter by examining an historic and path-breaking 1980s case on systemic discrimination: *CN v Canada (Canadian Human Rights Commission)*,[5] also referred to as the *Action travail des femmes* case,[6] after the name of the grassroots women's organization in Quebec that filed a human rights complaint with the Canadian Human Rights Commission alleging systemic gender-based discrimination at the Canadian National Railway Company (CN), specifically in the St Lawrence Region of Quebec. The case was litigated all the way to the Supreme Court of Canada. For the first time, the Court recognized the concept of systemic discrimination. The Court's decision also underscored the importance of crafting innovative and comprehensive remedies (including affirmative action) to prevent continued exclusion and discrimination. After explaining the factual and legal issues in the case, I use it to illustrate the multiple layers of inequality that constitute systemic discrimination.

Since this important case, there have been a number of other cases where the systemic dimensions of discrimination have been raised. They often involve a "series of incidents"[7] within an organization over time — sometimes many years. In each case, the *Action travail des femmes* case remains an important starting point. Yet, despite the fact that this case is now over thirty years old, courts and human rights tribunals continue to find systemic discrimination cases difficult, both in terms of identifying systemic discrimination and remedying it. Organizations often resist change, even in the face of legal orders to remedy past wrongs and prevent future discrimination. In some cases, despite winning in court, some individuals are never fully compensated for the long-lasting effects that the discrimination has on their well-being, sense of self, and feelings of belonging.

The CN Case: Women in the Rail Yards
Barriers to Entry and Under-Representation

RAILROADS HAVE BEEN at the heart of Canadian national identity, connecting us from east to west across vast expanses of mountains and plains, and CN is a large, well-known federally regulated corporation. The human rights complaint against CN in the *Action travail des femmes* case concerned the significant under-representation of women in jobs where men have been historically predominant, specifically "blue-collar" entry-level positions, including, for example, brake, signal, and switch operators; railway, bridge, and track-building workers; and track and coach maintenance jobs.[8] These entry-level positions often led to promotions and greater responsibility due to CN's tradition of development and promotion from within.

The sexism women encountered in accessing these entry-level jobs and the harassment women experienced on the job were recounted by the individual women who testified at the human rights hearings and were documented in various internal reports and studies produced by CN itself. For example, as noted in one of the reports:

> By the end of 1981, there were only 57 women in "blue-collar" posts in the St. Lawrence Region of CN, being a mere 0.7 per cent of the blue-collar labour force in the region. By contrast, women represented, in 1981, 40.7 per cent of the total Canadian labour force. At the time, women constituted only 6.11 per cent of the total work force of CN.[9]

Another internal report examined attitudinal bias towards women and concluded:

> One of the major reasons why women are not in positions of major responsibility within CN today is due to the unconscious, as well as the conscious, beliefs of male-dominated management in the many myths and stereotypes that exist about women as a group.[10]

The attitudes of male personnel towards women at CN included overt sexism and an unwillingness to accept women as co-workers, as these excerpts from the report demonstrate:

> Women are generally disruptive to the workforce.

> Women aren't tough enough to handle supervisory jobs. They fail miserably under pressure.

> The best jobs for women are coach cleaners — that's second nature to them.

One big problem adding women to train crews would be policing the morals in the cabooses.

Work in the yards is too physically demanding. The weather is too harsh.

Women cannot do the physical aspects of a CN conductor's job. There's too much handling of drunks, transients and undesirables.

Women have no drive, no ambition, no initiative.

A woman can't combine a career and family responsibilities....

Unless I'm forced, I won't take a woman.[11]

As the Supreme Court decision recognized, some male employees expressed more positive opinions about the presence of women:

Women are a vast, untapped resource we have over looked until now.

Women are the same as men — as long as they do the job, they should get hired, developed and promoted.

We are guilty of unconscious discrimination against women by never identifying and developing their talents.[12]

Some of the women who were hired into traditionally male jobs at CN experienced sexual and sex-based harassment, linked to a work culture that sexualized and denigrated women. Carla Nemeroff, who worked in non-traditional jobs at CN from December 4, 1978, to December 3, 1980, described the sexism and sexual harassment she experienced as the only woman in a totally male environment:

Some of them said "it is not a place for a woman, I would never let my wife or daughter work here". Some of them were threatened, they would say "now there is one, there is going to be 50". They were all kinds of rumors that many women were going to come, that women were stealing men's jobs, that that is why the economy was bad, because before in the old days the men worked and the women stayed at home, and the woman has her job in the home taking care of the family ... and the man brings in the money. Now, women want to be independent, they don't have kids, they come out in the work force, they take the jobs from the men, the men are unemployed, it screws up the nuclear family where the woman is at home. They were really upset by that....

Another time, a few guys — we were on break sort of hanging around outside because it was warm out; a few guys jumped me and pretended they were going to rape me. I found that quite offensive.

Then, another time, I was bringing a train into the shop — you see, I was not a cleaner anymore; I was signalling, and I was bringing a train into the shop. The boss yelled out something obscene to distract me from my work, and it was very dangerous. Nothing happened, but I could have had an accident. I could have really hurt myself.[13]

Her words attest to the psychological and physical effects of discrimination.

Findings of Discrimination and Remedies

After reviewing the extensive evidence submitted in the case, the Canadian Human Rights Tribunal concluded that CN had discriminated against women seeking traditionally male jobs in the railyards. It ordered CN to change a number of policies to eliminate barriers to women seeking access to non-traditional jobs. For example, it ordered CN to immediately stop using mechanical aptitude tests that examined skills that were not necessary to do the work and that had a negative impact on women. It also ordered CN to eliminate the welding experience requirement for entry-level jobs — another seemingly neutral requirement that adversely affected women applicants.[14] Foremen were also ordered to stop requiring female candidates to pass physical strength tests that male applicants were not asked to do (such as lifting a heavy piece of equipment).[15]

What was particularly innovative with respect to the Human Rights Tribunal ruling, however, was what it called *special temporary remedies*, which required CN to develop an affirmative action hiring program for entry-level jobs. Specifically, it ordered that one out of every four new hires be a woman until women represented 13 percent of those in blue-collar jobs at CN,[16] and CN was also required to submit progress reports to the Canadian Human Rights Commission regarding implementation of the special temporary measures. CN challenged the legality of the affirmative action remedial order all the way up to the Supreme Court of Canada.

In a landmark decision, the Supreme Court of Canada upheld the Canadian Human Rights Tribunal's affirmative action remedial order. Central to the Court's reasoning was its recognition of the concept of systemic discrimination:

> Systemic discrimination in an employment context results from *the simple operation of established procedures of recruitment, hiring and promotion, none of which is necessarily designed to promote discrimination. The discrimination is then reinforced by the very exclusion of the disadvantaged group* because the exclusion fosters the belief, both within and outside the group, that the exclusion is the result of "natural forces, for example, that women "just can't do the job." *To combat systemic discrimination, it is essential to create a climate in which both negative practices and negative attitudes can be challenged and discouraged.*[17]

As the Court explains, systemic discrimination involves a combination of direct discrimination based on negative stereotypes about the excluded group (in this case, women), as well as adverse impact discrimination, embedded in longstanding and seemingly neutral policies and practices that have disproportionately negative effects on excluded groups. The two are interconnected and reinforce each other. Affirmative action remedial initiatives were endorsed as important measures for addressing systemic discrimination. As the chief justice explained, "it is essential to look to the past patterns of discrimination and to destroy those patterns in order to prevent the same type of discrimination in the future."[18] Preventing discrimination in the future is one of the central goals of affirmative action initiatives.

Systemic Discrimination: A Multi-layered Approach

THE *ACTION TRAVAIL DES FEMMES* case is one of the most significant systemic workplace discrimination cases in Canadian anti-discrimination law. One way to think about systemic discrimination is by imagining multiple layers of inequality, including (1) individual-to-individual interactions, extending to (2) institutional or organizational-level inequities, and even beyond, to (3) deep societal and structural inequalities. I refer to these three levels as the *micro* (individual interactions and effects), *meso* (institutional or organizational rules, policies, norms, and culture), and *macro* (broader social, economic, and political inequalities and the effects of intergenerational inequities).

The Micro-level: Interactional Injustices

The first layer of systemic discrimination involves overt prejudice and direct discrimination in individual interactions. This type of discrimination is sometimes called "interactional injustice."[19] It includes discrimination caused by individuals in their everyday interactions with others, whether it be in the workplace, in educational institutions, or in public services (for example, policing). It may take the form of harassing, bullying, mistreating, undervaluing, or excluding individuals. Political theorists and sociologists often speak of interactional justice or injustice in reference to interpersonal treatment that either respects or undermines human dignity.[20] Similarly, people who perpetrate individual interactional injustices are subject to legal liability. Indeed, there is a significant body of anti-discrimination law and numerous statutory human rights cases that involve allegations of discrimination linked to interpersonal mistreatment. We tend to conceptualize these kinds of cases in terms of direct discrimination implicating differential treatment based on group-based stereotypes or prejudices. At CN, the historical and ongoing problems of gender-based exclusion and discrimination resulted in part from the overtly discriminatory attitudes or unconscious biases of supervisors, co-workers, and managers.

These interactional injustices, however, have systemic dimensions. First, when interactional injustices are widespread in an organization or workplace, they become systemic,[21] meaning that the discrimination is not an isolated exception. The discrimination and stereotyping are pervasive, institutionalized, and even considered normal, natural, or acceptable within broader society. With respect to this type of discrimination, it is often helpful to look to quantitative data about exclusion or mistreatment. Such data can reveal patterns of individual exclusion or mistreatment.[22] In some situations, individuals may not know whether the treatment they received is different from that of more privileged individuals in an organization. For example, a female employee may not know if she is being underpaid in relation to her male co-workers. Similarly, she may believe that her denial of a job or promotion is based on her individual shortcomings rather than a result of the systemic undervaluing of women's abilities and potential in the workplace.

Second, acceptance of the discriminatory norms or practices by the dominant majority group in the workplace reinforces their prevalence. As such, discriminatory attitudes become embedded in an exclusionary institutional culture.[23] When individuals who are outside the dominant group seek inclusion, they are perceived as a threat to institutional traditions, and often subjected to discrimination and harassment. The sexist attitudes and practices of many supervisors and co-workers at CN illustrate how women were seen as a threat to the traditional all-male workplace culture in the railyard. Indeed, it has often proved difficult to change workplace cultures and attitudes, even when they are overtly discriminatory and hostile to the inclusion of certain groups.[24]

Finally, individual interactions are shaped by structures of institutional power and privilege. Individuals have different degrees of power and privilege within organizations, and supervisors and employers have the institutional authority to make decisions that exclude or disadvantage other individuals.[25] Structural features of the workplace, such as income and job insecurity, also make some individuals more vulnerable to abuses of power and less likely to challenge violations of their rights. Two Ontario human rights cases illustrate these realities.

In the first case, *OPT v Presteve Foods Ltd*,[26] two migrant women workers from Mexico suffered discriminatory treatment and sexual harassment at the hands of their employer, the owner and manager of a fish processing plant. The Ontario Human Rights Tribunal adjudicator, Mark Hart, accepted the women's evidence, including their concerns about threats by their manager to send them back to their home country if they complained about the sexual harassment. The truth of these concerns was reinforced by expert evidence regarding the vulnerability of migrant workers and the unilateral discretionary power of managers. Expert witness Professor Kerry Preibisch explained that "the very threat of repatriation has the effect of causing migrant workers to do as they are told by their employers and not complain, given the significant consequences of being repatriated for workers and their families."[27] Thus, the sexual abuse and harassment was facilitated by the structural vulnerability of the migrant workers, embedded in the legal rules of the temporary migrant worker program.[28]

In the second case, *AB v Joe Singer Shoes Ltd*,[29] a woman who worked in a shoe store was subjected to sexual harassment and abuse by her employer, the owner of the store, over a period of many years. She had begun work at the store upon arriving in Canada as an immigrant from Thailand. She also rented an apartment (owned by her employer) above the store, where she lived with her son. Evidence supported the complainant's allegations of sexual harassment and assault, both in the store office and in her apartment:

> The applicant was vulnerable given she had no family here, was single, lived above the store and English was not her first language. I find that [the employer] Mr. Singer told the applicant she was stuck, that he had money and would get the best lawyers if she reported him while she would have to rely on community lawyers, and that she stayed because she felt she had no option.[30]

Thus, we see an employer preying on the vulnerability of a woman who is in a position of financial dependence, both at work and in relation to her housing. The individual misconduct is linked to the institutional power in the hands of the employer and landlord.[31] As these examples illustrate, we cannot completely separate individual interactional injustices from the institutional contexts within which they occur and the organizational norms that condone them. It is this institutional context that introduces a systemic dimension to cases involving individual interactional injustice.

The Meso-level: Organizational Rules, Policies, and Norms

A second level of systemic discrimination — the institutional or meso-level — includes institutional or organizational policies, rules, power structures, and norms within which individual interactions take place. Recognition of adverse impact discrimination represented an important moment that consolidated the importance of examining meso-level practices as potential sources of discrimination. Indeed, a significant body of anti-discrimination law focuses on the discrimination embedded within institutional policies and rules. Examples include the Saturday work rule that was found to discriminate against individuals whose Sabbath is Saturday,[32] or the aerobics test administered to all employees that was found to discriminate on the basis of gender.[33] To the extent that the focus in these anti-discrimination cases is on the institutional or organizational rules and policies, a shift to a more overtly acknowledged systemic approach is apparent. The discrimination is institutionalized or systemically embedded in apparently neutral rules and practices.

In the CN case, the welding experience requirement was found to have a disproportionately negative impact on women applicants; so too did the mechanical aptitude tests used in the screening process for entry-level jobs. Why are these apparently "neutral" entry-level requirements discriminatory and how are they related to systemic discrimination? As we saw in Chapter 2 on the rules regarding bowling, when rules or policies that appear neutral on their face have a negative impact on groups that have been disproportionately excluded from an activity or workplace, there is a risk that they are discriminatory. This was the case at CN with respect to the welding experience requirement and the mechanical aptitude tests, as neither are skills that were traditionally taught to women, but both could be easily attained through training. Nor were these apparently neutral requirements relevant to the effective assessment of entry-level candidates. In some cases, neutral requirements may screen out certain groups but nevertheless be necessary for the safe and effective performance of the job. For example, if the job were a full-time welding job, welding experience may well be a valid criterion for selection. But in the CN case, neither welding experience nor mechanical aptitude abilities were necessary for the entry-level jobs at the railyard. They had simply been used for many years and their discriminatory effects on women applicants had not been considered or assessed. In this situation, we see that systemic discrimination can sometimes occur when there is no overt intention to discriminate. Workplace policies that have been in place for many years, even if they are not necessary for the effective performance of the job, often remain in place and result in exclusion until they are challenged.

To the extent that many workplaces and institutions have numerous policies that respond to the needs and interests of those who have been in the dominant majority, such policies may unwittingly result in significant exclusion. This meso-level of systemic discrimination is complex because it is often invisible. The exclusion results from the equal application of apparently neutral policies. Everyone is treated the same, but the effects are different. The dominant policies are simply seen as the way things are and should be. Imagining alternative ways of doing things is difficult and often resisted by those who benefit from existing rules and institutional norms.

Although adverse impact discrimination is often associated with *unintentional* discrimination, it is important to note that unintentional discrimination may have an intentional component in two situations. First, an apparently neutral rule or policy may be used to screen out certain kinds of applicants intentionally. Second, once employers, supervisors, or co-workers become aware of the inequitable and exclusionary effects of a "neutral" rule, and do nothing to change it or to accommodate an individual adversely affected by it, what was once unintentional discrimination becomes much more intentional. Sometimes this happens when an individual who is negatively affected requests some accommodation or exemption.

Those who have the power to provide such accommodation or an exemption have a choice in many instances — they can say no, and insist that everyone abide by the rule, or they can allow for some flexibility. But once the adverse effects have been brought to their attention, the line between unintentional and intentional discrimination is blurred.[34] Moreover, beyond providing individual exemptions or accommodation, it becomes important to ask whether or not the rule should be changed for everyone. When rules or policies that have adverse effects on historically under-represented groups continue to be enforced without question or reconsideration, another aspect of systemic discrimination — one that is linked to overt institutional resistance to change — becomes apparent.

What is significant in terms of anti-discrimination law is that it doesn't matter if it is intentional or unintentional. The key issue is what effect the rule or policy has on the individual who experiences the discrimination. Both intentional and unintentional sources of discrimination are prohibited. As Justice La Forest wrote in an important decision involving sexual harassment, Canadian anti-discrimination law "is concerned with the *effects* of discrimination rather than its *causes* (or motivations)."[35] In that judgment, the Supreme Court of Canada also emphasized the importance of remedies aimed at the employer (rather than simply individual remedies against the harasser). The Court explained that "only an employer can remedy undesirable effects; only an employer can provide the most important remedy — a healthy work environment."[36] To deal with recurring systemic problems of discrimination and harassment, workplace environments and policies require change. It is not simply a matter of individual misconduct.

Both individual interactional discrimination and institutional discrimination are sometimes described as systemic when they are widespread or pervasive. Such is the case when there are numerous policies or rules that have discriminatory adverse effects, or, as noted above, when there are numerous incidents of individual misconduct and harassment.[37] Individual stories of discrimination may also help us to make connections between individual acts of discrimination (the micro), discrete institutional policies and practices that exclude or disadvantage (the meso), and the larger political and structural context (the macro).

Macro-level: Broader Societal and Legal Inequalities

The final layer of systemic discrimination is the macro level, which concerns the ways institutional exclusion is related to realities, histories, and inequalities *beyond* the boundaries of the institution and across the life cycle of the individuals affected. It is increasingly recognized that the institutional level alone does not go far enough. Institutions are situated within society, and what occurs inside an organization is deeply connected to the conditions and realities outside of that institution.

First, it is critical to recognize how discrimination in one institutional context is affected by experiences and realities in other institutions. For example, obligations and responsibilities in the family have an important impact on workplace equality or inequality, and access to affordable child care makes an enormous difference for parents in the workplace. Similarly, educational histories affect professional opportunities. Sometimes exclusion from workplace opportunities is related to prior educational inequalities or inequitable familial obligations. Yet our anti-discrimination laws focus on one institutional context — for example, the workplace *or* schools, but not the dynamic interaction between the two. There is some recognition of how what goes on outside of a workplace or educational institution may have an impact on individual circumstances or opportunities, but we tend to deal with discrete problems of discrimination in silos and without recognition of the cumulative effects of discrimination in individual lives.

Second, the effects of discrimination in one sector or institution at a particular time in an individual's life extend over an individual's life cycle. For example, if a woman experiences gender-based wage discrimination during her time in the paid labour force, this will have an impact on her economic and social well-being when she is older. The higher incidence of poverty among elderly women is partly linked to the discrimination and inequitable opportunities they faced in the labour force. Recognizing the ways inequality is a broader problem that impacts opportunities across a wide spectrum of society and over time reminds us of the limits of anti-discrimination law and the need for a wide array of integrated political and social responses.

A third element of a macro-level approach concerns the effects of public policies and laws. An array of governmental policies and regulatory provisions (at the municipal, provincial, federal, and international levels) set out the rules and regulations within which institutions must function. Indeed, anti-discrimination guarantees are part of this regulatory context. Occupational health and safety provisions, environmental regulations, pay equity, employment equity, and accessibility laws for persons with disabilities provide additional examples of laws that have important effects on workplace equalities. When the source of discrimination is related to governmental policies or laws, constitutional equality rights protections may be raised to challenge those policies or laws.

Developing a macro-systemic approach therefore requires an engagement with these broader historical, structural, legal, and political realities. Most legal cases, however, tend to focus on specific individual misconduct or specific institutional policies or rules; anti-discrimination law has difficulty addressing larger macro realities. Nonetheless, it is useful to keep these three levels in mind (and to consider the broader macro issues) when seeking to understand discrimination, particularly its systemic and dynamic dimensions. Examining systemic inequalities at multiple levels is also important when thinking about how to develop remedies that compensate for past discrimination and prevent future discrimination.

Conclusion

ACTION TRAVAIL DES FEMMES was a landmark case because the Supreme Court of Canada recognized the concept of systemic discrimination, for the first time, and affirmed the importance of remedies that would address and prevent the risks of future discrimination. Since the decision, there have been other cases involving systemic discrimination. Many have arisen in the workplace context, but educational institutions and government services are other important contexts where systemic discrimination has been challenged.[38] In some cases, the systemic dimensions of the discrimination have not been acknowledged and only individual remedies have been ordered;[39] in other cases, the litigation process has been very slow and has involved numerous procedural delays before a hearing on the merits of the case.

Given the difficulties of litigating systemic cases, there has been a shift towards enacting legislative initiatives that require workplaces and educational organizations to identify systemic inequalities and to develop proactive policies and programs to eliminate them.[40] Public inquiries and commissions have also been set up to identify persistent systemic inequalities and discrimination.[41] Regardless of the legal or policy strategy pursued, it remains vital to keep in mind the dynamic dimensions of systemic discrimination, and the ways in which it implicates micro-level human interactions, institutional policies at the meso-level, and dynamic macro or structural inequalities.

– 4 –

Taking Positive Steps:
Equity Initiatives

Systemic discrimination requires systemic remedies.

— JUDGE ROSALIE SILBERMAN ABELLA, EQUALITY IN EMPLOYMENT,
ROYAL COMMISSION REPORT, 1984[1]

CONCRETE STORIES OF exclusion, inequality, and injustice help us to understand why equity initiatives are important components of anti-discrimination law. This chapter does not focus on a specific individual story; rather, it explores a range of different types of pro-active equity initiatives and the underlying justifications for them. Equity initiatives are designed to remedy and to prevent discrimination by breaking cycles of historic and ongoing discrimination. They are borne of the realization that addressing discrimination retroactively on an individual case-by-case basis is an inadequate response to problems that are systemic, pervasive, and entrenched.

I begin by tracing the historical development of equity initatives in the employment and educational context. I then outline the defining features of an expansive approach to equity initiatives. On the basis of this broad definition of equity programs, I assess the ways in which such initiatives respond to both the historical inequalities and the current realities of systemic discrimination.

The Development of Equity Initiatives and Affirmative Action
Historical Preferential Treatment Policies

Some of the earliest preferential policy initiatives in Canada involved a number of special programs for returning veterans. Beginning in the aftermath of World War I, special veterans' preferences in land grants for farming, bank loans, and access to educational retraining were provided. In addition, veteran hiring preferences in the federal public service were introduced in 1918.[2] These preferences also advanced the rights of persons with disabilities, since many of the veterans had been disabled in war. Most people did not question the fairness of these special benefits and preferences for returning veterans. Because they risked their lives, and in many cases were permanently disabled, veterans were, and still are, generally viewed as deserving of some reciprocal benefits to recognize their sacrifices. This continuing chapter in our history provides important insights into why preferential treatment initiatives seem justified.[3] It also relates to current challenges faced by people with disabilities seeking equitable access to the workplace.[4]

A second wave of preferential hiring policies emerged in the 1960s and involved efforts to increase the hiring of Francophones in the federal civil service, particularly in upper level positions. In 1962, the *Royal Commission on Government Organization* recommended that the "federal government adopt active measures to develop bilingual capacities among its employees on a selective basis" and "intensify its efforts to attract and retain more of the highly qualified young people of French Canada capable of advancement to senior ranks."[5] A few years later, in 1967, the Royal Commission on Biculturalism and Bilingualism again identified under-representation in the federal civil service as a major problem:

> Other countries with two languages and cultures have seen clearly there can be no equal partnership without the active participation of both cultures in their administrations [i.e. public service]. Such participation rarely, if ever, develops on its own ... it is usually the

result of positive government measures affecting the structure of the civil service. [6]

As noted by John Carson, a visionary leader of the Public Service Commission, in his Annual Report of 1972:

> The existing application of the merit system has failed in one respect. It has not given us a representative public service. In the past, the service has been dominated by English speaking males. There are indications that this dominance exercises a subtle if unintended discrimination against other groups competing for jobs and careers in Canada's public service.[7]

Effective proactive hiring initiatives were introduced, along with increased bilingualism requirements for numerous government positions. As a result, by 1978, the under-representation of Francophones had been largely rectified.[8] Currently, given that bilingualism is required for many upper-level positions in the public service, there continues to be a fairly strong representation of Francophones; nevertheless, English continues to be the predominant working language.[9]

Discrimination against women in the workplace became a focus of equal-opportunity initiatives in the 1970s. The *Report of the Royal Commission on the Status of Women* documented discrimination against women in a wide range of sectors in society, including employment. The report recommended a variety of affirmative action programs, including that the federal government "increase significantly" the number of women named to a variety of federally appointed bodies and that the federal Public Service Commission (PSC) and federal departments "take special steps to increase the number of women appointed to occupations and professions not traditionally female."[10] The majority's strong recommendations in favour of affirmative action programs for women were not, however, taken up by the federal public service: "It was the view of the PSC at the time that the existing merit system, with no restrictions on women, was adequate to increase the representation of women."[11] The Abella Report in 1984 suggested that the programs that were implemented after the Royal Commission of the Status of Women were largely voluntary, and "had little impact on the composition of the public sector workforce."[12]

For racialized communities, prior to the reforms of the 1980s that are discussed below, there were only sporadic affirmative action initiatives. A few programs designed to increase the representation of Indigenous peoples in a variety of sectors began in the 1970s.[13] For example, the University of Saskatchewan developed the Native Law Program in 1973.[14] These programs, while seen as beneficial, did not have a widespread impact.[15] Proactive employment initiatives for the Black community first emerged in Nova Scotia, with the 1973 Black Employment Program in Halifax, which was designed to increase Black employment in the federal public service stationed in the province.[16] As the Abella Report documents, however, by 1982 the initiative had not succeeded in raising the representation of Black Nova Scotians in the federal public service in the region to even half their representation in the community at large.[17] Other racialized communities that had been subject to discrimination historically, including Chinese and Japanese Canadians, were not included in any early equity initiatives.[18]

In the United States, the historical context for affirmative action was quite different. It emerged primarily as a response to the civil rights movement and struggles by Black communities to end persistent racial inequalities in education and employment.[19] The term "affirmative action" initially emerged in the employment context in early labour legislation.[20] Shirley Wilcher, the executive director for the American Association for Access, Equity and Diversity, explains that "[t]o take an 'affirmative action' was to literally act affirmatively — not allowing events to run their course but rather having the government (or employers) take an active role in treating employees fairly."[21] While equal employment opportunities were the focus of some earlier presidential executive orders, President Kennedy was "the first president to marry the term 'affirmative action' with its modern-day connotation of a policy seeking to ensure racial equality."[22] He issued Executive Order 10925 in 1961, which required government contractors to "take affirmative action to ensure that applicants are employed and that employees are treated during employment without regard to their race, creed, color, or national origin."[23] A few years later, President Johnson issued Executive Order 11246,[24] requiring contractors "take affirmative action to ensure that applicants are employed, and that employees are treated during employment, without regard to their race, color, religion, sex or national origin."[25] In 2014, Obama signed another executive order to add sexual orientation and gender identity to that list.[26]

The Emergence of Employment Equity in the Contemporary Canadian Workplace

By the early 1980s in Canada, there was growing concern that certain groups, including women, persons with disabilities, Indigenous peoples, and racialized groups were not being accorded equal opportunities in the workplace. In 1983, the federal government appointed then Judge Silberman Abella to examine equality in employment for four groups in Canadian society — women, visible minorities, Indigenous peoples, and persons with disabilities. The Royal Commission on Equality in Employment was mandated "to inquire into the most efficient, effective and equitable means of promoting employment opportunities, eliminating systemic discrimination and assisting all individuals to compete for employment opportunities on an equal basis."[27] After consulting widely, Justice Abella issued her report, documenting barriers to equality and recommending the development of proactive employment equity initiatives. She recommended federal legislation to require federally regulated employers to develop employment equity programs. She also proposed contract compliance initiatives.[28] These initiatives consist of governmental policies to only purchase goods and services from businesses that agree to develop and implement employment equity programs — incentivizing equity in the private sector through government spending power.[29]

Concerned with negative reaction to "affirmative action" in the United States, she preferred the term "equity." As she explained:

> In devising their unique program, the Americans have called it
> affirmative action. In most people's minds, it has become associated

with the imposition of quotas. In creating our own program in Canada, we may not wish to use quotas and we should therefore seriously consider calling it something else if we want to avoid some of the intellectual resistance and confusion. It is not imperative that we do so, but it is worth considering.[30]

Justice Abella, therefore, endorsed what she called "employment equity."

Far from being limited to preferential treatment and quotas, Justice Abella's vision for employment equity was much larger. It began with the identification and elimination of discriminatory barriers at work and extended to pay equity and the provision of child care. Her objective was to develop a systemic and proactive approach to achieving equality.[31] She recognized that a retroactive individual complaints approach to legal enforcement works well when problems are isolated and rare. But when problems are deeply embedded in conscious and unconscious biases, as well as in policies and practices that appear neutral but that have adverse effects, a retroactive complaints model is ineffective. Instead, a proactive model that identifies barriers to inclusion and sources of adverse impact discrimination provides a much more promising model for remedying systemic institutional inequalities.

In the wake of Justice Abella's recommendations for proactive equity initiatives, in 1986 the federal government introduced the *Employment Equity Act*.[32] Expanded and strengthened in 1995, the legislation requires federally regulated private-sector employers, as well as many federal public-sector organizations, to develop employment equity plans to increase the representation of the four designated groups.[33] The federal law does not reach provincially regulated workplaces, and to date, the provinces have not enacted comprehensive employment equity laws. Legislated employment equity initiatives at the provincial level have generally been limited to public sector workplaces. The purpose of employment equity is clearly described at the outset of the federal Act:

The purpose of this Act is to achieve equality in the workplace so that no person shall be denied employment opportunities or benefits for reasons unrelated to ability and, in the fulfilment of that goal, to correct the conditions of disadvantage in employment experienced by women, Aboriginal peoples, persons with disabilities and members of visible minorities by giving effect to the principle that employment equity means more than treating persons in the same way but also requires special measures and the accommodation of differences.

Pursuant to the legislation, employers are required to:

- Identify and eliminate employment barriers that result from policies and practices; and
- Institute positive policies and practices and make reasonable accommodations to increase the representation of designated groups.[34]

The federal legislation has been in effect for over thirty years, and it is in need of modernization. There are concerns about ensuring more effective enforcement, the terminology used to describe the designated groups back in 1986 has changed, and there is widespread agreement that LGBTQ2S+ groups should be added.[35]

The federal government also established the Federal Contractors Program, which extends the reach of equity initiatives to provincial workplaces. It requires that all provincially regulated contractors with at least 100 permanent employees commit to implementing employment equity as a prerequisite to receiving federal government contracts or services of over $1 million.[36] The commitments under this program entail ongoing obligations: contractors must collect workforce information, conduct a workforce analysis, establish numerical goals, and make "reasonable efforts to ensure that reasonable progress towards full representation" are made. If found non-compliant, the contractors are ineligible for federal goods and services contracts, standing offers, and supply arrangements and may face the termination of existing contracts.[37]

Beginning in the late 1980s, pay equity laws were also introduced in some provinces.[38] Such laws are designed to redress gender-based inequities in wages by assessing the comparable worth of predominantly male and female jobs in relation to skill, effort, working conditions, and responsibilities.[39] The scope of each province's legislation varies: in some provinces, pay equity requirements only apply to public sector workers; in others, larger private sector employers are also required to develop proactive pay equity plans.[40] In 2018, the federal government enacted a new *Pay Equity Act*, which is intended to establish a proactive pay equity regime in the federal public and private sectors.[41]

Education Equity

Unlike in the employment context, equity initiatives to increase the representation of historically excluded groups in the education sector are voluntary and not mandated by any legislation. One domain where equity initiatives have played an important role is in the university context, particularly in relation to access to professional programs, such as law or medicine.[42] The Indigenous Black and Mi'kmaq Initiative (IB&M) at the Schulich School of Law at Dalhousie University provides one example of the kinds of initiatives that have emerged.[43] It is a wide-ranging program that includes admissions outreach, a pre-law preparatory course, financial and educational support, and assistance in career planning and job searches.

The IB&M Initiative is designed to redress discrimination and the historical under-representation of the Nova Scotian Black community and the Mi'kmaq people in legal studies and in the legal profession. It was developed at the time of the Royal Commission on the Donald Marshall Jr. Prosecution, which was tasked with examining the wrongful conviction of an innocent Indigenous man.[44] The Commission concluded that the wrongful conviction of Donald Marshall Jr was the by-product of systemic racism in the criminal justice system. One of its recommendations was to increase the representation of Black and Indigenous lawyers and judges in the criminal justice system. The Commission specifically recommended that the IB&M Initiative be supported with additional provincial and federal funding.[45] The IB&M Initiative was also designed to respond to the social justice needs of the Black and Mi'kmaq communities in Nova Scotia and beyond. It would contribute to ensuring that lawyers and judges would better reflect the demographic diversity of Nova Scotia and be knowledgeable and sensitive to problems of systemic racism. While the IB&M program is not limited to Black and Indigenous individuals from Nova Scotia, it is noteworthy that it was set up to address specific, local, contextual realities of exclusion and historical injustice. Note as well that the IB&M program was undertaken voluntarily; it was not a court-ordered remedy, nor was it mandated by legislation.

In the United States, many universities have also voluntarily developed affirmative action initiatives to redress historical under-representation of racialized communities and to increase student diversity.[46] These initiatives have been the focus of numerous court cases challenging the constitutionality of preferential treatment.[47] In an early important decision on affirmative action (*Regents of the University of California v Bakke*[48]) the pursuit of diversity was, despite a very fractured decision, established as a compelling justification for including considerations of race in the admissions process (among other dimensions of diversity). Allan Bakke had been refused admission to medical school despite scoring higher on the standardized test than some individuals admitted pursuant to the affirmative action program. Unlike the Canadian court decisions, historical subordination and exclusion of racialized groups was not accepted by a majority of the justices as a justification for affirmative action. Thus, as discussed further below, in the wake of the *Bakke* case, diversity became the touchstone for justification of affirmative action.[49]

Defining Features: More Than Just Group-Based Preferences

FROM THIS BRIEF historical overview of equity initiatives and affirmative action, it is possible to identify some recurring and defining features. One way of defining equity initiatives is simply to say that they are *proactive initiatives designed to redress historical and ongoing discrimination against individuals from group(s) that have experienced historical discrimination and that continue to experience exclusion and mistreatment.* Rather than waiting for individuals to file complaints about incidents of discrimination in a piecemeal and retroactive way, *equity initiatives engage in a proactive review of policies, practices, rules, and patterns of under-representation to identify barriers to inclusion and achievement.* They then set out to *address and redress these barriers.* Normally, equity initiatives are developed in specific institutional contexts, such as in educational programs or workplaces. The broad definition that I have set out above means that equity programs (or affirmative action) cannot simply be equated with group-based preferences or quotas. Special group-based preferences or even quotas may be part of some equity programs in certain circumstances, but there are lots of proactive equity initiatives that can be developed to address institutional inequities that do not involve preferential treatment.

As a *first step* to implementing an equity initiative, an institution must undertake *an assessment of the problems of inequality, discrimination, and barriers to equality that exist* within it. Once those are identified, *a second step* is the *elimination of inequitable institutional barriers* to the extent possible. The removal of barriers is thus a critical component of proactive equity initiatives that does not require any group-based preferences; rather, it is a matter of removing institutional sources of group-based disadvantages. Such a strategy does not involve any special treatment. It requires a change in the way things are done to make educational programs and workplaces more inclusive. For example, the IB&M initative involves community outreach as well as financial support for students.[50] Because they implicate changes in the institution for everyone, the elimination of barriers is actually quite radical — it is about transforming institutional policies and rules across the board. It goes beyond simply letting historically excluded individuals into an unchallenged institutional status quo.

A *third step* of proactive equity initiatives involves *identification of necessary, long-term, group-based differential treatment* as part of a policy of *reasonable accommodation.* Some policies and rules that are necessary for the safe, effective, or efficient operation of an educational institution, workplace, or profession may nevertheless fail to respond to the needs of certain minority groups. Take, for example, workplace schedules and religious observance: it may not make sense to change working hours if only a small minority of workers are affected by the need for time off for religious reasons; instead, we may leave the schedule intact but provide accommodation for the individual who needs time off for religious observance. Similarly, if an individual has a hearing impairment and needs to use a telephone for work, amplifying equipment may be required to ensure that the individual can use the telephone, but not all telephones need to be changed. Differential treatment in such circumstances responds to specific needs of an individual with a disability. These types of accommodations involve long-term differential treatment; they are sometimes ordered retroactively in the wake of a complaint before a human rights tribunal or court. But they may also be put in place as part of a proactive equity initiative. They exemplify situations where differential treatment secures equality of outcomes — a goal often associated with the idea of equity. These accommodations are not preferential treatment policies, but are simply designed to recognize and respond to group-based differences. From a fairness perspective, these types of policies are generally not controversial, or at least less controversial than affirmative action policies. Proactive reasonable accommodations are important (though often unacknowledged) components of equity initiatives.

In cases where there is significant under-representation and a well-documented pattern of historical discrimination in a specific employment, professional, or educational context, a *fourth step* and additional component of equity initiatives or affirmative action entails *group-based preferences to expedite the achievement of equality*.[51] These types of measures involve preferential treatment for individuals from groups that have been and continue to be subject to discrimination and exclusion. These measures are controversial because they use group-based categorizations to redress the effects of group-based inequalities — meaning that individuals are given priority based on their categorization, rather than individual circumstances. While I suggest below that these group-based preferential measures are justified in some contexts, I believe that they should only be relied upon once policies and practices that have discriminatory

effects have been revised and ameliorated. The reason it is so important to eliminate barriers and change institutional policies first is that
otherwise, you are developing preferential treatment without first
challenging the institutional history and the continuing status quo
that caused the inequality. What do I mean by this? If you start with
preferential treatment programs without changing institutional
policies or practices that contribute to the under-representation of
certain groups, you are not addressing the underlying causes of the
exclusion, and success therefore remains premised on a requirement of assimilation. Individuals labelled "different" must fit into
an institutional status quo that has been historically exclusionary
and unwelcoming. In addition, institutional policy changes can be
more effective at benefitting individuals who experience intersecting
forms of disadvantage: since the measures target the source of the
inequity, rather than prioritizing specific groups, they can help those
who need them the most.[52] As a result, this approach can also be less
controversial. Strangely, many affirmative action initiatives seem
to start with preferential treatment initiatives without identifying
and eliminating policies and practices that have contributed to and
will continue to result in exclusion and discrimination. Such transformative initiatives also avoid the need to identify which groups are
deserving of preferential treatment and which individuals fit within
particular identity groups in a world of increasingly complex and
hybrid identities.

As the above discussion suggests, equity initiatives and affirmative action entail much more than special group-based preferences.
As outlined in the *Action travail des femmes* case discussed in Chapter 3, after concluding that CN had engaged in persistent and widespread sex discrimination, the Human Rights Tribunal ordered two
things: first, a review of the barriers and the elimination of exclusionary policies not necessary for the effective performance of the
job (for example, a welding requirement for entry-level railyard
jobs); and second, hiring quotas for entry-level jobs (set up in relation
to the percentage of women in the labour market). The quotas were
endorsed as a necessary part of the remedies, given the particularly
egregious history of gender-based discrimination and the continuing

under-representation of women in blue-collar jobs at CN.[53] But they were part of a larger employment equity remedy that began with the revision of workplace policies. While a focus on institutional change reduces some of the controversy around affirmative action or equity programs and reduces the need for preferential group-based treatment policies, given the depths of historical and ongoing inequalities, it is sometimes necessary to take specific group-based measures to increase representation and inclusion. As Justice Harry Blackmun of the US Supreme Court put it in *Bakke*, the famous case involving a race-based preferential treatment program at a California medical school, "[i]n order to get beyond racism, we must first take account of race."[54] So are there justifications for giving individuals preferential treatment based on their group-based identities?

Continuing Controversies and Justifications

IN CANADA, EQUITY initiatives are mandated by legislation and endorsed both in human rights legislation and in our Constitution as necessary to ensure the attainment of equality for all.[55] They are understood as measures that advance rather than undermine equality. As Justice Abella explained in her Royal Commission Report, equity programs are not about "reverse discrimination"; they are "the beginning of equality."[56] While lawsuits alleging so-called reverse discrimination abound in the United States, there are relatively few here in Canada. Perhaps this is due to the explicit endorsement of affirmative action in the *Canadian Charter of Rights and Freedoms* in section 15(2). The equality rights protected in the *Charter* cannot be used to challenge laws, government programs, or initiatives that are aimed at "the amelioration of conditions of disadvantaged individuals or groups including those that are disadvantaged because of race, national or ethnic origin, colour, religion, sex, age or mental or physical disability." As noted by the Supreme Court of Canada, "the *Charter* seeks to protect efforts by the state to develop and adopt remedial schemes designed to assist disadvantaged groups."[57] Provided that the government can show that it developed the special program to assist disadvantaged groups, it does not violate the equality guarantees of the *Charter*. As Justice Abella has explained, the purpose of section 15(2) is to "save ameliorative programs from the charge of 'reverse discrimination'.... It protects ameliorative programs for disadvantaged groups from claims by those the program was not intended to benefit that the ameliorative program discriminates against them."[58] Similar provisions exist in human rights statutes at the provincial and federal levels.

The Supreme Court of Canada has further endorsed employment equity initiatives, including hiring quotas, when they are needed to redress historical discrimination and ongoing under-representation. In the *Action travail des femmes* case, Chief Justice Brian Dickson outlined three important justifications for employment equity programs:

> First, by countering the cumulative effects of systemic discrimination, such a program renders further discrimination pointless....
>
> Secondly, by placing members of the group that had previously been excluded into the heart of the work place and by allowing them to prove ability on the job, the employment equity scheme addresses the attitudinal problem of stereotyping....
>
> Thirdly, an employment equity program helps to create what has been termed a "critical mass" of the previously excluded group in the work place. This "critical mass" has important effects. The presence of a significant number of individuals from the targeted group eliminates the problems of "tokenism."[59]

In upholding the remedial order made by the Human Rights Tribunal, Chief Justice Dickson also stated:

> Systemic remedies must be built upon the experience of the past so as to prevent discrimination in the future. Specific hiring goals ... are a rational attempt to impose a systemic remedy on a systemic problem.

Although this case was decided a number of years ago, it remains one of the most robust endorsements of equity programs, including group-based quotas, by the Supreme Court of Canada and has been widely cited. In short, Canadian anti-discrimination laws, the Canadian *Charter*, and certain court decisions endorse the legality of special affirmative action programs and insulate them from being challenged in courts and tribunals. But how do these programs advance basic fairness and justice?

We live in a world built upon layers and layers of historical and continuing injustices. Children are born into circumstances of wealth, poverty, desperation, beauty, love, hate, desolation, peace, violence — that are far beyond their control. This is the world in which we must apply our laws that mandate equality and non-discrimination. Equal rights and anti-discrimination laws were first enacted with the underlying hope that we could simply treat everyone the same and achieve equality.[60] Yet we now realize that such an approach provides only formal equality — and fails to secure actual or substantive equality. To ensure equality in outcomes, it is necessary to recognize and address underlying inequities in society. Relying on a formal equality model or an individual treatment approach in a society of deeply embedded social and economic inequalities is a recipe for continued inequality. Those who are already privileged benefit, while those whose life circumstances are much more disadvantaged continue to lose or be left out.

For example, if you attend a prestigious private high school, your chances of accessing a selective university program are enhanced. And your educational privileges have likely better prepared you for the rigours of university studies, thus increasing the likelihood of success in accessing the next step along the way. In this way, cycles of privilege and disadvantage continue to accumulate, reinforcing the idea that people deserve what they achieve. It is of course true that individuals from privileged backgrounds merit what they achieve, but they have not achieved it alone. They have achieved it because of their access to financial, social, educational, and familial privileges, support, and resources. So when we think about achieving equality in a world of social and economic inequalities, we need to address the underlying inequalities in access to social, economic, psychological, community, and familial support and resources;[61] this recognition of inequitable starting points prompted the development of equity initiatives. Equity initatives advance the principle that those whose life circumstances are much less privileged than others deserve equitable access to the full panoply of educational, social, political, and employment opportunities. While the past and present are deeply intertwined, it nonetheless is useful to delineate justifications based on both historical and present injustices, as well as to identify other justifications prevalent in debates about affirmative action.

Redressing Historical Injustices and Inequalities

One important contributor to the debate regarding the fairness of affirmative action in the United States is Bernard Boxill, who wrote a book entitled *Blacks and Social Justice*.[62] In it, he develops an argument justifying the need to redress historical wrongs, even by those who did not engage in the wrongful conduct themselves. He observes that individuals who did not engage in the wrongful acts were nonetheless privileged by past wrongs. By analogy, according to Boxill, if you are given a stolen bicycle, you are ethically and morally required to give it back to its rightful owner even though you did not do anything wrong yourself.[63] In other words, you may be the beneficiary of past wrongs, and despite your innocence, you still have obligations to make reparations. Intergenerational justice requires taking past injustices and privileges into account in developing current policies and practices. Beyond affirmative action, debates about the need for reparations engage the connections between the present and the past.[64] One of the most compelling justifications of preferential treatment is the need to compensate for the ongoing effects of past injustices.

In some instances, the past wrongs can be linked to specific institutional policies or practices. In other cases, they involve broader societal inequalities that have inter-sectoral effects (for example, denial of educational opportunities impacts employment).[65] Developing preferential treatment to respond to specific documented discrimination in a workplace or educational institution (that is, explicit exclusionary policies in the past, or significant evidence of under-representation) is sometimes ordered as a remedy (as in the case of *Action travail des femmes* discussed in Chapter 3) or done voluntarily in response to a report or information documenting historical and continuing exclusion. Developing preferential treatment initiatives to respond to extra-institutional inequalities or societal inequalities at a more general level tend to be more controversial, since the connection between past inequalities and current institutional policies is less obvious and direct. Even when equity programs are adopted, the broader context is not always adequately considered. For example, Carol Aylward (former director of the IB&M program) has emphasized the importance of acknowledging the historical and continuing "struggle by Black and Mi'kmaq peoples to obtain an education despite forced assimilation, segregation, and oppression."[66] Redressing these historical inequalities and group-based patterns of under-representation remains one of the most compelling justifications for preferential treatment programs.

In the case of war veterans in Canada, there is widespread acceptance of the importance of preferential treatment. We understand that they have sacrificed their physical and mental well-being and we owe them special consideration in return. There is also growing recognition of the need for reparations to redress historic wrongs and the colonial policies that continue to impact Indigenous peoples. Similarly, it is generally acknowledged that persons with disabilities have been unjustly excluded from a whole range of social, political, and economic opportunities. However, other kinds of historic injustice confront greater controversy. When women are included in preferential treatment initiatives, there is often a sense that discrimination is a thing of the past and that preferential treatment provides unjustified assistance to economically privileged women. Race-based exclusions (other than those linked to Indigenous peoples) have never been fully recognized in Canada in the same way that they have been in the United States. Though slavery existed in Canada, its smaller numbers made it invisible to many.[67] The need for equity initiatives to redress anti-Black racism has only recently gained momentum in the wake of the social mobilization of Black Lives Matter.[68] As we can see, the justifications for equity initiatives based on historic injustices can be controversial even in the Canadian context, but they are a compelling reminder of our collective responsibility to connect the past to the present.

Redressing Current Injustices and Inequalities

While the recognition of past injustices in society that have caused deeply embedded systemic and structural disadvantages to particular groups provides a compelling rationale for equity initiatives, it is also important to recognize ongoing injustices as an additional justification for preferential treatment. The legacies of past injustices continue to infuse the present. Injustice and unfair treatment resulting from non-recognition of skills, potential, and abilities; undervaluing; stereotyping; and conscious and unconscious bias are unfortunately alive and well in our everyday institutions. Why is it that we continue to have such a significant under-representation of women; racialized individuals; persons with disabilities; and openly lesbian, gay, or trans individuals in positions of institutional and political power?

Justice requires that we account for continuing sources of inequality that compromise fairness and equal opportunity. If we can identify ongoing sources of bias and inequality, then some preferential treatment may well be justified. Indeed, failure to provide such preferences leaves the hidden biases unremedied. Social science research has documented the continued risks of exclusion linked to both conscious and unconscious stereotypes and prejudices.[69] While these biases are integrally connected to histories of under-representation and inequitable institutional norms, they continue in the present and constitute often imperceptible sources of discrimination. Inequalities borne of conscious and unconscious biases linked to sexism, racism, able-bodyism, heterosexism, Islamophobia, and antisemitism continue to infuse institutional decision making. Recognition of these biases sustains the call for equity initiatives based on *continued* inequities — rectifying, for example, not only historical inequality, but also current under-representation in decision-making processes. In short, justifications for equity programs and affirmative action are rooted in the need to remedy both past and continuing wrongs that are linked both to individual acts of exclusion and to deeply embedded systemic and structural inequalities.

Policy-Based Justifications

The justifications of historical and current injustice are important; they connect the fairness of preferential treatment to the groups directly affected by them, both in terms of historical inequalities and continued conscious and unconscious sources of bias. However, there are also other justifications for equitable initiatives, linked to the need to address certain societal concerns. Such justifications tend to view equity initiatives as temporary exceptions to the principle of equality that are necessary to advance important public policy goals. For example, institutional diversity has been accepted as an important policy objective for educational institutions that justifies the consideration of race, national or ethnic origin, gender, and other sources of diversity for student admissions, or staff hiring or promotions.[70]

Another policy-based justification for equity initiatives that is sometimes advanced is the importance of having professionals and service providers from the communities they are to serve. For example, some have argued that police forces that are representative of their communities will be better able to respond to the needs of the citizenry they are to serve and protect — particularly in the context of arrests, prosecutions, and the use of force.[71] The Royal Commission on the Donald Marshall, Jr., Prosecution pressed for more representation of members of racial minorities in occupations like correctional system guards and administrators, justices of the peace, juries, and police forces.[72] Similar arguments have also been advanced with respect to other aspects of government and the public service. To meet the needs of the public, the diversity of the public must be reflected in the institutions making and implementing policy.[73]

A further policy justification for equity initatives is the need for role models who reflect the diversity of society. According to this logic, increasing the representation of individuals from historically excluded or under-represented groups functions to provide individuals from these groups with someone to look to as a role model and potentially a mentor.[74] It is crucial to recall, however, that a focus on individual role models may be premised on tokenism and may "eclipse attention to the systemic nature of exclusion."[75] Despite this important caveat, the policy goal of providing role models continues to be an important justification for preferential treatment programs.

Conclusion

EQUITY INITIATIVES CHALLENGE institutional actors to take proactive measures to redress historical and continuing exclusion and inequitable treatment. Yet one persistent problem with many equity initiatives is their tendency to leave the institutional status quo intact.[76] Individuals from historically under-represented groups are required to fit into an institution that has been shaped and informed by the values and norms of more privileged and dominant groups in society. Definitions of success are biased in favour of traditional ways of being. It is important, therefore, to ensure that equity initiatives challenge norms and assumptions within institutions.

Another challenge for current equity initiatives is their focus on inequalities within one specific institutional context, such as a workplace or educational setting. While it is critical to examine institutions as sites of discrimination and revise policies to make them more equitable and welcoming of diverse communities, institutional discrimination is situated within a broader structural context of societal inequality. Inequality occurs across different institutional sectors of our lives, across life cycles and generations. Iris Marion Young refers to this matrix of injustice — for which there is no particularly identifiable wrongdoer — as structural injustice.[77] For example, the IB&M initative responds to legacies of colonialism and ongoing societal inequalities. The university is not necessarily the cause of all of these inequities, but it certainly is an institution in which they can be partially remedied. Understanding the ways in which inequalities generated from outside of an institution impact inequalities within it is essential for developing effective institutional equity policies. At the same time, it is important to recognize that institutionally based equity initiatives must be supplemented by initiatives in other institutions and in society at large. By building equity initiatives into the institutions of everyday life, we can contribute to the larger project of ending structural injustices. Day-to-day engagements with building equity into institutional policies and practices are not a panacea to the complex and multiple problems of discrimination and inequality. Still, they are a tangible and important component of the larger quest for a more equitable society.

5

Equitable Freedom and Dancing Shoes

I love getting all dressed up. I do. I love my pretty dresses. I love the way my heels sound as I walk (or strut) around my apartment. I love the Beyoncé pump-up music my friends and I listen to as we get ready to head out. I feel carefree and unburdened by my thoughts and worries. I don't see anything wrong with me sincerely enjoying these simple, gendered clichés of womanhood, as long as they don't limit my self-expression. I understand where these norms originate.

Every so often, when I've decided to put on one of my sexy dresses and go out on the town, my critical feminist perspective slithers in unannounced and bites the head off my "carefree" night.

— AYLA LEFKOWITZ, "DRESSES, DRINKS AND MISOGYNY: A NIGHT AT THE ANNUAL RUGBY BANQUET," 2012[1]

Yeohee Im was 23 when she left her hometown of Busan, South Korea, to travel halfway across the world to work with Verdu, a renowned electrical engineering professor.

...

When they arrived at Verdu's home, Im says they poured some drinks and turned on the movie. Im says she sat at the edge of one of the two couches in Verdu's living room. Verdu chose to sit on the same couch and sat "right next to [her]" with their "arms touching at least some of the time," according to Im.

While the movie was playing, Im says Verdu asked if she had a boyfriend and put his arm around her shoulder for "a short time." Im says she was very confused and started to panic.

"It was happening in his home," she said. "And right in front of me there was a photo of him and his daughter. I was panicking, can this be sexual harassment? I know that his daughter is a similar age to me. I was wondering, is he doing this because I am a similar age to his daughter? In that moment, I was just panicking."

— ALANNA VAGIANOS, "GRAD STUDENT SAYS PRINCETON PROF WHO SEXUALLY HARASSED HER WAS GIVEN SLAP ON THE WRIST," 2017[2]

"Going into it, I felt like I trusted the police," says Ava ... "I had no reason not to trust the process."

Looking back, she describes an abrupt loss of faith.

"I started to put it together that I wasn't necessarily being believed," she says. "It was like the floor opened up underneath me. I felt like I was sinking."

— AVA WILLIAMS, UNIVERSITY OF WESTERN ONTARIO STUDENT WHOSE SEXUAL ASSAULT FILE WAS CLOSED AND LABELLED "UNFOUNDED," 2017[3]

The capacity to think independently, to take risks, to assert ourselves mentally is inseparable from our physical way of being in the world, our feelings of personal integrity. If it is dangerous for me to walk home late of an evening from the library, because I am a woman and can be raped, *how self-possessed, how exuberant can I feel as I sit working in that library?*

— ADRIENNE RICH, "TAKING WOMEN STUDENTS SERIOUSLY," 1979[4]

THESE SHORT AND selective quotes (there are thousands of others) raise concerns about sexual assault and harassment in the post-secondary educational context. In the first quote, Ayla Lefkowitz speaks out about her experience of sexual harassment during a university sports banquet to which she had worn high-heeled shoes and a "sexy" dress. Her words remind us of how women may blame themselves or be treated as partly responsible for sexual harassment or abuse. The second quote raises the troubling question of why a brilliant young graduate student like Yeohee Im, studying far away from her home country, has to worry about sexual advances from her professor. In

Ava Williams's case, a criminal investigation into her allegations of sexual assault made her feel victimized again when the police doubted the truth of her story because she had been drinking and partying when the sexual assault occurred. Finally, Adrienne Rich's insights remind us of how the fear of something as mundane as going home from the library at night can undermine educational pursuits.

While protection from, and prevention of, sexual violence and harassment are generally associated with equality rights, embedded in each of the above quotes is a yearning for freedom: a freedom to be and live in a world that is not pervasively and structurally constrained by the risks and realities of sexual violence.[5] This freedom means that when you travel thousands of kilometres to study with a world-renowned professor, you should not have to endure sexual advances or conduct that makes you feel uncomfortable; it means you should be free to work late at the library, without having to worry about getting home safely. It is not about freedom in the abstract, but rather about enhancing freedom in the everyday moments that constitute our daily lives. It is about equality in the exercise of freedom or what I call "equitable freedom." Equitable freedom denotes a freedom to be safe in our everyday lives — to be creative, to be ourselves, to experiment, to explore, to laugh and express ourselves; to study, work, and learn without fear of sexual violence, belittling, harassment, violation. Equitable freedom means that people are free to wear whatever they choose, without risk of sexual assault; freedom even means that individuals are free to drink too much without fearing or risking rape, knowing that others will help them get home safely. And so, this chapter is about equitable freedom.

In focusing on freedom, I have been inspired by the feminist work of Nancy Hirschmann in her book *The Subject of Liberty: Toward a Feminist Theory of Freedom.*[6] Her approach to "liberty" resonates with my idea of equitable freedom. For Hirschmann, liberty does not mean that you are to be left alone to fend for yourself in an unequal world. It is not defined in negative terms, whereby freedom means non-intervention by governments. Rather, Hirschmann speaks of positive freedom, situating it in its social context and examining the systemic and institutional conditions that make freedom possible.

From this perspective, we experience greater freedom and autonomy when we are supported in our endeavours and needs. As she explains:

> [F]reedom of education is rather hollow if you cannot afford tuition or get into the building where instruction is offered. Adopting a more contextual and communal notion of the self, positive liberty is able to view individual conditions such as disability, as well as social conditions such as poverty, as barriers to freedom that can be overcome by positive action, that is, the provision of conditions the individual cannot create on her own.[7]

Jennifer Nedelsky develops a similar idea in her work on relational autonomy.[8] We are more autonomous when we are in supportive relationships and communities — autonomy is not enhanced by isolation. Building on Hirschmann's concept of positive feminist freedom and Nedelsky's idea of relational autonomy, therefore, I suggest that we need to ensure and build (through our laws, institutional policies, and everyday practices) equitable freedom.

In this chapter, I explore the idea of equitable freedom in the context of the increasingly documented problem of sexual violence in universities. I begin by highlighting the ways in which sexual assault and harassment may be understood through the lens of direct, adverse impact, and systemic discrimination. In the second part of the chapter, I focus on university responses to sexual assault and harassment. What happens in the wake of an incident of harassment or assault? Are there fair, effective, and timely complaints processes in place, and are there tangible remedies for survivors that make it possible for them to continue their studies without fear or risk? I then turn to prevention. Once a sexual assault or harassment occurs, the long-term effects of the harm are often very difficult to remedy. The poisoned atmosphere of fear and violation persists; access to a safe and joyous educational environment is undermined. Preventing sexual violence, therefore, is a critical institutional and collective imperative of our times. I conclude by highlighting a few examples of innovative programs and policies that are working effectively to reduce sexual assaults and harassment on campus. In short, this chapter explores how sexual violence on campus raises issues of equality and systemic discrimination at the micro, institutional, and macro levels. As such, institutional and systemic responses are needed.

Inequality and Freedom: Sexual Violence as Discrimination

PERHAPS THE MOST important starting point for thinking about equitable freedom is to recognize the current inequalities in the exercise of freedom in this world. With respect to sexual violence in universities, empirical studies reveal that it is a deeply gendered phenomenon. For example, a report on Quebec universities reveals that "89.7% of sexual harassment, 86.6% of non-consensual sexual behaviour and 84.3% of sexual coercion [cases] are perpetrated by men against women or men."[9] Sexual violence on campus disproportionately affects young women's lives, and men are the perpetrators in the vast majority of cases, even in those cases where men are themselves the victims.

Violence is a denial of equality, an offence to human dignity, and a violation of physical and psychological well-being. As Justice Claire L'Heureux Dubé noted in an important decision on rape myths and criminal law, sexual assault "is an assault upon human dignity and constitutes a denial of ... equality."[10] Similarly, in an important decision confirming sexual harassment as a form of sex discrimination, Chief Justice Brian Dickson described sexual harassment as "a demeaning practice, one that constitutes a profound affront to ... the dignity and self-respect of the victim."[11] As noted by the Ontario Human Rights Commission, sexual harassment can diminish "morale, decrease productivity and contribute to physical and emotional effects such as anxiety, depression and posttraumatic stress disorder."[12] The Commission referenced the United Nations' *Declaration on the Elimination of Violence Against Women*, which includes "sexual harassment and intimidation at work, in educational institutions and elsewhere" in its definition of violence against women.[13] Additionally, the Commission draws on the research of sociologist Sandra Welsh, noting:

> Sexual harassment and violence reflect negative attitudes about girls and women. Inappropriate sexual behaviour (sexual jokes, innuendo and unwanted gestures of "affection") often develops over time and, if left unchecked, may progress to more serious forms.... Physical or sexual assault may be the culmination of ongoing acts of harassment.[14]

The escalation from small incidents of harassment to more serious incidents of sexual assault is deeply troubling and has important implications for those responsible for ensuring that educational spaces are safe for all.[15]

It is also important to recognize that some individuals are more vulnerable to sexual violence than others. The risks and realities of sexual violence are disproportionately experienced by women, particularly young women, racialized women, foreign students, Indigenous women, women with disabilities, and LBGTQ2S+ individuals.[16] Think of Yeohee Im, twenty-three years old and far away from her family and friends in South Korea. Having come halfway around the world to work with a renowned professor, she finds herself feeling deeply uncomfortable and at risk of sexual harassment rather than intellectually energized and engaged. Think of young Indigenous women, living far from their home communities to pursue their education, encountering sexual violence without a family or community support system.[17] Think of a young trans woman, who is beginning to feel free in her gender identity, and yet knows she is at higher risk of sexual abuse and harassment.[18]

The disparities in risks of sexual assault and harassment between, for example, women (including cis and trans women) and men raise questions of inequitable freedom and discrimination. Inequities in the risk and incidence of sexual violence may be understood as a form of direct discrimination. Individuals are directly targeted for abuse or harassment because of stereotypes and prejudices about their identity(ies).[19] In addition to direct discrimination, apparently "neutral" institutional policies, practices, and norms may result in adverse impact discrimination.[20] For example, alcohol and drinking policies during orientation week; policies regarding social media posting;

supervision practices that give significant discretionary power to professors, supervisors, or tutorial leaders; grading policies; dormitory or residential housing policies; lighting on university campuses; and the physical design of exterior and interior facilities — to name but a few — may have inadvertent but disproportionately negative effects on women and increase the risk of sexual misconduct. The effects may be even more problematic for more vulnerable individuals; for example, if the wheelchair-accessible entrance is in an isolated part (or even the basement) of a building, individuals who use wheelchairs are at heightened risk of sexual assault. Similarly, young students working late at the library or at an event, for whom taxis are too expensive, are more at risk travelling home late at night. While these institutional policies or practices are not necessarily designed to discriminate, they still need to be examined to assess whether or not they have unintentional discriminatory effects. If so, they need to be re-evaluated and changed to secure equality.

While discrete institutional policies or practices may need revision, the impact of these policies, combined with direct discriminatory practices, often results in a problem that is cumulative, dynamic, and pervasive within an institution. To address institutionalized problems of sexual violence and discrimination, a systemic approach is needed. As Justice Abella explained in her Royal Commission Report:

> Rather than approaching discrimination from the perspective of the single perpetrator and the single victim, the systemic approach acknowledges that by and large the systems and practices we customarily and often unwittingly adopt may have an unjustifiably negative effect on certain groups in society.[21]

There is growing recognition in Canadian law that discrimination goes beyond isolated, exceptional acts of misconduct; it is a complex, systemic phenomenon, embedded in institutional policies and practices. The institutional phenomenon of sexual violence is also connected to broader societal inequalities. Therefore, to redress sexual violence on campus, it is important to be attentive to societal and intergenerational sources of vulnerability and risk, such as being in a foreign environment, living with a disability, being in a sexual minority community, or being economically vulnerable.

Responding to Sexual Violence

WHILE IT REMAINS absolutely essential to focus on preventing sexual misconduct, universities and educational institutions must also develop effective, fair, and equitable processes for responding to misconduct when it does occur. An institution's response to incidents of sexual misconduct is of utmost importance in creating a culture that makes survivors feel believed, safe, and supported. It ensures fairness and confidentiality, accountability and effective remedies. Research studies have revealed that "institutions have the potential to either worsen post-traumatic outcomes or become sources of justice, support, and healing."[22]

The harm caused by individual perpetrators may also be aggravated by institutional responses to the incident. Think of Ava Williams's experience. When she recounted it to the police, she was faced with the trauma of skepticism: "I started to put it together that I wasn't necessarily being believed ... It was like the floor opened up underneath me. I felt like I was sinking."[23] If complaints mechanisms are ineffective or insensitive to the needs and realities of survivors, there is a significant risk of revictimizing survivors of sexual abuse. Reporting on Ava Williams's case, Robyn Doolittle writes:

> When complaints of sexual assault are dismissed with ... frequency, it is a sign of deeper flaws in the investigative process: inadequate training for police; dated interviewing techniques that do not take into account the effect that trauma can have on memory; and the persistence of rape myths among law-enforcement officials.[24]

Survivors may actually be dissuaded from filing complaints, which is a widespread problem.[25] In the wake of her experiences, Ava Williams initiated a class action lawsuit, alleging rights violations by the London police in their sexual assault investigation processes.[26] She is speaking up and urging other survivors of sexual assault to join in her class action lawsuit for damages and systemic change.

Institutional policies that provide fair, effective, accessible, and supportive processes for survivors, therefore, are critical to securing equality and freedom[27] — this includes police processes and the complaints processes at universities and colleges. A useful starting point is a 2014 report published by METRAC, an organization in Toronto that works to end violence against women and children, titled *Sexual Assault Policies on Campus: A Discussion Paper*. This report identifies some of the key components of an effective institutional response to sexual violence. First, the importance of a "stand-alone policy," which is attentive to the rights of both complainants and respondents, is highlighted.[28] Second, it is essential to have "robust processes for reporting, investigating and adjudicating" cases involving allegations of sexual misconduct.[29] Third, there need to be "interim measures to protect and support the complainant."[30] Too often, a complaint is filed and then months pass without any decision or institutional response; in some cases, complainants do not even receive information about the outcome of their case.[31] Fourth, the importance of ensuring specialized expertise is emphasized, involving trained responders with expertise in dealing with the complexities and realities of sexual violence.[32] Finally, there should be comprehensive and timely reporting requirements to track progress and ongoing problems.[33]

Traditionally, legal responses to sexual misconduct have been premised on what has been called a "perpetrator perspective" — a focus on the perpetrator's intent rather than the effects on the survivor.[34] The misconduct is defined in terms of a lack of consent, which is measured by assessing whether or not the perpetrator knew or should have known that the sexual conduct was unwelcome. A finding of wrongdoing by the perpetrator leads to punitive measures — either criminal punishment or institutional disciplinary action. This classic legal response is an important component of the legal response to sexual violence. But currently, many policies are limited to punishment or disciplinary measures against the perpetrator. They do not provide concrete remedies to the survivor of the sexual violence or attend to the policy changes needed to prevent future violence. If an institution's focus is exclusively on punishing wrongdoing, there is a risk that the victims of sexual violence will be left without any compensation or remedy. Moreover, there is no attention given to the ways in which institutional policies or practices might have contributed to increased risks or incidents of sexual violence.

What would it mean to focus institutional attention on the experiences and needs of the survivors of sexual misconduct? Human rights laws, which focus on compensating the harm experienced by the survivor rather than on punishing the wrongdoer, provide insights in this regard. As recognized by the Supreme Court of Canada, the primary objective of human rights laws is "not to punish the discriminator, but rather to provide relief for the victims of discrimination."[35] Yet these kinds of remedies have been almost completely non-existent in the university context. Numerous policy reforms in universities could be developed to respond to the needs of survivors of sexual violence. For example, as noted above, the outcome of a complaint could include compensation and remedies for the survivor of the sexual misconduct; similarly, additional preventive policies (canvassed below) could be implemented. While the focus of institutional policy makers has been on developing policies that define sexual misconduct clearly and set out processes and procedures for filing, investigating, and adjudicating complaints, there is a growing recognition that institutions need to develop more innovative initiatives for preventing sexual violence to ensure that students experience an educational environment of equitable freedom.

Preventing Sexual Violence

A key reason why campuses remain unsafe for women is the absence of administration-led systemic change.

— ANNE FORREST AND CHARLENE SENN, UNIVERSITY OF WINDSOR [36]

WHAT CAN UNIVERSITIES and schools do to ensure that sexual misconduct does not occur? What policies and programs have been developed to prevent sexual violence? In a societal context of growing awareness of the problem of sexual violence on university campuses and beyond, there have been some innovative programs that are making a difference.

Safety Audits and Campus Climate Surveys

To address the risks of sexual assault, York University carried out a comprehensive safety audit performed by METRAC. Four inter-related dimensions of the university were assessed:

1. **Physical features and infrastructure**: building design and lay-out, landscaping and planting, maintenance, lighting, signage, sightlines, secluded areas, accessible routes, access enhance-ments and graffiti.

2. **Security provisions**: safety patrols, emergency phones, cam-eras, escort programs, mirrors, reporting mechanisms, security protocols, threat and risk assessments tools, protected spaces and critical incident systems.

3. **Social dynamics**: perceptions, experiences, attitudes and behaviours and social relations between groups.

4. **Institutional policies and programs**: University policies and operational protocols for setting standards to enhance personal and community safety with respect to fostering non-violence and addressing discrimination and harassment on campus. They include the availability and utilization of a full range of resources and structured supports to prevent and respond to violence on campus and to promote safety at York.[37]

Following a two-year audit process (which included surveys, focus groups, consultation meetings, submissions, and research), numerous recommendations were made to improve the social environment, campus security services, and the physical space. The recommendations were comprehensive and far-reaching, including, to cite just a few examples:

1.1. The president should issue a statement that describes York's commitment to achieving a safe campus and outlines action steps to address violence against women, hate incidents and systemic inequities. Upon release of this report and at the beginning of every semester.

1.2. The university should continue to allocate eight million dollars to support physical security and prevention of violence and crime on campus. . . .

2.1. Security staffing levels should be increased to improve campus patrols, night-time coverage, response time to calls and coverage at special events (e.g. Pub Nights). . . .

3.1. Review and strengthen the multi-year lighting program to incorporate environmentally friendly white light. . . .

3.22. Install safety mirrors in all areas where there is:

- a turn where one cannot see ahead; and
- an obstruction that interrupts a line of sight within 25 metres or creates an area where someone can hide. . . .

3.30. Review safety programs to ensure they are accessible for people with disabilities. Ensure Counselling and Disabilities Services, the Access York Advisory Committee and other stakeholders are included in the review.[38]

As these few selective examples reveal, the safety audit addressed a wide range of institutional policies and practices that would help to prevent sexual assault. It would seem that such a safety audit would be an essential starting point for all universities seeking to prevent sexual violence.

Other proactive surveys have focused on attitudes and experiences of sexual violence. For example, in 2014, the University of Ottawa conducted a "Campus Climate Survey,"[39] which included questions designed to identify:

- Harmful beliefs about women and sexual violence
- Experiences of harassment and violence online and in face-to-face situations
- The impact of these experiences, help-seeking and satisfaction with help received
- Willingness to intervene to prevent harassment and violence

Such institution-wide surveys are essential for identifying problems that do not surface within the individual complaint process since survivors often do not file complaints with university authorities.

Bystander Initiatives

A second innovative program is the University of Windsor's Bystander Initiatives. Its co-founders, Professors Anne Forrest and Charlene Senn, began teaching workshops "designed to help students understand the importance of speaking out against social norms that support sexual assault and coercion, recognize and safely interrupt situations that could lead to sexual assault, and be an effective and supportive ally to rape survivors."[40] The program was developed to target students most at risk of sexual assault:

> Studies consistently tell us that the most at risk are first- and second-year students, and as many as 1 in 4 women will experience sexual assault before graduation. Recent research shows high rates of sexual assault against members of LGBTQ+ groups and international students. Men generally report sexual assault in lower numbers, and those who come forward deserve to be believed and supported. In most cases, perpetrators are likely to be men. Many of these encounters are not reported and do not appear in official statistics.

The purpose of the initiative is clearly described:

> The long-term goal of the Bystander Initiative is the creation of an anti-rape campus ethos supported by a critical mass of students who are willing and able to shut down rape jokes, challenge rape myths, and disrupt sexual assaults in-the-making. To produce this shift in campus culture, we must commit to sustainability. Sexual assault prevention cannot be a one-time, one-cohort intervention — every fall, we welcome to campus a new group of students for whom sexual and gender-based violence is normalized by the wider culture.

The pilot program began in the fall of 2017 and research into its impact is ongoing. However, there are some concerns related to implementing a bystander initative. The founders wanted to ensure "that the content and approach did not limit women's freedom nor remove responsibility from the male perpetrator."[41] As Senn further explains, focusing on bystander interventions created a "tension between individualizing the experience to make it relevant for the individual participant at the expense of looking at the cultural/systemic/structural issues giving rise to widespread sexual violence."[42] A short workshop does not provide enough time to examine the larger structural and systemic causes of gendered violence. Nonetheless, bystander initiatives have been making a real difference in preventing the escalation of sexual violence. If we think again about Ava Williams's experience, had there been effective bystander intervention training, perhaps the sexual assault could have been prevented.

Policies That Acknowledge Structural Inequalities

A third domain of innovation concerns institutional policies regarding structural power imbalances and risks of sexual harassment. Professors have significant power over the future career and well-being of students. Sexual harassment in such a context can be devastating to a student who experiences not only the immediate fear and harm of the misconduct, but the long-term harm to their education and career. Universities recognize how the risks of abuse may be accentuated in relationships of inequitable power and privilege. As Yale University's policy on teacher-student consensual relationships acknowledges at the outset, the "unequal institutional power inherent in this relationship heightens the vulnerability of the student and the potential for coercion."[43]

Accordingly, professors at Yale "must avoid sexual relationships with students over whom they have or might reasonably expect to have direct pedagogical or supervisory responsibilities, regardless of whether the relationship is consensual."[44] It is important to underline at this point that consent is not a justification for having a relationship with a student with whom a professor has a professional teaching relationship. Indeed, the policy at Yale goes on to prohibit any relationships between professors and undergraduate students, regardless of whether they are in a teaching relationship. The reason is stated simply: "Undergraduate students are particularly vulnerable to the unequal institutional power inherent in the teacher-student relationship and the potential for coercion, because of their age and relative lack of maturity."[45] Regarding Im's situation at Princeton, there too, the university policy prohibits romantic or sexual relations between a supervising professor and graduate student.[46] Unfortunately, the presence of a policy on paper does not ensure compliance with it in practice. Still, clear policies that prohibit sexual conduct between professors and their students are critically important and there should be significant consequences for their violation.

Sexual Violence: A Public Health Approach

Examining sexual violence through the lens of public health represents a promising preventive approach. The Sexual Health Initiative to Foster Transformation (SHIFT) at Columbia University is "a comprehensive research project that examines the many factors that shape sexual health and sexual violence for undergrads at Columbia."[47] What is particularly innovative about the SHIFT approach is its commitment to finding out about the daily realities of student lives in relation to sexual health and sexual violence in the context of universities. Researchers did extensive work studying the everyday lives and interactions of college students, in effect performing an ethnography of sexual practices and encounters. On the basis of these research findings, a series of recommendations were made that included both educational and more policy/structural initiatives, such as:

> (1) comprehensive sexuality education; (2) more participatory and skills-based consent education; (3) alcohol policy changes to reduce the harms of drunk sex; and (4) space planning to build safer campuses.[48]

The educational initiatives included evidence-based recommendations. For example, the participatory consent education was to be designed to "actually transform behavior by engaging students in critical reflection and providing a space for them to discuss their own practices, rather than teaching them the right answer."[49] The harm reduction strategies included, for example, reducing binge drinking and drunk sex by providing food and water in places where students normally drink, and reducing factors that prompt students to engage in binge drinking (such as financial or academic stress). Finally, institutional space planning issues were also raised; for example, colleges should provide students with "spaces that create opportunities for students to socialize without alcohol."[50] These kinds of initiatives, with their focus on harm reduction, are an important component of a university's response to preventing sexual misconduct.

Addressing Small Things to Prevent Big Problems

One final innovative approach to sexual violence in the university context focuses on addressing small incidents of disrespect or sexism that create a culture of complacency about sexual misconduct. Whereas most sexual harassment and sexual violence policies emphasize the need to define the line between acceptable and unacceptable social conduct — or consensual versus non-consensual sexual inter-action — some scholars of institutional change have observed that focusing on the threshold between acceptable and unacceptable conduct may not be the most effective strategy. Conflict often emerges over difficult cases where it is challenging to know with certainty whether the line between acceptable and unacceptable behaviour was crossed. Instead of focusing on the precise situations where conduct becomes misconduct, it has been suggested that it is important to develop effective and prompt institutional responses to conduct that contributes to an inequitable culture, even if that conduct does not amount to sexual misconduct.

Drawing on research into organizational culture and change, Brian Rubineau and Nazampal Jaswal explain that management theory provides some useful insights that may be fruitfully applied to sexual misconduct at work and in educational contexts. They highlight "the importance of attending to and addressing the more common and milder forms of the kinds of behaviors that are to be prevented."[51] Thus, rather than focusing exclusively on identifying and punishing sexual misconduct after it occurs, creating a culture of respect by attending to everyday interactions and relationships is critical. One example of such an approach is the CREW (Civility, Respect, and Engagement in the Workplace) initiative, which works towards enhancing relations in everyday interactions at work, rather than focusing on individual instances of wrongdoing.[52]

Such an approach resonates with Susan Sturm's work on what she calls "second generation discrimination."[53] Whereas first generation discrimination refers to clear cases of overt bias, exclusion, and unfair treatment, second generation discrimination entails "a more subtle and complex form of bias,"[54] often involving unconscious biases, the aggregated effects of numerous small incidents of exclusion and stereotyping, demeaning organizational cultures, and structural inequities. Unlike in overt and egregious cases of sexual harassment that lend themselves more readily to retroactive legal enforcement in the courts, women are much less likely to file complaints about small everyday acts of discrimination.[55] One is unlikely to file a human rights complaint in the wake of a small incident, a casual sexist remark, a feeling of fear or non-belonging. Still, if we think again about the quotations at the outset of this chapter, we see that these small incidents contribute to institutional cultures of sexism and create a climate in which there is an increased risk of sexual misconduct.

The importance of addressing problems of institutional culture before they escalate into harmful and damaging incidents of sexual abuse or harassment was underscored in *Online Sexual Harassment: Report of the Task Force on Misogyny, Sexism and Homophobia in Dalhousie University.*[56] The extent of the harm caused to female dentistry students by the male students' Facebook posts of graphic, sexually demeaning, and violent acts was clearly described in the report. Female students were shocked and hurt when they realized that "fellow students, with whom they had worked and socialized for more than three years, had objectified and sexualized them."[57] Moreover, the report emphasized that the Facebook incident that caused considerable harm was not isolated. Rather, it appeared that it was common for female students to experience sexist comments and treatment by instructors in their clinical work to the point where "sexist comments had become normalized and went unnoticed."[58] Recommendations included improving complaints processes as well as changing the institutional culture of the dentistry faculty. Indeed, although the report focused on the specific incident of online harassment at Dalhousie University, similar problems of sexual harassment are widespread and have occurred in other universities.[59]

Conclusion

THERE IS GROWING recognition that universities should take proactive measures to create a positive and safe learning environment and a non-sexist organizational culture. In Ontario, for example, Bill 132, *Sexual Violence and Harassment Action Plan Act (Supporting Survivors and Challenging Sexual Violence and Harassment), 2016*[60] requires colleges and universities to put in place a sexual violence policy and imposes reporting obligations regarding the occurrence of sexual violence on campus.[61] Similarly, in 2017, Quebec passed Bill 151, *An Act to prevent and fight sexual violence in higher education institutions.*[62] Its purpose is to "prevent and fight sexual violence in higher education institutions and to help foster a healthy and safe living environment for students and personnel members."[63] In addition to providing for individual assistance in the wake of sexual violence, the legislation puts an emphasis on "prevention, awareness-raising, accountability, [and] support."[64] Also of significance in the Quebec legislation is the requirement that the policy "take into account persons at greater risk of experiencing sexual violence," including LGBTQ2S+, racialized, Indigenous, and foreign students, as well as students with disabilities.[65] Beyond ensuring effective, timely, and supportive complaints processes to allow survivors of sexual misconduct to seek redress, there is a growing trend towards recognizing the need for a more proactive response. Let's hope that these emerging legislative and institutional initiatives take us forward towards a world of equitable freedom — a world where young women are free to wear whatever dancing shoes they wish — with joy, without fear, and in safety.

6

Caring about Equality in Indigenous Communities

They came for the children.

— TRUTH AND RECONCILIATION COMMISSION OF CANADA[1]

ONE WAY TO assess if a society is respecting equality rights is to look at how it cares for its most vulnerable members. As Indigenous scholar and teacher, Patricia Monture, taught us, "only when we understand caring will we understand equality."[2] Thinking about caring asks us to explore the real human relations, emotions, and respect we need to draw on to work towards substantive equality. This chapter explores two important cases where First Nations children were denied equitable treatment in government funding for health and child welfare services. The stories in these cases highlight the inequitable treatment of children, as well as their caregivers and communities. We begin with the story of Maurina Beadle and her son, Jeremy Meawasige, who were refused the funding they needed to continue in-home healthcare services for Jeremy.[3] The second case involves a challenge to the chronic underfunding of child welfare services on First Nations' reserves[4] and in the Yukon. The case was initiated and led by Cindy Blackstock, a social worker who had witnessed the devastating effects of inadequate child welfare services on the lives of First Nations children.[5]

Both cases illustrate the power of individuals and communities when they stand up for their rights and contest inequities. The cases also reveal the continued risks of institutionalization facing Indigenous children — either in long-term healthcare facilities or in foster homes. Finally, they provide concrete examples of how complex governmental funding policies for basic health and social services have significant and discriminatory impacts on the lives of children, families, and communities. Similar to how it plays out in workplaces and educational institutions, discrimination also occurs in the provision of health and social services. The harmful effects of inequitable access to health and social services perpetuate cycles of systemic discrimination in Indigenous communities at the micro, meso, and macro levels.

Maurina Beadle's Story: Underfunding as a Violation of Jordan's Principle

MAURINA BEADLE WAS a Mi'kmaq woman from Pictou Landing First Nation in Nova Scotia. Her son, Jeremy Meawasige, has multiple disabilities and healthcare needs as a result of hydrocephaly, cerebral palsy, spinal curvature, and autism. As his mother and primary caregiver, Maurina Beadle attended to Jeremy's daily home care needs without financial or other assistance until 2010, when she had a stroke and could no longer do so. After her stroke, the Pictou Landing Band Council provided additional financial and health services support. Given the significant costs, in 2011, the director of the Pictou Landing First Nations Health Centre, Philippa Pictou, contacted the federal government to seek additional funding to ensure continued home care for Jeremy. The request for funding was denied.[6]

Healthcare services in Nova Scotia, including support for home care, are generally provided by the provincial government. For Indigenous individuals and families living on reserves in Nova Scotia, however, many healthcare services are paid for by the federal government.[7] The state of shared responsibility for providing health-related services to Indigenous people has led to jurisdictional disputes between the federal and provincial governments over which government is responsible for which services and who should pay.[8]

At this point, Jeremy's story intersects with the story of a young Cree boy, Jordan River Anderson from Norway House First Nation in Manitoba. Born with significant health needs, Jordan died in hospital at the age of five. Jordan spent his short life in hospital because of a funding dispute between the federal and provincial governments; neither government would assume responsibility for the costs that would have allowed Jordan to move out of the hospital into a home setting.[9] While the jurisdictional dispute continued, Jordan was forced to remain in the hospital. In the wake of Jordan's death, the federal House of Commons unanimously endorsed a motion providing that "the government should immediately adopt a child first principle, based on Jordan's Principle, to resolve jurisdictional disputes involving the care of First Nations children."[10] This motion, now referred to as "Jordan's Principle," requires that the first governmental agency or department approached for services should provide the necessary services and resolve any disputes about funding or jurisdictional responsibilities afterwards.

In Jeremy's case, the Pictou Landing First Nations Health Centre director formally requested additional funding for home healthcare services from the federal government on the basis of Jordan's Principle. She maintained that off-reserve residents would be entitled to special provincial funding in situations similar to Jeremy's. The federal government official responsible for administering Jordan's Principle funding requests in Atlantic Canada, however, declined the request, even though the amount requested was less than what the government would have to pay if Jeremy were institutionalized. In the face of the federal government's refusal of additional funds, the Pictou Landing Band Council and Maurina Beadle went to court. They maintained that the denial of increased funding violated constitutional equality rights and was inconsistent with Jordan's Principle.[11]

Federal Court Justice Mandamin agreed with the Pictou Landing Band Council and Maurina Beadle and ordered additional funding on the basis of Jordan's Principle. He found that an individual with multiple disabilities living off-reserve in Nova Scotia would be eligible for additional funding for in-home care services, while

Jeremy, an on-reserve teenager "in similar dire straits," was being denied funding.[12] Justice Mandamin found that this type of inequity "engages consideration under Jordan's Principle, which exists precisely to address situations such as Jeremy's."[13] He concluded that the federal government's refusal to provide additional funding was unreasonable. As Justice Mandamin explained, the denial of funding would result in Jeremy's "institutionalization and separation from his mother and his community.... He, like sad little Jordan, would be institutionalized, removed from family and the only home he has known. He would be placed in the same situation as was little Jordan."[14] Maurina Beadle and the Pictou Landing Band Council won their case and additional funding was immediately provided. The law worked to provide a concrete remedy to keep Jeremy at home, with his mother, brother, and community.

What is so striking about this case is how the years of home care that Maurina Beadle provided for her son did not become visible until she was no longer able to offer the same level of care after her stroke — it was only at that point that the costs and value of those years of home care became more apparent. Suddenly, it would cost about $8,000 a month to provide the family with the same health care services that Maurina Beadle had been performing without any financial compensation. To care for Jeremy in an institutionalized hospital setting would cost closer to $10,000 per month.[15] We should not have to monetize everything we do to understand its value; yet, doing so underscores the historical and continued undervaluing of unpaid care work.[16] Although there has not been much research into Indigenous home care work, the authors of one important study published in 2004 maintain that:

> Aboriginal women have always played a central role as caregivers and healers in their communities.... While women in Canada provide about 80 percent of caregiving, including both paid and unpaid work, the gender discrepancy is arguably even higher in Aboriginal communities, due to a number of factors including cultural values of caring for family members, lack of services and lack of professional training opportunities.[17]

The authors note that Indigenous women are "one of the most politically, socially and economically marginalized populations in Canada," with higher levels of "chronic diseases, poverty and systemic discrimination."[18] Despite these realities, Indigenous women have "unique knowledge and expertise, based on traditional holistic understandings of health."[19] Indeed, as Justice Mandamin recognized, "Ms. Beadle and her son have a deep bond with each other. His mother is often the only person who can understand his communication and needs. She spent many hours training him to walk and helping him with special exercises." He further underscored how she had discovered Jeremy's love of music, how she sings to him when he is upset or uncooperative, and how her "voice calms him and can make him desist in self-destructive behaviour."[20] How could he ever find that kind of care in a long-term care institution? Moreover, if we fail to support caregivers, it will cost us much more in the long run — not only in monetary terms, but in terms of the loss of humane, loving care in families that can make such a difference in the quality and well-being of individuals. For Jeremy, this meant singing and dancing — participating, with his mother and brother, in the joy of his community's traditions — rather than sitting in an institution while looking through a window across the seasons, from summer to fall to winter and beyond.

Child Welfare in First Nations Communities: Underfunding as Race Discrimination

In *First Nations Child and Family Caring Society et al v Attorney General of Canada*,[21] the Canadian Human Rights Tribunal concluded that underfunding child welfare services on reserves and in the Yukon had resulted in race discrimination against Indigenous children and had contributed to their overrepresentation in foster care. After outlining the adverse effects of the numerous and complex funding formulas for child welfare services, tribunal chairperson Sophie Marchildon wrote, "it is only because of their race and/or national or ethnic origin that they suffer the adverse impacts outlined above in the provision of child and family services."[22] One problem identified by the Tribunal was the failure of the federal government to provide sufficient funding to secure services for Indigenous children on reserves that were comparable to services provided to off-reserve children. This underfunding, therefore, resulted in discrimination against Indigenous children on reserves, just as the underfunding of health services had discriminated against children like Jeremy and Jordan.

In its lengthy and comprehensive decision, the Tribunal examined the challenging child welfare issues facing First Nations children and families on reserves:

> For First Nations, the main source of child maltreatment is neglect in the form of a failure to supervise and failure to meet basic needs. Poverty, poor housing and substance abuse are common risk factors on reserves that call for early counselling and support services for children and families to avoid the intervention of child protection services.[23]

Therefore, to ensure that children have more effective protection, it is clear that the larger issues of poverty, housing, and the health of Indigenous *parents* need to be addressed. We cannot isolate child welfare from the welfare of families and the community at large.

Beyond the failure to address the larger sources of child neglect, such as poverty or poor housing, the underfunding of child protection services on reserves often resulted in a retroactive crisis intervention approach rather than a more proactive *preventive* approach that would be more likely to keep families together. After its lengthy review of the funding formulas for how the provinces and territories coordinated child protection services on reserves, the Tribunal concluded that the services "are structured in such a way that they promote negative outcomes for First Nations children and families, namely the incentive to take children into care."[24] While best practices in social work emphasize the need to intervene early and to make every effort to keep families together, such an approach was not being used on reserves. Instead, child welfare authorities would intervene only once a child protection crisis was extreme, and the only option was taking the child away from the home. The Tribunal also recognized the ways in which inadequacies in child protection policies and funding "perpetuate historical disadvantages suffered by Aboriginal peoples, mainly as a result of the Residential Schools system."[25] Finally, the Tribunal emphasized the importance of an outcomes-oriented approach, based on the concept of real or substantive equality. It was not enough to simply match provincial and federal funding. Given the "higher service needs of many First Nations children and families living on reserve, along with the higher costs to deliver those services in many situations," the focus should be on equitable services, not equal funding.[26] To secure equitable services for Indigenous children on reserves, it may be necessary to provide more funding than that which is provided for off-reserve services. The Tribunal emphasized that equitable outcomes rather than simply equal treatment provide the most meaningful measure of substantive equality.

In addition to ordering the federal government to cease its discriminatory funding policies, the Canadian Human Rights Tribunal ordered the federal government to take measures to immediately implement the full meaning and scope of Jordan's Principle.[27] The Tribunal recognized the close connection between Jordan's Principle, non-discrimination, and equitable treatment for children living on and off reserves. Even though the First Nations Caring Society won its case before the Canadian Human Rights Tribunal, there continue to be problems with implementing the decision. According to the First Nations Caring Society, underfunding of child welfare services persists. Since the Tribunal's important decision on the merits in January 2016, where it concluded that the federal government's funding policies were racially discriminatory, the Tribunal has had to issue numerous remedial orders, demonstrating ongoing inadequacies in the provision of child and family services.[28]

Common Threads: Tapestries of Injustice and Resilience

REFLECTING ON THESE two cases reveals common threads that weave a tapestry of injustice — of loss, racism, sexism, and inequities perpetrated by those who are untouched by the everyday realities in Indigenous communities. The common threads ask us to consider how historical injustices are connected to current injustices, and how achieving equal outcomes for Indigenous children is integral to remedying the effects of colonialism in Indigenous communities as a whole. Yet, the two cases also reveal a tapestry of resilience, of communities surviving despite the odds, of the strengths of children and of communities caring for each other, celebrating their history, and making their future.

Continuing Risks of Institutionalization

Decades of federal and provincial governmental policies have resulted in Indigenous children being taken away from their homes, families, and communities for both child welfare and health related reasons. The removal of children began with the assimilationist and colonial residential schools policy, which persisted for over a hundred years and removed Indigenous children from their communities.[29] The devastating effects of the residential schools have been widely documented and acknowledged. Despite the closure of the last residential school in 1996, the harm caused by residential schools continues.[30] Most recently, the National Inquiry into Missing and Murdered Indigenous Women and Girls concluded that one of the legacies of the era of residential schools is the breakdown of the child protection system for Indigenous children and the disproportionately high removal of Indigenous children from their families.[31]

From the 1950s onward, child welfare policies replaced residential schools as the major public policy mechanism for removing children from their communities. Child welfare policies and practices continue to result in a serious overrepresentation of Indigenous children in foster homes — the children having been removed from their families by child protection authorities. As Cindy Blackstock explains, the number of children taken out of their communities as a result of child protection policies is currently higher than at the height of the residential schools era.[32] Government census data from 2016 indicates that "Indigenous children represent 52.2% of children in foster care, in private homes in Canada, despite accounting for only 7.7% of the overall population of children under 15."[33] There is no dispute about the high risks of institutionalization facing Indigenous children; numerous studies and reports confirm this tragic reality and its negative effects on individual children, parents, families, and communities.

The absence of adequate local healthcare services has also resulted in children being forced to leave their communities for treatment and healthcare. While this affects both Indigenous and non-Indigenous individuals living in rural communities away from specialized health services, cases like those of Jeremy Meawasige and Jordan River Anderson demonstrate how institutionalization may occur when children require long-term health support services that are not available on reserves. These cases poignantly illustrate the importance of ensuring that Indigenous children can be cared for by their families and communities as much as possible with supportive home care treatment and healthcare support. One pathway for reinforcing the well-being of Indigenous children is to support and address the health and well-being of the mothers, fathers, families, and communities who care for Indigenous children and give them their sense of belonging, history, identity, and pride.

Discretionary Power and Discrimination

Another parallel between Jeremy's case in *Pictou Landing* and the Caring Society's challenge to the provision of child welfare services is the critical significance of discretionary decision making by governmental officials, social workers, and others in positions of authority. Those empowered to make decisions that impact the lives of Indigenous children and their families often do so by exercising discretion, which itself may be a source of discrimination or perpetuate historical legacies of discrimination. Discrimination can result when decisions are guided by vague or culturally biased stereotypes, when decision makers have no personal involvement with the communities their decisions impact, or when they do not take the time to learn about the communities that their decisions affect.

Over the years, thousands of social workers have made discretionary decisions about whether to take children out of their homes based on an assessment of whether the children are in need of protection. The principle guiding these decisions — "the best interests of the child" — is vague and subject to multiple interpretations.[34] Similarly, federal guidelines for applying Jordan's Principle are subject to a range of discretionary interpretations. The federal government has publicized a commitment to using an equitable outcomes-based approach to Jordan's Principle applications, which is rooted in substantive equality.[35] Nonetheless, considerable uncertainty persists. For instance, the administrative decision not to provide additional funding for home care for Jeremy flowed from a government official's erroneous conclusion about the level of services available to off-reserve individuals. The official then concluded that Jordan's Principle was not relevant to Maurina Beadle's request and that no additional funding for home care should be provided. It is troubling that this government official approved funding to pay for institutional care, even though it would be more expensive.[36] The decisions made in these cases lead us to ask hard questions about discretionary power. How do we ensure humane, equitable, and accountable discretionary decision making that is not mired in bureaucratic, fragmented funding policies, or based on cultural or class-biased assessments of what is best for Indigenous children?

It is critically important to enhance non-discriminatory decision making that is attentive to the realities and needs of Indigneous communities. As we saw in the *Pictou Landing* case, governmental decisions are subject to judicial oversight if they are not exercised fairly and reasonably. Going to court to ensure discretionary fairness, however, is expensive and time-consuming, and comes with no guarantee of success. It depends on the understanding, knowledge, and sensitivity of judges to the needs of Indigenous children and communities.[37] It seems more effective to ensure that discretionary decisions are equitable and fair in the first place.

How can government discretion be exercised across a divide of difference in a way that is fair, humane, and sensitive to the realities of Indigenous communities? Lorne Sossin has called for an "intimate approach to fairness, impartiality and reasonableness."[38] He asks, "[w]hat if decision-makers had a chance to know the people whose lives they shape, rather than the pieces and fragments of their lives which appear in application forms and case files?"[39] Sossin suggests that the "act of exercising discretion ... should be seen as a medium of communication between the bureaucrat and the citizen."[40] The communication should be a two-way process whereby individuals and communities share information and knowledge with the government official, who in turn shares information about the criteria for making decisions. The idea of transparent governance resonates with Sossin's idea of a two-way dialogue between governmental decision makers and individuals. If we think about the decision to deny funding to Maurina Beadle and Jeremy Meawasige, the government official responsible for administering Jordan's Principle did not seem at all connected to the concrete circumstances and realities in the Pictou Landing First Nation. The official was willing to endorse a decision that would result in Jeremy's institutionalization, which, in addition to perpetuating historical inequities, would also be more expensive for the federal government. How was this decision made? A different and more humane outcome would surely have resulted if a "model of intimacy in administrative relationships" based on "trust, vulnerability and a sharing of knowledge" had existed.[41] But sadly, administrative intimacy is not the norm and discretionary decision making about the lives of Indigenous children continues to occur across divides of bureaucratic power and knowledge.

Beyond thinking about ways to ensure the equitable exercise of discretion, structural self-governance provides for a more transformative solution. Rather than having non-Indigenous government officials and social workers make decisions about the lives of Indigenous children, health and social services decision making should be vested in members of the community as much as possible.[42] Indeed, child welfare and health services on reserves are increasingly being organized and controlled by Indigenous communities themselves.[43] Keeping child protection decision-making power within the community is one way to ensure better outcomes for Indigenous children. In response to the *Caring Society* decisions and general advocacy for the need for change, the federal government introduced the *Act respecting First Nations, Inuit and Métis children, youth and families*, which recognizes that the inherent constitutional right of self-government includes "jurisdiction in relation to child and family services."[44] It also clarifies that child welfare decisions must be informed by the principle of substantive equality, which makes space for the voices of Indigenous children, family members, and community members to be heard.[45] Decisions made by those in the community, who know and care for the children and families, supported with adequate funding and capacity building, would result in more equitable results.[46]

Systemic Discrimination

A further thread that weaves throughout both cases is the larger systemic and structural dimensions of the inequalities experienced. If we think back to our micro, meso, and macro framework for analyzing systemic discrimination,[47] we can see that government funding operates at the macro level. Funding policies and federal laws regulating health and social services on reserves are developed outside of Indigenous communities. These funding policies and laws, however, have a critical impact on the kinds of child welfare and health services provided; they impact the meso or institutional level. For example, are there early intervention family support services to identify children at risk? Is adequate funding available to support home health-care services? Federal underfunding contributes to inequitable social work interventions in child protection because social workers with limited resources intervene in crisis situations, and they lack the resources to develop early intervention initiatives for families at risk. There is also lack of funding for communities to provide protection services themselves. In the health services domain, despite endorsement of Jordan's Principle, time and again, Indigenous children and their families are denied the funding they need.

Children and their families experience the real effects of government policies, laws, and funding decisions at the micro level. Government officials are often unable to see how these funding decisions reinforce patterns and histories of inadequate services, and how they may have life-and-death consequences on individuals, families, and communities. These consequences remind us that broader macro- and meso-level policy decisions have a direct micro impact on individual children, resulting in heartbreaking tragedies in some cases.[48]

Systemic discrimination traverses time and space. It involves direct and indirect forms of discrimination and exclusion built into the very fabric of government and other institutions. Systemic discrimination arises from both conscious and unconscious biases about certain groups, as well as laws and policies that have discriminatory effects on groups. In the case of Indigenous children in the child welfare and healthcare contexts, the causes of discrimination are rooted in colonialism and attempts to assimilate Indigenous peoples. Perhaps residential schools no longer exist, but the underfunding of services relating to Indigenous children can produce similar results by denying them the care of their communities and the opportunity to remain connected to their cultures and languages. Indigenous communities need to be empowered to address child welfare and healthcare. Systemic discrimination cannot be tackled without acknowledgement of historical and continuing injustices. Failure to act leaves systemic inequalities unchecked and unremedied. We must approach the quest for substantive equality for Indigenous children with acceptance that it might cost more to provide children in Indigenous communities with the same level of services available to non-Indigenous children, or that it will involve empowering Indigenous communities to revitalize self-governance. Failing to do so leaves in place the ongoing impacts of discrimination and leaves Indigenous children in the vulnerable position of being institutionalized in foster care.

Conclusion

BOTH CASES THAT we have focused on in this chapter involved legal challenges to government funding choices. In the first case, underfunding was found to be in violation of Jordan's Principle; in the second, it was found to be discriminatory. But both cases were focused on government underfunding. In the *Pictou Landing* case, increased funds were needed to pay for assistance in caring for Jeremy at home. In the *First Nations Child and Family Caring Society* case, increased funds were needed to provide comprehensive child protection services that would address prevention and early intervention for families at risk. In both cases, legal action was initiated in the wake of a refusal of funding; in both cases, it is significant that the remedies ordered required the federal government to increase its funding for services needed by First Nations children. These remedial orders effectively tell the government to allocate more resources to First Nations children and their families. Courts and tribunals are often reluctant to tell governments how to spend public funds; they consider those types of questions to be determined by political choices rather than by legal rights and entitlements. Yet, in these cases, underfunding is understood to directly violate rights and principles, and as such, it is deserving of a legal remedy.

Questions of funding also raise larger questions about who decides how funds are spent and who decides how services are delivered. While these legal challenges resulted in monetary remedies for additional funding, in both the health services and child welfare domains, there is a growing recognition that providing funding without more fundamental change in governance and decision making in Indigenous communities will provide mere "band-aid" solutions that fail to address underlying structural inequalities. [49] While legal cases before human rights tribunals and courts generally address only one specific problem, it is nevertheless important to situate them within a larger context of societal change. We tend to think of services as unrelated to larger transformative justice and governance questions; they are simply provided to respond to individual needs. But how services are provided is a deeply political issue; services reflect how we relate to each other in society. The provision of services tells us a great deal about conceptions of citizenship and belonging, and about responsibility to those without power or privilege in communities. With respect to child protection, it is not simply a matter of funding (important as that may be) — it is a matter of respecting the self-governance and self-determination of Indigenous peoples and communities. These cases, therefore, are important for understanding the broader struggles for justice and equality in Indigenous communities.

7

Seeking Justice and Belonging: The Complexity of Identity

LAWS DO NOT emerge in a social vacuum. Legal protections are usually the product of significant social struggles by groups that have been wronged and are seeking legal redress for those wrongs. In the Canadian context, the first anti-discrimination laws were aimed at prohibiting overt exclusions based on race, national or ethnic origin, sex, and religion in employment, education, and housing. But laws crafted to address specific problems of discrimination may not be capable of responding to new or previously unacknowledged forms of discrimination. Therefore, a second wave of anti-discrimination reform was necessary to add new grounds, such as sexual orientation, disability, family status, and pregnancy, as well as explicit prohibitions of grounds-based harassment.[1] A few jurisdictions have added the grounds of social condition and being in receipt of social assistance to address poverty and economic disadvantage.[2] Most recently, gender identity and expression and genetic-based discrimination have been the focus of human rights reform.[3] Accordingly, one of the most important and dynamic developments in anti-discrimination law has been the expansion of anti-discrimination protections to recognize additional grounds of discrimination.

However, creating new grounds of discrimination does not address all of the challenges of using group-based categories to advance equality. In many cases, discrimination is more complex than the traditional grounds-based protections suggest. One source of complexity arises in relation to individuals who are part of more than one group that has historically been subjected to discrimination. For example, a racialized woman may be subjected to discrimination that cannot be simply categorized as sex and/or race discrimination; it is the combination of both that results in the discrimination. The idea of "intersectionality," developed by Kimberlé Crenshaw in 1989, provides us with a way of thinking about the specificity of Black women's experiences of discrimination.[4] Crenshaw's analysis focused on employment discrimination cases where Black women's experiences of exclusion and discrimination were rendered invisible by reliance either on race-based or sex-based data. In the cases she analyzed, there were no statistics on exclusion based on the combined effects of sex and race; as a result, Black women's experiences of disadvantage and discrimination risked being overlooked. Intersectionality is not the same as what we might call additive discrimination (for example, sex plus race discrimination); instead, it describes discrimination that is unique to a particular group at the intersection of multiple identities. As noted in the International Labour Organization's global report on equality at work, intersectionality recognizes that the "interplay of identities results in experiences of exclusion and disadvantage that are unique to those with multiple identities."[5]

A further limitation of traditional categories of anti-discrimination law flows from the fact that people in the same group-based category may live their identities in dramatically different ways. For example, one lesbian may be a feminist queer activist, while another has not told anyone about her sexual orientation. One individual from a racialized community may be active in the Black Lives Matter movement,[6] while another is not active in any social movements.[7] The discrimination faced by these individuals may be very different and will not always be captured by existing categories of law. Some have referred to this as discrimination related to the "performance of identity."[8] This concern about categories also raises fundamental issues about invisible sources of discrimination. With respect to sexual orientation, gender identity, race, and mental health disabilities, for example, a critical issue is the extent to which individuals feel free to disclose how they are different from dominant majorities. When do they conceal their differences? When does disclosure lead to discrimination and stigmatization? What are the risks and harms of non-disclosure?[9]

Beyond the limitations of single-category analyses that fail to embrace the multiplicity of identities or the different ways in which individuals live their identities, some have critiqued existing group-based categories altogether and articulated new and more complex understandings of identity. One important example of this phenomenon is the identification and celebration of non-binary gender identities; another is the recognition that many individuals do not fit exclusively into one identity category — they are mixed race, they have parents of different religions or ethnicities, or they may have more than one first language. They are not, for example, Black *or* white, Christian *or* Muslim, French *or* English, non-Indigenous *or* Indigenous — they are both. Just as there exist non-binary gender identities, here we see non-binary racial, ethnic, religious, and linguistic identities. They live the richness of what some have called *métissage* — a kind of cultural mixing.[10] How does the law deal with individuals who do not fit easily into traditional categories?

Given the complexity of identifying with multiple categories, individuals sometimes choose to focus on one identity category. Alternatively, they may assert their affiliation with multiple identity categories at the same time. In some instances, individuals seek to define new identity categories. In this chapter, I explore how individuals and groups contest traditional identity categories in their quest for acknowledgement of the dynamic complexity of human identity. While categories are needed to engage in legal analysis and are often important as celebratory markers of identity, I maintain that legal categories must be continually questioned and challenged. Law itself constructs categories of identity; in doing so, it must be sensitive to the myriad ways that identities are lived, and be flexible enough to ensure that categorical rigidity does not impede quests for justice, dignity, respect, and belonging.

Intersectionality and Discrimination

THERE HAS BEEN a growing recognition of intersectionality in Canadian courts and tribunals. As Justice L'Heureux-Dubé of the Supreme Court of Canada wrote:

> [C]ategorizing ... discrimination as primarily racially oriented, or primarily gender-oriented, misconceives the reality of discrimination as it is experienced by individuals. Discrimination may be experienced on many grounds, and where this is the case, it is not really meaningful to assert that it is one or the other. It may be more realistic to recognize that both forms of discrimination may be present and intersect.[11]

The story of Levan Turner, who claimed discrimination based on race, national and ethnic origin, colour, age, and perceived disability provides an example of how intersectionality operates. He maintained that it was not just one of these grounds that resulted in his exclusion; it was the combination of all of them. After numerous legal proceedings, the Canadian Human Rights Tribunal concluded that Levan Turner had been stereotyped as an older Black man who was overweight, and that he was subjected to discrimination based on age, race, and perceived disability (connected to his weight).[12] Had the grounds in his case been treated independently of one another, his discrimination claim would present only a partial and fragmented picture. To fully appreciate the exclusion he experienced requires us to think about how discrimination arises at the intersection of multiple grounds — in this case, at the intersection of age, race, and perceived disability.

Turner's case has entailed multiple tribunal and court proceedings and decisions.[13] In his initial human rights complaint, Turner maintained that he had been discriminated against on the basis of race and age, but did not specify disability or perceived disability. During the first tribunal hearing, however, the ground of perceived disability, linked specifically to his weight, was raised in oral argument. Following this first hearing, the Canadian Human Rights Tribunal dismissed Turner's complaint. Of significance is the Tribunal's failure to examine the intersectional effects of the grounds of discrimination; instead, it assessed each alleged ground of discrimination in turn. In doing so, it found no convincing evidence of any age discrimination against individuals over the age of thirty-five (Turner was thirty-seven at the time he applied). With respect to the race-based claim, it found that the "raft of scattered, confusing and inconclusive statistical evidence" did not substantiate any claim of racial discrimination.[14] Finally, the Tribunal did not address the perceived disability claim since it was not in the initial complaint. Examining exclusion based on each ground separately did not reveal patterns of discrimination based on either race or age alone. But for Turner, it was the combined effects of race, age, and his weight that, he maintained, prompted his discriminatory treatment.

Following his initial loss at the Canadian Human Rights Tribunal, Levan Turner and his union challenged the ruling in court. In May 2012, the Federal Court of Appeal agreed that the Tribunal's decision should be set aside since it did not consider whether or not there was discrimination on the basis of "perceived disability";[15] nor did it give enough weight to the argument that the discrimination might have resulted from a combination or intersection of the grounds of race, age, and disability. As noted by Justice Robert Mainville of the Federal Court of Appeal, "though the primary focus of a complaint of discrimination may be race, the analysis of that primary ground must not ignore the other grounds of complaint, such as disability, and the possibility that compound discrimination may have occurred as a result of the intersection of these grounds."[16] He further explained the idea of intersecting grounds of discrimination as follows:

> [W]hen multiple grounds of discrimination are present, their combined effect may be more than the sum of their individual effects. The concept of intersecting grounds also holds that analytically separating these multiple grounds minimizes what is, in fact, compound discrimination. When analyzed separately, each ground

may not justify individually a finding of discrimination, but when the grounds are considered together, another picture may emerge.[17]

Thus, Turner's story provides us with a concrete example of a case that does not fall neatly into one ground of discrimination. Adjudicators are tasked with assessing the combined effects of more than one category of potential discrimination.

In the wake of the decision of the Federal Court of Appeal, Turner's case went back to the Canadian Human Rights Tribunal. After reviewing all of the evidence again and assessing perceived disability as well as intersectional discrimination, the Tribunal decided in Turner's favour, as noted above. At the outset of his decision, Adjudicator Wallace Craig acknowledged that in cases of race discrimination, there is often no direct evidence available. Instead, adjudicators need to rely on what is called "circumstantial evidence" (indirect evidence) and assess what has been called the "subtle scent of discrimination."[18] As explained in an earlier race discrimination case:

> Discrimination is not a practice that one should expect to see displayed overtly. A tribunal should therefore consider all circumstances in determining if there exists what has been described as the *subtle scent of discrimination*. In cases involving circumstantial evidence, an inference of discrimination may be drawn where the evidence offered in support of it renders such an inference more probable than the other possible inferences or hypotheses.[19]

The Tribunal then affirmed that discrimination on the basis of a perceived disability is protected in the *Canadian Human Rights Act*, noting, "discrimination on the basis of disability can occur even in the absence of an actual physical or mental limitation on activities, based solely on societal perceptions of one's limitations."[20] Finally, the importance of considering the possibility that the discrimination involved a combination of grounds was recognized, specifically that "tribunals should be alive to the 'interrelationship between a number of intersecting grounds of discrimination.'"[21] Following a detailed review of the evidence, the Tribunal found that there was discrimination on the basis of age, race, and a perceived disability of obesity,[22] and a substantial remedy for lost wages and moral damages was ordered. The inequality in Levan Turner's case does not fit easily into only one category of discrimination; it cannot be linked exclusively to race, age, or perceived disability. It is the combination of all of these identity markers that potentially interacted to result the job being denied to him. His case is just one among many that raise discrimination issues at the intersection of identity markers.[23]

Although the number of grounds of discrimination protected in national and international human rights documents has gradually increased, courts and adjudicators often fail to incorporate the insights of intersecting inequalities. Even when legal protections and institutional processes allow multiple and intersecting discrimination claims, courts and tribunals still have difficulty analyzing such claims, and tend to revert to legal reasoning that is rooted in traditional single-group categories of anti-discrimination law. The predominant approach continues to focus on a single ground of discrimination rather than on multiple, intersecting grounds. This tendency is further reinforced by the fact that most social science research does not provide comparative statistical data that takes into account intersectional identities.[24] Anti-discrimination law, therefore, has been critiqued for the ways in which it promotes an "atomized" conception of human identity that divides complex identities into discrete group-based claims, even when individual lives are characterized by membership in multiple groups that have been subjected to discrimination.[25]

In short, questions of intersectionality arise when individual discrimination (a single occurrence of discrimination) occurs at the intersection of more than one ground of discrimination (or numerous grounds), such as race and sex, or religion and sex, or disability and sexual orientation. Yet too often, anti-discrimination laws require individuals to choose a single ground when proceeding with a human rights complaint. In so doing, there is a real risk that intersecting forms of discrimination will not be recognized, and individuals whose exclusion results from a combination of identity markers will be left without a remedy.

Living Identity Differently: "Identity Performance"

IN THEIR ARTICLE, "The Fifth Black Woman," Devon Carbado and Mitu Gulati explain that individuals with similar identity markers often live their lives or "perform their identities" in significantly different ways.[26] In addition to looking at intragroup differences in terms of intersectionality, they outline the need to examine "identity performance." They tell a fictional story of five Black women in a corporate law firm seeking to become partners. Four of the Black women are promoted, and one is rejected for partnership. Although she receives excellent evaluations for her work at the firm, the one Black woman who is refused partnership performs her racial identity differently than the others. For example, she wears her hair in locs instead of relaxing it; she has advocated for the need to increase the hiring and retention of women and minorities in the law firm; she tends not to participate in the firm's social events; she does not golf or play tennis; she is a member of the local Black bar association; she is a single mother; and she did not attend an Ivy League college.[27] Carbado and Gulati use this example to emphasize that "intra group distinctions based on identity performance implicate workplace discrimination."[28] Yet anti-discrimination law tends to overlook differences based on identity performance, focusing instead simply on identity status.

This idea of "identity performance" resonates with concerns that many have expressed about the pressures that individuals feel to assimilate by emulating the norms, culture, and practices of those who dominate within an institution. It has been characterized by some as "trait discrimination" rather than "status discrimination."[29] Kenji Yoshino speaks of "covering," which he explains involves toning down "a disfavored identity to fit into the mainstream."[30] Indeed, historical definitions of discrimination based on sameness of treatment often comprised an unstated assimilation requirement. Individuals from historically under-represented groups within an institution were to be treated the same as those from the dominant groups, on the condition they conformed to dominant norms and ways of being. For example, a woman would be hired into a traditionally male job, provided she could "act like a man." She could not have child care obligations or demonstrate stereotypical "female" traits. To enter a traditionally male domain meant accepting traditionally "male" ways of being, working, acting, and interacting. Patricia Hewlin has done extensive work on what she calls "facades of conformity" in the workplace.[31] She explores the pressures experienced by under-represented groups to conform to the dominant norms of the work-place culture, and yet believes that thriving at work requires that we celebrate and share our "authentic selves."[32] An important compon-ent of inclusion without assimilation involves both accommodation of differences in institutional settings and the revision of dominant norms to eliminate their negative effects.

The different performance of identities also raises fundamen-tal issues about invisible sources of discrimination. With respect to sexual orientation, gender identity, race, and mental health disabil-ities, for example, a critical issue is the extent to which individuals feel free to disclose their differences from dominant majorities.[33] For some, their differences from the dominant groups are evident and cannot be hidden. Others, however, may choose to hide their differ-ences. Yoshino characterizes the hiding of one's identity as "passing." Martha Minow's insightful work on what she calls the "difference dilemma" clarifies the problem.[34] She explains that in many situations, to identify oneself as different from the majority is to risk being stig-matized. However, if one does not identify one's differences, there is a risk of non-recognition or non-accommodation. Sometimes, indi-viduals fearing stigma, exclusion, and discrimination will hide their differences and not disclose important dimensions of their identity. Others may choose to disclose their differences, and may experience discrimination or stigma in the wake of doing so. The difference dilemma, therefore, is closely related to the idea of identity perform-ance. Thus, it is critical to recognize that those with similar identities may express them differently, depending on context, community, circumstances, and power relations.[35]

Rejecting Categories: Creating New Identities

Je n'ai pas plusieurs identités, j'en ai une seule, faite de tous les éléments qui l'ont façonnée.

— AMIN MAALOUF, *LES IDENTITÉS MEURTRIÈRES*[36]

AS AMIN MAALOUF explains, individuals do not experience their identity in terms of discrete and separate compartments. In his book, he explains that he is half French and half Lebanese, which he explains does not make him any less French or less Lebanese. When asked about his origins, he refuses to choose one or the other; he is both.[37] To take another example, if you are bilingual in French and English, you do not speak less English or less French by virtue of speaking both languages fluently. In many situations, to have multiple identities does not reduce your affiliation with any one of those identities. The cultural and social contexts of your life and the communities in which you live may make one of your affiliated identities more prominent, but being both does not equal being less of one or the other. Sometimes individuals choose to identify with one of the dimensions of their identity more than others; sometimes they claim both or multiple identities simultaneously; sometimes they create new categories. As Megan Gannon has observed, the "rigidity of racial and ethnic categories does not reflect Canadian society, which is filled with rich human diversity."[38]

How does law create categories of identity? How do we deal with complex identities that defy neat categorization? One approach is to focus on how individual people are treated, rather than on their biological or visible identities. For example, when biracial individuals are subjected to racial exclusion or prejudice, they experience discrimination on the basis of race,[39] even though, in some cases, their racial identity may not be apparent. They may have family histories that include a Black parent and grandparents, but they may look white or Hispanic as a result of their other non-racialized parent and grandparents' genetics (or genetic makeup/composition). Even siblings may have different genetic traits that make them more or less likely to be subjected to racial discrimination. Additionally, regardless of how individuals look to others, their lives are deeply shaped by their familial and cultural histories.

In some instances, we may use the terminology of "racialized" to refer to "the process by which societies construct races as real, different and unequal in ways that matter and affect economic, political and social life."[40] In the United States, for example, segregation policies historically applied to all mixed-race individuals — labelled Black in a world where the two dichotomous choices were Black or white.[41] In Canada, Islamophobia has been understood to implicate the racialization of religion and Muslim identities, illustrating how racism evolves and emerges in new circumstances[42] and how racialization can be socially constructed. Racialization is linked to how individuals and groups are perceived and treated as "other."[43]

The arbitrariness of racial categories is illustrated by the treatment of Indigenous women by the Canadian government. In the 1870s, a patrilineal definition of "Indian status" was included in the federal *Indian Act*.[44] Having one's identity as an "Indian" formally recognized by the federal government under this Act brought individuals within the administration of the Act, and granted rights such as being able to live and receive housing on reserve, participate in governance, and receive federally funded healthcare. Historically, if a First Nations woman married a white man she would lose her Indian status, and her children would not be recognized as "status Indians"; whereas if a white woman married a status Indian, she would gain Indian status.[45] Here, we see a racialized identity category, "Indian status," constructed in law in ways that do not necessarily align with any biological or genetic reality, nor with belonging to a community. Instead, it is a product of patriarchy, sexism, and the colonial destruction of Indigenous communities. Patrilineal nationality rules have long histories in Western legal traditions, with a married woman's nationality dictated by that of her husband. It was only after significant legal struggles at the domestic and international levels that the exclusionary and patriarchal Indian status rules were reformed.[46] Ongoing issues of non-recognition of Indigenous identity status continue to impact the children and grandchildren of women who lost their Indian status through marriage.

The complexity of identity has also resulted in the emergence of new identities at the interstice of two historic identity categories. For example, the Métis emerged as a distinctive Indigenous people resulting from the intermarriage of European male fur traders and Indigenous women. The story of the Métis illustrates the dynamic and evolving dimensions of group-based identities. As James Tully notes, "cultures are not internally homogeneous. They are continuously contested, imagined and reimagined, transformed and negotiated, both by their members and through their interaction with others."[47] The emergence of new identity categories reflects the importance of focusing on — rather than ignoring — the dynamic components of identity, which often arise in the space between the polar opposites of traditional categories.

Another area where traditional identity categories are being questioned concerns gender. One important example of this phenomenon is the identification and celebration of non-binary gender identities. For many, the binary division of the world into men and women is so engrained into our psyches and experiences that it is hard to imagine a world where our binary genders are not apparent. And yet, the emergence of trans and intersex voices are revolutionizing how we think about gender identity.[48] Stories that reject traditional gender categories remind us to celebrate each individual's unique identity, with all of its complexities. As Ivan Coyote writes, "My new shirt. Plaid on the outside, but with flowers on the inside. Just like me."[49] Coyote's gender identity is non-binary. Using the "they" pronoun instead of either she or he, Coyote provides insights into the complexities of gender identity in the context of family, community, and work. Their deeply humanistic stories break down divides of misunderstanding, urging us to build a more accepting and just society.

A human rights complaint in British Columbia provides further illustration of how gender identity categories are being challenged in fundamental ways. In this case, complainants filed a complaint against birth certificate sex identification policies that required parents to identify the sex of their baby, even though the birth certificate could be changed in the future if the child's lived gender did not reflect the original identification.[50] The BC government responded by offering to "amend its policies and procedures to allow for a third designation option of 'x' on birth certificates, in addition to the existing 'male' or 'female' option."[51] The x option would be "available to trans or intersex individuals for whom the 'male' or 'female' sex designation does not reflect their lived gender."[52] The response of the BC government aligns with shifts in policy on gender identification by other governments. The Canadian federal government now allows individuals to use a third gender identifier, x, on their passports, even though some countries may not recognize this emerging category. In Ontario, individuals may choose x rather than using male or female sex markers on drivers' licences and health cards.

While the emergence of a third category in addition to male or female is still in its early phases, in the BC case, the complainants did not accept the settlement offer based on the shift to an x sex identification marker. They were concerned that putting x as an identity marker would "increase rather than decrease the marginalization experienced by non-binary people because it 'will "out" them to anyone who requires a birth certificate and thereby expose them immediately to the prejudice, stereotypes and marginalization experienced by trans people.'"[53] Additional concerns that would not be addressed simply by adding a new x sex category included the following:

a) the marginalization experienced by a person between the development of their gender identity and the change to the gender on their birth certificates, which could be a matter of years;

b) a situation of gender variant children whose guardians may not support their gender identity or permit them to change their gender identity on the birth certificate;

c) a situation where a child's parents or guardians do not agree with each other about whether a child should be permitted to change their gender; or

d) a situation where people do not have access to changing their gender because of poverty, lack of access to a certifying professional, or lack of access to paperwork.[54]

All of these concerns raise fundamental questions about the whole idea of gender identity categories and whether it is even necessary to include gender or sex labels on government documents. Despite the complexity of these arguments and the challenges they present to our traditional ways of categorizing the world, it seems important to be open to new approaches to and understandings of identity — to honour and respect the varied and evolving experiences of diversity at the heart of humanity.

Conclusion

IN THIS CHAPTER, I have questioned the traditional legal categories of anti-discrimination law — categories that have proven to be inadequate in addressing some of the most pressing contemporary issues of exclusion and stereotyping. Rather than dispensing with categorical analysis altogether, however, it is helpful to understand categories as tentative and open to revision and continued challenge. Reliance on categories should be combined with a recognition of their limits, as distinct categories are "permeated by other categories, fluid and changing, always in the process of being created and recreated by dynamics of power."[55] Sometimes we choose a category, or multiple and overlapping categories; sometimes we reject existing categories and create new ones. While categories continue to be central to evolving understandings of identity and are important legal and analytical tools, they must be treated as partial, provisional, and dynamic. In this way, we may contribute to the possibility of resisting conformity and celebrating the dynamic complexity of human identities.

– 8 –

When Speech Hurts:
Conflicting Freedoms

Sticks and ſtones may break our bones, but words will break our hearts.

— ROBERT FULGHUM,

ALL I REALLY NEED TO KNOW I LEARNED IN KINDERGARTEN, 1988[1]

IMAGINE YOU ARE an elderly gay man, living with your partner in a quiet residential neighbourhood in Saskatoon. When you check the morning mail, you find anti-gay flyers in your mailbox, which have been distributed by a group called the Christian Truth Activists. The flyers, which depict your sexual orientation in very negative terms, upset your sense of belonging and well-being, and make you fearful that you may even be at risk of violence. This is what happened to James Komar.[2] Other Saskatchewan residents also received the anti-gay flyers in their mail, and four individuals (including Komar) decided to file complaints under the *Saskatchewan Human Rights Code*, which prohibits discriminatory public speech that "exposes or tends to expose to hatred."[3] Although they won their case before the Saskatchewan Human Rights Tribunal,[4] the Christian Truth Activists appealed to the courts on the question of whether the prohibitions on hate speech in the *Saskatchewan Human Rights Act* violate freedom of expression and religion in the *Canadian Charter of Rights and Freedoms*. One way of understanding this case is to view it as a conflict between equality rights and freedom of expression. However, before we accept this way of framing the issue, it is important to think about alternative ways of understanding the dilemma at the heart of this case. Rather than understanding it only in terms of a conflict between rights and freedoms, we could recognize that it is also a conflict between two freedoms — the freedom to live in this world without fear of violence or hate, versus the freedom to say whatever you want, even if it causes fear or harm, or is hateful. We discussed the idea of equitable freedom in Chapter 5, and here we can extend it to include not only freedom from sexual violence, but also from violence more generally. Conceptualizing this story of hateful flyers in terms of *conflicting* freedoms means that, no matter the outcome of the legal challenge, someone's freedom is undermined. Rather than recognizing only one freedom and framing the analysis as one of "freedom" versus "equality," it seems more accurate to understand the dilemma as one involving equality and contested freedoms. Human rights laws should endeavour to protect equality, and in so doing also protect freedom equitably.[5]

In this chapter, we examine what I call "harmful speech" to draw out the idea of equitably balancing conflicting freedoms. Harmful speech is an umbrella term that includes overlapping types of speech, such as "hate speech," "dangerous speech," and "discriminatory hurtful speech." Legal responses to harmful speech must consider the contexts within which speech occurs, power dynamics between the speaker and audience, and an understanding of why people engage in hateful speech. Beyond legal responses, we might also imagine a world where individuals take care to recognize the impact of their words and to speak in ways that do not intentionally cause harm.

How Speech Hurts
Harms to Individuals and Groups

There are two main types of harm experienced as a result of speech. The first is actual physical violence against the targeted group; the second is the psychological and emotional effects of speech on the targeted group. In one of the leading criminal cases on hate speech, *R v Keegstra*, Chief Justice Dickson recognized both types of harm.[6] The case involved a high school teacher who engaged in repeated anti-Semitic speech in his classroom. With respect to the risk of physical harm, Chief Justice Dickson noted:

> The threat to the self-dignity of target group members is thus matched by the possibility that prejudiced messages will gain some credence, with the attendant result of discrimination, and perhaps even violence, against minority groups in Canadian society.[7]

Concerns about the actual physical harms of speech are central to Harvard University's Dangerous Speech Project.[8] The Project defines dangerous speech as including "expression (e.g. speech, text, or images) that can increase the risk that its audience will condone or commit violence against members of another group."[9] The term "hate speech" is not used because it is a nebulous term that is often difficult to define and identify. The initiative focuses specifically on increased risks (not necessarily actual causation) of physical violence or bodily harm. The Dangerous Speech Project has examined the historical links between dangerous speech against specific groups and the subsequent violence and genocide in numerous countries and contexts. By analyzing the various elements of dangerous speech — including the speaker, the audience, the message, the historical and social context, and the medium — it is possible to predict the risk of violence. This is a critical first step in preventing violence resulting from dangerous speech. It can "serve as an early warning indicator for violence between groups" and it can be countered by educating people about its harmful and false messages.[10]

In addition to physical violence, speech may cause psychological, emotional, and physiological harm. In *Keegstra*, the Supreme Court stated, "It is indisputable that the emotional damage caused by words may be of grave psychological and social consequence."[11] In explaining the effects of hateful speech, Chief Justice Dickson found that the "derision, hostility and abuse encouraged by hate propaganda ... have a severely negative impact on the individual's sense of self-worth and acceptance."[12] In the *Whatcott* human rights case in Saskatchewan, Gens Hellquist, who was the executive director of Gay and Lesbian Health Services in Saskatoon at the time the leaflets were distributed, was an expert witness at the human rights tribunal hearing. He had received numerous complaints about the leaflets and testified that they undermined self-esteem and "had the potential to be very devastating on gays and lesbians, especially amongst the youth."[13] Mari Matsuda has enumerated the "real and immediate" psychological, emotional, and physiological effects of hate speech:

> Victims of vicious hate propaganda have experienced physiological symptoms and emotional distress ranging from fear in the gut, rapid pulse rate and difficulty in breathing, nightmares, post-traumatic stress disorder, hypertension, psychosis, and suicide.[14]

These significant and often long-term effects of speech have been recognized in numerous human rights cases.

Another important and controversial case that demonstrates the psychological and emotional harm of speech involved jokes made by a comedian targeting a young boy with a hearing disability. [15] Jérémy Gabriel was born with Treacher Collins syndrome, an illness that made him nearly deaf by the age of three (though it had no other effects on his health or life expectancy). When he was six, an implanted hearing device reduced his hearing loss significantly and he began to pursue his dream of becoming a singer. At the age of nine, he appeared on television and sang the national anthem at the Bell Centre before a Montreal Canadiens hockey game. One year later, he was invited to sing with Céline Dion in Las Vegas and before the Pope in Rome. This success led to the creation of an autobiography and his participation in a documentary about Treacher Collins syndrome — all before the age of thirteen. It was at this time that comedian Mike Ward began using Jérémy as the target of jokes in his comedy shows, which he performed live, made into DVDs, and posted online as videos. His jokes about Jérémy included making fun of his disability and singing abilities, as well as criticizing his appearance. When Jérémy saw the videos, they upset him deeply.

Jérémy and his parents filed a discrimination complaint with the Quebec Human Rights and Youth Rights Commission. After investigating the complaint, the Commission took Jérémy's case before the

Quebec Human Rights Tribunal. Jérémy's reaction to the jokes was described by the Tribunal in its decision:

> He withdrew and lost confidence and hope. For two years, he did not want to go out, sing, or even exist anymore.
>
> At school, other students repeated the jokes they heard in Ward's videos. Jérémy felt ridiculed and sad. He developed suicidal thoughts.... In his testimony, Jérémy said he felt lost, fragile and isolated.[16]

Judge Scott Hughes of the Quebec Human Rights Tribunal concluded that Ward's comments and jokes about Jérémy were discriminatory and targeted him based on his physical disability. While acknowledging the countervailing values of freedom of expression, the Tribunal nonetheless found that they did not insulate Ward's discriminatory comments in this case.[17]

Harms to Society

Beyond the specific harms to individuals, in *Keegstra*, Chief Justice Dickson concluded that another "harmful effect of hate propaganda which is of pressing and substantial concern is its influence upon society at large."[18] As he explained, "the active dissemination of hate propaganda can attract individuals to its cause, and in the process create serious discord between various cultural groups in society."[19] In undermining social cohesion and inclusion, hate speech interferes with the effective and equitable functioning of democratic institutions. As Justice Marshall Rothstein explained for the Supreme Court of Canada in the *Whatcott* decision, hateful speech undermines democracy by impeding the equitable participation of groups:

> [A] particularly insidious aspect of hate speech is that it acts to cut off any path of reply by the group under attack. It does this not only by attempting to marginalize the group so that their reply will be ignored: it also forces the group to argue for their basic humanity or social standing, as a precondition to participating in the deliberative aspects of our democracy.[20]

Since one of the widely acknowledged justifications for freedom of expression is the enhancement of democratic self-governance, the undermining of democratic participation has been viewed as a justification for limits on speech.

Context Matters: Power, Privilege, and Speech

RECOGNITION OF THE different kinds of psychological, emotional, and even physical harm that speech may cause is an important starting point for thinking about how to protect individuals and groups from harmful speech. But simply recognizing the harm does not provide any clear answers about whether there should be some limits on freedom of speech. It may depend on a variety of different and sometimes conflicting factors; in other words, it depends on the context.[21]

First, it may depend on how hateful, hurtful, or dangerous the speech is, and on whether the speech threatens the actual physical and psychological safety or well-being of a specific individual or group. Does the speech perpetuate or contribute to discrimination against specific groups? Deciding to limit speech may depend on the nature of the speech and the risks of it causing harm — if it is not that damaging or dangerous, we may not want to limit freedom of expression. As elaborated below, Canadian criminal and human rights laws have generally taken this approach — limiting criminal and civil regulation of harmful speech to extreme cases of vilification and group-based denigration or denials of human dignity.

Second, it is important to recognize that harmful speech undermines not only the rights of those in the targeted group, but also their freedoms. It potentially violates their freedom to live without fear or denigration, to participate equitably, and to express themselves. Recognizing that we are dealing not only with the freedom of one person (the speaker), but also the freedom of the person against whom the harmful speech is directed, underscores the fact that we are faced with a situation of conflicting freedoms, in addition to a conflict *between* rights and freedoms. Reframing the dilemma in terms of contested freedoms is useful because it challenges the idea that it is only the freedom of the speaker that is at stake in debates about freedom of expression. The freedom of targeted individuals and groups is undermined as well, impacting their freedom to live in safety without threats of violence, harm, belittling, or denigration, and their freedom to participate fully as democratic citizens in a world where each person and diverse communities are respected and valued.

A third contextual consideration is the vulnerability of the individual or group targeted by the harmful speech. How much power or privilege do they have in the institution or in society? Are they in a position to "talk back" or to contest the hateful or harmful speech? Speech does not begin from a neutral starting point; it is embedded in a matrix of institutional and societal inequalities that give more power to some than others. Often, individuals with significant societal power are in a position to cause harm through their speech, and even to cause harm with impunity or without consequences. Those with less power in particular institutional or social contexts do not have that same level of freedom of expression or do not have the same power to cause harm through their speech. In some cases, an individual's institutional power means that speech directed against that individual does not cause significant harm; some individuals are insulated by their institutional and social power. For example, a situation where an individual citizen lashes out verbally against a police officer is very different from a situation where a police officer is verbally aggressive towards an individual citizen.[22] The police officer in most cases has significant power, whereas the individual citizen does not and may in fact be powerless and at risk of institutionalized violence. When the individual and group targeted by the hateful speech is in a precarious, vulnerable, or marginalized situation, hate speech causes greater risks to their health and well-being. In short, whether we believe speech should be curtailed or allowed may depend on the circumstances and the dynamics of power between the individuals or groups involved. Catharine MacKinnon has cautioned that the "law of equality and the law of freedom of speech are on a collision course"[23] in which "the less speech you have, the more the speech of those who have it keep you unequal; the more the speech of the dominant is protected, the more dominant they become."[24] In other words, freedom of expression must be analyzed in relation to the actual conditions of equality and inequality in our society.

Another dimension of the power dynamics of speech concerns access to platforms for expressing ideas. Too often, those with power, privilege, money, or connections to large, organized interest groups disproportionately speak in our society. Another dimension of the power dynamics of speech concerns access to platforms for expressing ideas. Too often, those with power, privilege, money, or connections to large, organized interest groups have a disproportionately large platform to speak in our society. In some cases, it has been recognized that we need to limit certain speech to advance more equitable freedom of speech generally; for example, election spending laws are designed to ensure that democratic choices are not skewed by inequitable access to the means of communication by wealthy or well-funded candidates.[25] The impact of the internet and social media is also changing access to communication channels in complex and challenging ways — in some cases, enhancing more equitable freedom of expression, but in other contexts, accentuating problems such as harmful speech and cyberbullying.[26]

Finally, we need to assess why people engage in harmful speech. Is it linked to an intentional desire to hurt someone or denigrate a group in society? Is it being used to exert power or privilege over an individual or community? Is it based on an unwitting microaggression against a particular group? Is it based on a negligent disregard for how speech may harm others? Is it speech that inadvertently causes harm, even though the speaker did not realize the speech was harmful? The appropriateness of different legal and social responses depends on the answers to these questions. If there is respect and goodwill between individuals and groups, an apology, a retraction, or a teaching moment may address the harm. In many situations, once individuals realize the harm they are causing, they will voluntarily change how they speak to respect the well-being, as well as the rights and freedoms, of others.[27] In other situations, individuals who become aware or who are already well aware of the harm their speech is causing may insist on their right to continue to engage in the harmful speech. Their speech may be linked to religious or other individual beliefs, or simply to the belief that they are entitled to exercise their freedom of speech without restrictions. These more difficult cases are where context, rights, and principles need to be applied to mediate harm and freedom.

In short, a contextual approach to harmful speech underscores the fact that speech does not occur in the abstract. It involves real people, with different degrees of power and privilege in society — where historical and ongoing inequalities and unequal freedom affect the harm speech may cause. The context of harmful speech is an important starting point for assessing how to deal with it. When those engaging in harmful speech have significant power and privilege, there is a greater likelihood that they will increase the risks of physical harm to the targeted individuals and group; at the same time, they also have more power to inflict psychological and emotional harm. A contextual approach also allows us to determine what is really at stake. What are the underlying interests and concerns? Does the speech create significant risks of physical, psychological, or emotional harm, or undermine the equality of historically disadvantaged groups in society? Would curtailing the speech undermine democratic debate, personal self-actualization, and robust discussions of community and societal well-being?[28] More practically, is it possible to control the speech without creating other harms and risks to the safety of society? What is the best approach to regulating harmful speech? And is law capable of regulating speech fairly and effectively?

Regulating Harmful Speech: Criminal, Civil, and International

THERE ARE NUMEROUS legal limits on harmful speech and expression. In its guidance to governments, the *International Covenant on Civil and Political Rights* provides that "[a]ny advocacy of national, racial or religious hatred that constitutes incitement to discrimination, hostility or violence shall be prohibited by law."[29] Similarly, the *International Convention on the Elimination of all Forms of Racial Discrimination* urges states to make it an offence to disseminate "ideas based on racial superiority or hatred."[30] Prohibitions on hate speech, therefore, have been an important part of the post–World War II international human rights revolution, with the recognition that they must be balanced with protection of freedom of expression.

In Canada, as is the case in many countries around the world, there are both criminal and civil law restrictions on hateful speech. The *Criminal Code of Canada* prohibits "public incitement of hatred" and the "wilful promotion of hatred" (other than in private conversation) against certain identifiable groups, including those "distinguished by colour, race, religion, national or ethnic origin, age, sex, sexual orientation, gender identity or expression, or mental or physical disability."[31] It is quite rare for individuals to be criminally prosecuted, though there have been a few high-profile cases.[32] If convicted, individuals may be sentenced to up to two years in prison.[33] It is important to note, however, that with respect to the offence of the wilful promotion of hatred, there are a number of defenses. Section 318(3) states:

(3) No person shall be convicted of an offence under subsection (2)

a. if he establishes that the statements communicated were *true*;

b. if, in good faith, the person expressed or attempted to establish by an argument an opinion on a *religious subject* or an opinion based on a belief in a religious text;

c. if the statements were relevant to any subject of *public interest*, the discussion of which was for the public benefit, and if on reasonable grounds *he believed them to be true*; or

d. if, in *good faith*, he intended to point out, *for the purpose of removal, matters producing or tending to produce feelings of hatred* toward an identifiable group in Canada.[34]

These criminal law provisions have been challenged in the courts. While they have been found to violate constitutional protections of freedom of expression, they have generally been upheld as reasonable limits to those constitutional rights, pursuant to section 1 of the *Charter*.[35]

In addition to criminal law prohibitions, human rights legislation has been used to contest hateful speech. In some jurisdictions, there are specific provisions that prohibit hate speech. For example, as we saw in James Komar's case about anti-gay hate speech, the

Saskatchewan Human Rights Code prohibits publishing or displaying in public, any statement, symbol or expression that "exposes or tends to expose to hatred . . . any person or class of persons on the basis of a prohibited ground."[36] The *Canadian Human Rights Act* prohibits the publication or public display of "any notice, sign, symbol, emblem or other representation that (a) expresses or implies discrimination or an intention to discriminate, or (b) incites or is calculated to incite others to discriminate."[37] Similarly, the *Quebec Charter of Human Rights and Freedoms* provides that "no one may distribute, publish or publicly exhibit a notice, symbol or sign involving discrimination, or authorize anyone to do so."[38]

Even in the absence of prohibitions on hate speech, existing protections against discrimination and harassment may be interpreted to prohibit harmful discriminatory speech, particularly when it occurs in specific institutional settings, such as the workplace or schools. Individuals may file complaints of discrimination or harassment based on the group-based harm caused by speech. Harassment may take the form of words, comments, or other types of expression. For example, in what has been called "the longest-running human rights case in Canadian history," Michael McKinnon, who was employed as a correctional officer at the Toronto East Detention Centre, was the subject of persistent racial slurs linked to his Indigenous ancestry.[39] The repeated racial slurs were found to contribute to a workplace culture that tolerated pervasive racial harassment at the provincial detention centre where he worked; numerous other racialized individuals testified that they had been subjected to racial slurs.[40] Similarly, the Quebec Court of Appeal recognized that racially derogatory remarks made by an employer, wrongly accusing Chinese workers of uncleanliness, were discriminatory and undermined the human dignity of the workers in violation of the Quebec *Charter of Human Rights and Freedoms*.[41] Sensitive to the social and economic context of the Chinese workers, Justice Paul Vézina noted:

> The complainants had recently immigrated to Canada from China, with hopes of living a better life, if not for themselves, at least for their children. With few resources, little knowledge of the language,

they are vulnerable individuals. They are between the ages of 35 and 45, have university degrees, but must begin again at the bottom of the employment ladder, earning only minimum wage at the company.[42]

In both of the above examples, the speech is causing harm to the point of constituting discrimination or harassment against groups protected in human rights legislation. Thus, discriminatory or harassing speech based on grounds such as race, national or ethnic origin, disability, gender, gender identity, sexual orientation, and religion is subject to human rights law prohibitions.

At the same time, harmful speech that targets individuals in ways that are not connected to their group-based identities is not prohibited in human rights legislation. Nevertheless, this kind of speech is still subject to important restrictions when it is untruthful and harms the reputation of individuals. The common law tort (or civil wrong) of defamation protects an individual's character and reputation.[43]

The criminal and human rights laws described above address alleged violations of hate speech prohibitions after they have occured; the harm has already been done. It may then take many years to obtain redress in human rights tribunals and courts. The legal processes may actually extend the harms of the speech, as it is repeated and debated in the legal proceedings and may even give hatemongers a platform for expression to a certain extent. Furthermore, this traditional retroactive approach is not always effective in preventing hate speech. Although the traditional approach is motivated by the idea that individuals will be reluctant to wilfully promote hatred or cause harm if they risk criminal or civil liability, or institutional disciplinary action, it is worth asking if there are other ways to address the harms of speech or to prevent harmful speech. While we cannot prevent all harmful speech before it happens (and indeed, we may not even wish to try, given the importance of freedom of expression), in thinking about the role of law in responding to such speech, we need to understand the harms that speech may cause and the inequitable social contexts within which speech occurs.

Alternative Approaches to Preventing and Responding to Harmful Speech

DESPITE THE ARRAY of legal provisions that endeavour to prohibit hateful and dangerous speech, it is difficult to regulate such speech. In some instances, legal intervention may amplify hateful speech in ways that seem counterproductive to the protection of the survivors of the harmful speech or the good of society at large.[44] Given the difficulty and risks of relying on retroactive human rights complaints and criminal prosecutions, it is important to think creatively about what various institutional actors could do to prevent harmful, discriminatory speech. It is critical, therefore, to think about the role of law in developing alternative approaches to preventing and responding to harmful speech.

Equitable Communication: Amplifying Voices and Democratizing Speech

One important structural strategy for countering the negative effects of harmful speech is to bolster the freedom of expression for those targeted by hateful speech. Ensuring equitable access to modes of communication and amplifying the voices of those who are too often silenced in our society are strategies based on the adage of "fighting speech with speech." These strategies also reinforce power, resilience, and survival rather than the victimization that is often emphasized in the courtroom. Beyond that, they attest to a belief in genuine exchange and learning across divides of difference, and reinforce our hope for human connection through communication.

Promoting more equitable expression also reinforces democracy. Since democratic self-governance is closely linked to effective dialogue, communication, and debate, ensuring that diverse communities participate equitably in decision making over issues central to their daily lives is critical.[45] This idea of equitable participation rights, however, has not yet been endorsed in Canadian law. In *Native Women's Assn of Canada v Canada*, for example, the Supreme Court of Canada did not accept the argument that the government had any positive duty to fund an Indigenous women's organization to enhance the participation of Indigenous women in an important constitutional debate.[46] Mary Eberts, Sharon McIvor, and Teressa Nahanee, in criticizing this decision, endorse the need for a "constitutional norm" that affirms the importance of participatory democracy and an entitlement for Indigenous women "to speak for themselves."[47] As they explain, it is through speech that "Aboriginal women [can] rebuild and reclaim their recognized position of equality in Aboriginal societies and promote their equality within Canada." They go on to say:

> Aboriginal women's equal right to speak requires that they be able to speak for themselves on an equal basis with Aboriginal men and not be compelled to speak through men or bargain with those men, from a position of unequal power, for the expression of their concerns.[48]

Institutional Engagement Against Hate Speech

Institutional codes of conduct at workplaces and in educational institutions have been another important development in the struggle to reduce harmful speech, particularly when it arises as a dimension of discrimination or harassment.[49] It is also important to remember that constraints on freedom of speech are embedded in institutional roles and responsibilities. For a teacher, professor, student, employer, or supervisor, there may be limits on expression that do not apply to communication between two individual citizens outside of an institutional context.[50] Institutional disciplinary measures are sometimes invoked, generally in more extreme cases, when speech clearly crosses the line of acceptable conduct and causes harm to co-workers or students, and when limits on freedom of expression are more readily justified.[51]

In cases that are less extreme, however, resorting to formal legal processes is less fruitful and generates more controversy about interfering with freedom of speech than about the initial harm of the speech itself. One strategy would be to work towards an institutional culture of respect and dialogue, without resorting to formal legal channels.[52] Rather than invoking institutional disciplinary procedures, institutional leaders and citizens can contest the speech with speech — condemning its message and place in the institution. For example, if a sexist remark is made about a woman or a transgender person, bystanders (of any gender) should challenge it and make clear that it is not welcome. While one would not likely initiate a sexual harassment complaint due to one sexist comment, leaving it unchallenged is also problematic.[53] The impunity of one sexist comment builds into a culture of sexism. To stop this negative dynamic, institutional leaders and the institutional community must make clear that such sexist comments are unacceptable and hurtful. In so doing, a message is conveyed that can contribute to a more equitable institutional culture. Individuals making sexist comments are condemned by institutional leaders and by their peers. They learn that such speech is neither acceptable nor funny, making it less likely that they will make sexist remarks in the future.

Social Media

The internet is a challenging arena that has seen an escalation of hate speech in recent years. Social media has allowed for an explosion of unaccountable speech, which has proven difficult to regulate through traditional legal channels. Two strategies have emerged: one favours more speech and dialogue to combat harmful speech; the other aims to neutralize speech by removing it from the internet or censoring those who engage in it.

The self-regulation of social media networks (either through legislation or through codes of conduct),[54] the use of artificial intelligence,[55] and civil society techniques like "naming and shaming"[56] tend to view censorship and the removal of content as the best strategy for combatting hate speech. Media initiatives that focus on education and media literacy, along with some civil society initiatives, tend to view increased expression and communication as a more viable solution.[57] Likely, a combination of these strategies will be needed to address harmful speech online.

One innovative civil society initiative, Project Someone (**So**cial **M**edia **E**ducati**on** **E**very day), originated from Professor Vivek Venkatesh of Concordia University.[58] It is an online, educational platform that applies principles of social pedagogy and artistic expression to combat hate speech and curb radicalization. For example, projects include:

- **#visualizingempathy**, which encourages youth to make and share visual representations of their daily lives
- **Learning to Hate: An Anti-Hate Comic Project**, which has academics translating anti-hate scholarship into comic book form to connect with youth
- **Literary Peace Project**, which uses blogging and literature to encourage civic dialogue in English classrooms
- **Adult Ed & Online Hate**, which implements adult education models, technology, and interactive activities (for example, participatory theatre) to encourage community members to openly and respectfully discuss contentious issues
- **Theatrics of Hate Speech**, which analyzes the prevalence of hate speech in social media and the complicity of online subcultures and underground music scenes in its propagation[59]

The project's alternative approach to combatting hate speech has earned it many accolades, and it is expanding to other countries, including the United States, Belgium, Denmark, Finland, France, Germany, Norway, Sweden, and Lebanon.[60]

Preventing Violence and Acts of Hate

Another important alternative to trying to regulate harmful speech is to focus instead on redressing and preventing acts of hate, harassment, and violence. As one commentator from the United States has noted:

> Free speech issues have often overwhelmed the problem of ethno-violence on our college and university campuses. In formulating policy, university administrators and legal counsel are now considering free speech issues as much, if not more, than the race conflict issue itself.[61]

This comment reminds us of the need to address both speech and actual acts of violence directed at certain groups.

Conclusion

We encounter each other in words, words
spiny or smooth, whispered or declaimed,
words to consider, reconsider.

— ELIZABETH ANDERSON, *PRAISE SONG FOR THE DAY*:
A POEM FOR BARACK OBAMA'S PRESIDENTIAL INAUGURATION, 2009[62]

IT IS HARD to understand why some people insist on engaging in speech that has a harmful impact on others. No doubt, individuals often say hurtful things inadvertently, negligently, or in the heat of a debate. But once they realize that their speech is harming others, why would someone choose to continue to use such speech? In some of the cases we have seen, speakers insist, based on principle, on their freedom to say whatever they wish, even when they know it is causing harm to others — they insist on their freedom in isolation from others. This conception of individual freedom — which does not take into account the impact of one's acts or speech on others in the community — is deeply problematic. At the end of the day, it is impossible and even undesirable for the government to try to regulate the harmful aspects of a wide range of human communication. It is, instead, a responsibility that each one of us needs to assume. For beyond all of the possible creative interpretations of legal doctrine, potential justifications for limitations on freedom of expression, or legal remedies for harmful speech, the most effective way to reduce harmful speech may be found not in law, but in the quality of our human relations.[63] As noted in the Dangerous Speech Project, "No one has ever been born hating or fearing other people. That has to be taught."[64] Attending to our human relations, our educational journeys, and our communities may be just as important as all of the laws we might enact to restrain, contain, or punish hateful speech.

The work of James Komar and his colleagues in Saskatchewan, speaking up as members of their community to identify the harms of hateful speech, has had an impact. A 2019 poll conducted by the University of Saskatchewan for the CBC found that "78 per cent of 400 respondents said they either somewhat or strongly agreed that Saskatchewan has become more welcoming to the LGBTQS2+ community in the last five years."[65] Members of the LGBTQ2S+ community explain that "small changes are making them feel like the tide is slowly turning toward more acceptance of the LGBTQ community in Saskatchewan"[66] — a shift that provides the groundwork for belonging, well-being, and safety, as well as enabling equality and freedom to flourish.

conclusion

With Glowing Hearts

With glowing hearts, we see thee rise

— "O CANADA"[1]

WORKING TOWARDS EQUALITY and inclusion is a collective project. "With glowing hearts, we see thee rise," part of Canada's national anthem, speaks to the sense of well-being that is evoked when we all rise, as a community and as a society. Equality is not a project that is only relevant for those who have been subjected to discrimination and exclusion; it requires change and engagement from everyone; it occurs in and through our relations with others. In changing how we respond to inequality and injustice, we do not lose; we gain. Advancing equality is our collective obligation. "With glowing hearts, we see thee rise" is also a positive phrase that evokes a feeling of equality and inclusion. It has symbolic significance, as part of the Canadian national anthem.[2] It conveys a hopeful message: we can be a society that is more equitable and less discriminatory. But both the melody and the lyrics of the national anthem also contain phrases that evoke feelings of exclusion and inequality, reminding us of continuing struggles for inclusion and representation. The history of the anthem contains insights about who has the power to represent a country, about colonialism, and about divides across language, gender, and race.

The Melody: Racism and Blackface

THE MELODY FOR "O Canada" was composed in the 1880s by Calixa Lavallée, a French Canadian musician who spent a considerable part of his musical career in the United States.[3] While Lavallée has been portrayed by some historians as "a humble, patriotic French Canadian," Brian Thompson's book, *Anthems and Minstrel Shows: The Life and Times of Calixa Lavallée, 1842–1891*, examines Lavallée's extensive involvement in blackface minstrel shows.[4] Minstrel groups performed satirical skits and songs that featured the impersonation and stereotyping of Black people. Minstrel shows were, at the time, a leading form of entertainment in North America, and Lavallée rose to fame as a result of their popularity.[5] Many Canadians today, however, have never heard of Lavallée's contribution to the national anthem; nor are they aware of Lavallée's involvement in blackface minstrel shows.[6] Indeed, before working on this chapter, I was completely unaware of the historical link between our national anthem and blackface. I was shocked to read about it in an article written by Laila El Mugammar, entitled "The Hidden Racist History of 'O Canada.'"[7] As she poignantly explains:

> What does it mean to sing the melody of a man who wore me as a costume? Lavallée made a name for himself in reducing Blackness to a monolith for cheap laughs. Though he was not the lyricist of our anthem, his melody remained through the many English and French drafts that predated Parliament's official words. His legacy still comes to life in my Black voice. I've tried to excise blackface from the body of his work, but it had metastasized long before the scalpel fell from my hand.[8]

I had been focusing on the debates about the lyrics of "O Canada" when I realized that this little-known history renders the melody itself problematic. At this moment in our history, when Black individuals and communities are increasingly speaking out about the realities of racism, learning about the connection between "O Canada" and blackface reminded me of how racism is both deeply embedded and yet invisible in our national historical narratives.

In his work on the racist underpinnings of blackface, Phillip Howard notes that "[t]here are few studies of contemporary blackface, and almost none about contemporary blackface in Canada."[9] He points out that while some claim that blackface is not racist, scholarship has "addressed how racist discourse comes to be passed off as non-racist through humour and costuming, and the claim that humour cannot be racist has long been debunked."[10] Howard further explains that "by caricaturing Black bodies and appropriating Black culture, white men constructed representations of Blackness against which they could know themselves as white."[11] He also points out that blackface minstrelsy echoes the history of slavery, as it involves white people using Black bodies for their pleasure.[12] The exploitative nature of minstrelsy is particularly evident when white composers such as Calixa Lavallée not only financially benefit from blackface, but receive acclaim and elevated social status.

Rather than just a relic of history, blackface incidents have had a resurgence in Canada in recent decades.[13] Debates about blackface emerged in the media during the election campaign of 2019, when photos from 2001 of Prime Minister Justin Trudeau in blackface and brownface were published in the national press. Trudeau apologized for the harm that he caused,[14] but what stood out in the national debate was the powerful message of the leader of the New Democratic Party, Jagmeet Singh, the first Sikh person to be the leader of a national political party in Canada. He described the impact of blackface images on Canadian children of colour:

> The kids that see this image, the people that see this image, are going to think about all the times in their life that they were made fun of, that they were hurt, that they were hit, that they were insulted, that they were made to feel less because of who they are and I want to talk to those people right now....
>
> I want to talk to all the kids out there ... You might feel like giving up on Canada. You might feel like giving up on yourselves. I want you to know that you have value, you have worth and you are loved and I don't want you to give up on Canada and please don't give up on yourselves.[15]

Blackface performances and costumes are now widely acknowledged as racist, unacceptable, and offensive. Still, as Laila El
Mugammar writes, "[e]very time I stand for the Canadian national
anthem, I think about blackface."[16] The knowledge we now have
about the historical connection between blackface and our national
anthem means that we can no longer sing the anthem in the same
way. Perhaps this knowledge will remind us that racism not only
has a history in our country, but continues in our present, everyday lives — and that we must recognize and contest it. Perhaps we
should change the melody as a way to remedy the continued harm it
risks causing. And if we have difficulty remembering the new melody, it is because change is hard. It requires both individual and collective work, rooted in solidarity and a recognition of the importance
of the pursuit of racial justice.

The Lyrics: Continuing Controversies

THE LYRICS TO "O Canada" also contain lessons about inequality and
exclusion. They were first written in French by Sir Adolphe-Basile
Routhier,[17] and the French version has not been revised. They were
written to celebrate the French presence in North America; Canada
(an Indigenous word)[18] was initially used to refer to what we now call
Quebec. "O Canada" was first sung at the Saint-Jean-Baptiste celebration in Quebec City on June 24, 1880 — a celebration that began
as a day to celebrate French Canadians, and that more recently has
become a day to celebrate Quebec nationalism.[19] The lyrics speak to
the French military presence, Catholicism, and the colonization of
New France. It is significant that Canada's national anthem has deep
roots in the French-Canadian community.

The English version is not a direct translation. Various English
versions of "O Canada" were written in the early years of the 1900s.
In 1908, a national weekly magazine held a competition for the best
English lyrics of "O Canada," receiving over 300 entries. Mercy E
Powell McCulloch won the competition; however, her version did not
become the official version.[20] Instead Stanley Weir's version, written
as a poem in 1908, became the most popular English version. In 1980,

the federal government officially endorsed Stanley Weir's English lyrics (with some minor modifications) as well as the original French version as the official national anthem.[21] Unlike the French version, the English version does not use religious symbols (for example, carrying the cross, or in French, *porter la croix*); nor does it refer to the strength of religious faith (*foi trempée*) although it does reference "God." Finally, it does not refer to the protection of our homes and rights (*protègera nos foyers et nos droits*).

The 1980 official version in English was not entirely true to the first version Stanley Weir had written. Whereas Weir's original 1908 version had begun "O Canada! Our home, our native land. True patriot love, thou dost in us command," the version approved as the official anthem was a more gendered version, which stated, "in all thy sons command." This version emerged on the eve of World War I and was perhaps revised to resonate with the patriotism and emotion of a society where young Canadian men were preparing to go to war.[22] While young Canadian women had not fought in World War I, about 2,500 went overseas to serve as nurses and some lost their lives.[23] In World War II, women's divisions were created in all three sections of the Canadian military, and around 50,000 women joined the military.[24] Women also assumed critically important roles in the war effort on the home front. The exclusion embedded in the gendered lyrics was felt more poignantly after World War II, particularly in families that had lost a daughter in the war.

Post–World War II Canada was changing rapidly, with an expanding social welfare state, emerging human rights protections, an end to overtly discriminatory immigration policies, and the birth of Canadian citizenship separate from the British subject status of our colonial past. The 1960s also witnessed the creation of the Canadian flag, another sign of growing Canadian nationalism. As noted above, the national anthem, though widely used throughout the twentieth century, was only officially established by law in 1980. The major constitutional reforms of the early 1980s included the passage of the *Canadian Charter of Rights and Freedoms* and the constitutional entrenchment of Aboriginal rights. The contours of these constitutional rights were shaped by the women's movement, advocates for persons with disabilities, Indigenous peoples, minority linguistic communities, and the increasingly multicultural character of Canadian society.

It was within this changing social landscape that concerns arose about the phrase "in all thy sons command." It seemed to reinforce an erasure of women as citizens, even though they too had given their lives in the military and were contributing to Canadian society in other critically important ways.[25] Some people just started singing it differently — singing "in all of us command" — making the lyrics inclusive.[26] But when the national anthem became official, the legislated version was not gender neutral. It would require further legislation to amend the lyrics of the official national anthem from "in all thy sons" to "in all of us" command.

Now, one might have thought that this small change in the lyrics would not be too controversial, particularly since Stanley Weir's original version in English had been gender neutral. All that would be needed was a quick amendment to the legislation, rectifying a historical anomaly and ensuring gender-inclusive lyrics. Alas, such was not the case. It took almost thirty years to get that one phrase changed. In 1990, the Toronto City Council voted for the federal government to change the wording of "O Canada" from "in all thy sons command" to "in all of us command."[27] At the federal level, Vivienne Poy, the first Canadian senator of Asian descent, introduced the first bill in Senate to change the lyrics in 2002. During her tenure in the Senate, Poy did not succeed in having the lyrics changed.[28] Nevertheless, two other senators, Nancy Ruth and Frances Lankin, continued to push for the change. In 2010, Governor General Michaëlle Jean proposed to have the original gender-neutral wording of the anthem reviewed by Parliament.[29] Further popular mobilization emerged in 2013 in the wake of the reluctance of lawmakers to change the lyrics; the "Restore Our Anthem" campaign strategically framed the issue in terms of a return to the original gender-neutral wording.[30] Ultimately, a private member's bill was presented in the House of Commons in 2016 by Mauril Bélanger.[31] He had advocated changing the lyrics for many years but sadly died before it was passed into law. It took another two years and extended debates in the Senate for the gender-neutral lyrics to be officially adopted in 2018.[32] As Member of Parliament, Mona Fortier, the successor to Bélanger, noted, "[w]e can bring this new version to recognize who we are internationally, nationally and locally."[33] Since 2018, therefore, the official lyrics in English, are the following:

> O Canada!
> Our home and native land!
> True patriot love in all of us command.
> With glowing hearts, we see thee rise,
> The True North strong and free!
> From far and wide,
> O Canada, we stand on guard for thee.
>
> God keep our land glorious and free!
> O Canada, we stand on guard for thee.
> O Canada, we stand on guard for thee.[34]

Securing gender equality in the lyrics of the national anthem is only a symbolic victory. It doesn't change anything in the everyday lives of those excluded by the previous lyrics. Still, words and symbols do matter, and messages of exclusion or inclusion take hold of our psyches and imaginations — impacting our conscious and unconscious biases — limiting or expanding our visions of belonging and of citizenship.

The gender inequalities embedded in the phrase "in all our sons command" are not the only concerns that have been voiced about the national anthem. As Judith Sayers, president of the Nuu-chah-nulth Tribal Council (NTC)[35] and a member of the Hupacasath First Nation, explains, when she sings "O Canada," she does not sing "Our home *and* native land"; she sings "Our home *on* native land":

> Canada was built on First Nations lands and became wealthy off First Nation resources. First Nations were displaced off their territories and put on reserves and many are living in third world conditions. Canada took lands and resources without any compensation to First Nations and without legal right to do so. This remains unresolved.[36]

Indigenous peoples have criticized the phrase "our home and native land" for its failure to make clear that Canada was populated by self-governing Indigenous communities prior to the arrival of European settlers. Immigrants to Canada have also felt excluded by the phrase "home and native land" because for them, their native land is their original homeland. In response to both of these concerns, some have suggested replacing "Our home and native land" with "Our home and cherished land." Finally, the reference to God is questionable in a multicultural, multi-faith, and secular society.[37]

Final Thoughts

SO, WHAT DOES this exploration of Canada's national anthem teach us? And how does it relate to the themes of this book? First, it reminds us of the importance of addressing discrimination, exclusion, and inequality in our national symbols, history, and everyday lives. The stories of discrimination detailed in the previous chapters illustrate larger theoretical and conceptual issues about inequality and discrimination. They tell us that discrimination can be direct or overt, occurring when individuals are treated differently because of their actual or perceived membership in certain groups. Beyond direct discrimination, sometimes apparently "neutral" rules, policies, and practices in the institutions of everyday life, such as the workplace, educational institutions, or community organizations, disproportionately exclude or disadvantage individuals from certain groups, causing adverse impact discrimination. It is important to assess the impact of everyday rules and practices that appear neutral and fair but may not be in practice. When the inequitable effects of such rules are identified, there are two remedial options: either the rule or policy may be changed across the board to remove its discriminatory effects, or individuals impacted by the rule or policy may be accommodated to ensure that they are not excluded or harmed.

Furthermore, in almost every case of discrimination that is discussed in this book — from racial profiling to exclusions in the workplace, schools, or community activities — individual cases of discrimination occur within institutional and societal contexts that are complex and shaped by histories of inequality and structural injustice. As we have seen, inequities at the micro, meso, and macro levels often intersect, making discrimination a systemic rather than individual problem. Legal cases, however, tend to isolate one particular moment — one problematic source of exclusion or prejudice in one specific institutional context — but to understand the systemic dimensions of discrimination, we need to situate the exclusion or harm within its larger context across the different sectors of our lives, across life cycles and generations. In looking at the exclusionary effects of the simple phrase "in all our sons command," we see before us a history of patriarchy, militarism, colonialism, and hierarchy. Embedded in the familiar melody is a history of harm, stereotyping, prejudice, and denial of equitable well-being. Every seemingly small example of inequality is just one part of a much larger story of social injustice.

In addition to illustrating different types of discrimination, the story of the national anthem provides a second lesson. It reminds us that while we may raise specific issues of discrimination — such as gender-based exclusions — we should be attentive to other sources of discrimination that are also implicated. In the case of the national anthem, the initial focus was on gender-based exclusion in the lyrics, but as individuals from Indigenous, Black, immigrant, and religious minority communities have noted, there are additional ways in which both the lyrics and the melody of the national anthem risk overlooking or excluding some. Anti-discrimination law continues to operate using group-based categories, usually one at a time. To change laws and challenge discrimination, it is sometimes necessary to work with specific categories that speak to only one source of exclusion or disadvantage. Challenging every type of inequality at the same time may be impossible. Still, one of the lessons of this book is the importance of trying to be as inclusive as possible in working towards a more equitable society. Working in solidarity across differences, celebrating identities while recognizing that they are always changing, and focusing on those who are most vulnerable and marginalized in society are potential strategies of how to do so. One of the critiques of anti-discrimination law is its tendency to push individuals from historically disadvantaged groups to conform to the dominant norms in society. Expanding anti-discrimination law to secure the inclusion of individuals who do not conform to dominant norms will provide the basis for a much more transformative vision of Canada's societal institutions and communities. In terms of the national anthem, it means changing the gendered lyrics while also addressing the concerns of Indigenous peoples, immigrant communities, and those related to religious diversity. Regarding the melody of the anthem, knowledge of its connection to the racism of blackface means that we cannot sing it without thinking of that reality, and being reminded in turn of the need to work towards racial justice.

Exploring the national anthem also teaches us about how change happens in society and the importance of perseverance in seeking change. It is not easy to challenge exclusion. There will be resistance to change and this resistance should be anticipated. In the case of the national anthem, it took thirty years to do something as seemingly non-controversial as replacing "in all thy sons" with "in all of us." Changing the melody remains a task for the future.

As in many of the examples in this book, the initial push for challenging the national anthem came from individuals — individuals with agency, stamina, insight, and a determination to contest exclusion or mistreatment. Indeed, the individuals who challenged discrimination and unfairness are the heroes of this book: they refused to accept mistreatment or exclusion, bringing human rights complaints or initiating other types of action for change; and they persisted, even in the face of extensive delays, obstacles, and failures. Even when they won, they often had to continue struggling to make equality a reality in their everyday lives; even if they lost, they had tried to make a difference and have their voices heard. But they did not do it alone: there were parents, partners, colleagues, friends, activists, community-based organizations, lawyers, adjudicators, and judges working to understand experiences of exclusion and create pathways to equality. And if one individual's struggle did not succeed, others often took up the challenge and continued.

One final lesson from the national anthem story concerns participation. We are entitled to seek and demand change to make our society equitable and fair. When Vivienne Poy reflected on her efforts to change the lyrics to "O Canada," she stated, "I remember people saying, how can you as an immigrant, come into this country and change our national anthem?" She would respond, "But the national anthem is for every Canadian!"[38] She rejected a vision of Canadian society that entitles only some to speak to the content of national symbols and values. We live in a country where old patterns of privilege and entitlement need to be challenged and disrupted. To celebrate diversity, to promote inclusion, to take difference seriously, to rethink how we do things, to listen, to acknowledge Indigenous ways of being — all of these challenges are central to an inclusive and engaged understanding of citizenship and belonging. For as Jérémy Gabriel taught us,[39] we can defy the odds and refuse to accept limitations on what we can be or do — and we can sing — sing together — sing in our own language, sing a melody that affirms all of us, sing our chosen lyrics, sing in our own voices. We can sing boldly and with glowing hearts.

Notes

preface

1   When referring to race throughout this book, Black is capitalized and white is not. For a discussion of why this choice has been made, please see Nancy Coleman, "Why We're Capitalizing Black" *New York Times* (5 July 2020), online: www.nytimes.com/2020/07/05/insider/capitalized-black.html.

introduction

1   Donovan Livingston, "Lift Off — The Remarks of Donovan Livingston, Ed.M.'16, Student Speaker at HGSE's 2016 Convocation Exercises" (25 May 2016) at 03m:04s, online (video): *Harvard Graduate School of Education* www.gse.harvard.edu/news/16/05/lift.

2   Lexico, "Coercion" (nd), online: *Lexico* www.lexico.com/en/definition/coercion.

3   For an overview of Canadian anti-discrimination law, see Colleen Sheppard, "Anti-discrimination Law in Canada and the Challenge of Effective Enforcement" in Marie Mercat-Bruns, David B Oppenheimer & Cady Sartorius, eds, *Comparative Perspectives on the Enforcement and Effectiveness of Antidiscrimination Law: Challenges and Innovative Tools* (New York: Springer International Publishing, 2018) 83.

4   Part 1 of the *Constitution Act, 1982*, being Schedule B to the *Canada Act 1982* (UK), 1982, c 11 [*Canadian Charter*]. See, in particular, section 15, which provides:

> 15. (1) Every individual is equal before and under the law and has the right to the equal protection and equal benefit of the law without discrimination and, in particular, without discrimination based on race, national or ethnic origin, colour, religion, sex, age or mental or physical disability.
>
> (2) Section (1) does not preclude any law, program or activity that has as its object the amelioration of conditions of disadvantaged individuals or groups including those that are disadvantaged because of race, national or ethnic origin, colour, religion, sex, age or mental or physical disability.

5   For a more extensive discussion of formal, substantive, and inclusive equality, see Colleen Sheppard, *Inclusive Equality: The Relational Dimensions of Systemic*

Discrimination in Canada (Montreal: McGill-Queen's University Press, 2010). For a general review of Canadian equality law, including the major Supreme Court decisions, see Colleen Sheppard, *The Principles of Equality and Non-Discrimination: A Comparative Analysis — Canada* (European Parliamentary Research Service, 2020), online: www.europarl.europa.eu/RegData/etudes/STUD/2020/659362/EPRS_STU(2020)659362_EN.pdf.

6   *Nassiah v Peel (Regional Municipality) Services Boards*, 2007 HRTO 14.

7   *McLeod v Youth Bowling Council of Ontario*, (18 July 1988) Ontario BOI 88-015 (Ontario Board of Inquiry) [*McLeod BOI*]. See also *Youth Bowling Council of Ontario v McLeod* (1994), 20 OR (3d) 658; 121 DLR (4th) 187 (Ontario Divisional Court).

8   *Canadian National Railway v Canada (Canadian Human Rights Commission)* [1987] 1 SCR 1114, 40 DLR (4th) 193 (SCC) [*Action travail des femmes*].

9   *Action Travail des Femmes v Canadian National Railway*, 1984 CanLII 9 (CHRT).

10   Judge Rosalie Silberman Abella, *Equality in Employment: A Royal Commission Report* (Ottawa: Supply and Services Canada, 1984) at 9, online: www.bakerlaw.ca/wp-content/uploads/Rosie-Abella-1984-Equality-in-Employment.pdf.

11   See Colleen Sheppard, "Jordan's Principle: Reconciliation and the First Nations Child" (2018) 27:1 *Constitutional Forum* 3; Colleen Sheppard, "#MeToo Canada: Towards a Culture of Equality" in Ann Noel et al, eds, *The Global #MeToo Movement: How Social Media Propelled a Historic Movement and the Law Responded* (2020), online: www.globalmetoobook.com.

12   *Pictou Landing Band Council v Canada (Attorney General)*, 2013 FC 342 at para 6 [*Pictou Landing*].

13   *First Nations Child & Family Caring Society of Canada et al v Attorney General of Canada (representing the Minister of Indigenous and Northern Affairs Canada)*, 2016 CHRT 2.

14   *Turner v Canada (Border Services Agency)*, 2014 CHRT 10 at para 216.

15   See Sumi Cho, Kimberlé Williams Crenshaw & Leslie McCall, "Toward a Field of Intersectionality Studies: Theory, Applications, and Praxis" (Summer 2013) 38 (4) *Signs: Journal of Women in Culture and Society* 785.

16   See Devon W Carbado & Mitu Gulati, "The Fifth Black Woman" (2001) 11 *Journal of Contemporary Legal Issues* 701 at 703; Kenji Yoshino, *Covering: The Hidden Assault on Our Civil Rights* (New York: Random House, 2007).

17   For a discussion of the importance of collective political responsibility for social justice, see Iris Marion Young, *Responsibility for Justice* (Oxford: Oxford University Press, 2011).

one | Be Careful Going Shopping: Racial Profiling in Everyday Life

1   *Nassiah v Peel (Regional Municipality) Services Board*, 2007 HRTO 14 [*Nassiah*]. Details outlined in this chapter about the case are based on the review of the facts included in the decision of the Ontario Human Rights Tribunal.

2   *Elmardy v Toronto Police Service Board*, 2017 ONSC 2074 (a Black man is stopped by the police while walking down the street); *Johnson v Sanford and Halifax Regional Police Service*, (2003) 48 CHRR D/307 (Nova Scotia Board of Inquiry) [*Johnson*] (a driver who is Black is stopped).

3   *Shaw v Phipps*, 2012 ONCA 155 (a replacement mail carrier who is Black in wealthy Toronto area is singled out by the police for interrogation).

4 *Radek v Henderson Development (Canada) and Securiguard Services (No 3)*, 2005 BCHRT 302 [*Radek*] (racial and disability profiling of a disabled Indigenous woman by a shopping mall security guard).

5 *R v Campbell*, [2005] QJ No 394, 2005 CarswellQue 243 (Black man racially profiled while riding in a taxi in Montreal).

6 For a discussion of the meaning of the term "racialized," see Ontario Human Rights Commission, "Policy and Guidelines on Racism and Racial Discrimination" (Toronto: OHRC, 2005), online: www.ohrc.on.ca/en/policy-and-guidelines-racism-and-racial-discrimination (s 2.1). As noted (at 12):

> When it is necessary to describe people collectively, the term "racialized person" or "racialized group" is preferred over "racial minority," "visible minority," "person of colour" or "non-White" as it expresses race as a social construct rather than as a description based on perceived biological traits. Furthermore, these other terms treat "White" as the norm to which racialized persons are to be compared and have a tendency to group all racialized persons in one category, as if they are all the same.

7 *Nassiah*, above note 1 at para 9.

8 *Ibid* at paras 10–13.

9 *Ibid* at para 16.

10 *Ibid* at para 70. Jacqueline Nassiah could have also filed a complaint against the security guard and the store; however, she limited her complaint to the police officer.

11 *Ibid* at para 166.

12 *Ibid* at para 134 [emphasis in the original].

13 *Ibid* at para 166.

14 *Ibid* at para 212.

15 Jacqueline Nassiah, quoted in Christian Cotroneo, "A Victim of Racial Profiling" *Toronto Star* (18 May 2007).

16 *Nassiah*, above note 1 at para 112.

17 See, for example, Ontario Human Rights Commission, *A Collective Impact: Interim Report on the Inquiry Into Racial Profiling and Racial Discrimination of Black Persons by the Toronto Police Service* (November 2018), online: www.ohrc.on.ca/en/public-interest-inquiry-racial-profiling-and-discrimination-toronto-police-service/collective-impact-interim-report-inquiry-racial-profiling-and-racial-discrimination-black; Scot Wortley & Akwasi Owusu-Bempah, "The Usual Suspects: Police Stop and Search Practices in Canada" (2011) 21:4 *Policing & Society* 395; Jim Rankin, "Race Matters: Blacks Documented by Police at Higher Rate" *Toronto Star* (6 February 2010).

18 See the background paper prepared by Michèle Turenne, *Racial Profiling: Context and Definition* (2005) (Cat 2.120-1.25) at 13. The Quebec Human Rights Commission also published a study on the results of its consultation on racial profiling: see *Racial Profiling and Systemic Discrimination of Racialized Youth* (2011), online: www.cdpdj.qc.ca/publications/Profiling_final_EN.pdf. The Ontario Human Rights Commission currently has a similar definition, defining racial profiling as "any action undertaken for reasons of safety, security or public protection that relies on stereotypes about race, colour, ethnicity, ancestry, religion or place of origin — rather than on reasonable suspicion — to single out an individual for greater scrutiny or different treatment." See Ontario Human Rights Commission, *Under Suspicion: Research and Consultation Report on Racial Profiling in Ontario* (2017),

online: www.ohrc.on.ca/en/under-suspicion-research-and-consultation-report-racial-profiling-ontario (at 16, noting the importance of recognizing the systemic dimensions of racial profiling).

19 Nova Scotia Human Rights Commission, *Working Together to Better Serve All Nova Scotians: A Report on Consumer Racial Profiling in Nova Scotia* (May 2013) at 17 [NSHRC, *Working Together*]. On consumer profiling based on disability, see Catherine Frazee, "Exile from the China Shop: Cultural Injunction and Disability Policy" in Mary Ann McColl & Lyn Jongbloed, eds, *Disability and Social Policy in Canada*, 2d ed (Concord, ON: Captus University Publications, 2006) at 357.

20 NSHRC, *Working Together*, above note 19 at 25.

21 *Ibid* at 100.

22 The term was coined by psychiatrist and Harvard University professor Chester M Pierce in 1970 to describe insults and dismissals he regularly witnessed non-Black Americans inflict on Black Americans.

23 *Nassiah*, above note 1 at para 129.

24 As Anthony Greenwald and Linda Hamilton Krieger explain, "Implicit biases are especially intriguing, and also especially problematic, because they can produce behavior that diverges from a person's avowed or endorsed beliefs or principles." See Anthony G Greenwald & Linda Hamilton Krieger, "Implicit Bias: Scientific Foundations" (2006) 94 *California Law Review* 945 at 951.

25 See, for example, Wortley & Owusu-Bempah, above note 17; Rankin, above note 17.

26 Greenwald & Krieger, above note 24 at 963.

27 *Nassiah*, above note 1 at para 112. See also Carol Tator & Frances Henry, *Racial Profiling in Canada: Challenging the Myth of "A Few Bad Apples"* (Toronto: University of Toronto Press, 2006).

28 *R v Parks*, 15 OR (3d) 324, [1993] OJ No 2157 at para 43.

29 For a helpful overview of racism and race discrimination, see Ontario Human Rights Commission, "Policy Guidelines on Racism and Racial Discrimination" (2005), online: www.ohrc.on.ca/sites/default/files/attachments/Policy_and_guidelines_on_racism_and_racial_discrimination.pdf.

30 Ontario Human Rights Commission, *Count Me In!: Collecting Human Rights-Based Data* (2010), online: www.ohrc.on.ca/en/count-me-collecting-human-rights-based-data.

31 *Nassiah*, above note 1 at para 172.

32 *Ibid* at para 126.

33 *Ibid* at para 130.

34 *Peart v Peel Regional Police Services*, 43 CR (6th) 175, [2006] OJ No 4457 at para 96 ("[T]he indicators of racial profiling recognized in the literature by experts and in the caselaw can assist a trier of fact in deciding what inferences should or should not be drawn and what testimony should or should not be accepted in a particular case").

35 *Nassiah*, above note 1 at para 129.

36 In one important case, the Supreme Court of Canada concluded that there had not been any racial profiling, despite the Quebec Human Rights Tribunal's finding to the contrary: see *Quebec (Commission des droits de la personne et des droits de la jeunesse) v Bombardier Inc*, 2015 SCC 39 [*Bombardier*]. For a more detailed discussion of the difficulties of proving racial profiling in that case, see Colleen Sheppard & Mary Louise Chabot, "Obstacles to Crossing the Discrimination Threshold:

Connecting Individual Exclusion to Group-Based Inequities" (2018) 96 *Canadian Bar Review* 1, online: https://cbr.cba.org/index.php/cbr/article/view/4448.

37 For a review of key cases on racial profiling, see David M Tanovich, *The Colour of Justice: Policing Race in Canada* (Toronto: Irwin Law, 2006). See also Vic Satzewich, "Racial Profiling: Dimensions of Black Experience" in *Racism in Canada* (Oxford: Oxford University Press, 2011), ch 6. For a discussion of recent Supreme Court of Canada decisions on racial profiling, see Meryl Friedland, "Supreme Court of Canada Finally Addresses Racial Profiling by Police" (26 June 2020), online: http://ablawg.ca/wp-content/uploads/2020/06/Blog_MF_RacialProfiling.pdf (discussing the significance of two recent cases: *R v Le*, 2019 SCC 34 and *R v Ahmad*, 2020 SCC 11).

38 Quoted in Maureen Brown, "In Their Own Voices: African Canadians in the Greater Toronto Area Share Experiences of Racial Profiling" (African Canadian Community Coalition on Police Profiling: March 2004), ch 7, online: www.diversitytrainersplus.com/wp-content/uploads/2010/09/In_their_Own_Voices-16902.pdf, in Tator & Henry, above note 27 at 166.

39 See Maureen Brown, *ibid* at 151–83.

40 See *Anti-Racism Act, 2017*, SO 2017, c 15, Preamble. See also *Bombardier*, above note 36.

41 See House of Commons, Standing Committee on Canadian Heritage, *Taking Action Against Systemic Racism and Religious Discrimination including Islamophobia* (February 2018) (Chair: Hon Hedy Fry), online: www.ourcommons.ca/Content/Committee/421/CHPC/Reports/RP9315686/chpcrp10/chpcrp10-e.pdf.

42 For a review of racism against Indigenous peoples, see Samantha Loppie, Charlotte Reading & Sarah de Leeuw, "Aboriginal Experiences with Racism and its Impacts" (2014) National Collaborating Centre for Aboriginal Health, online: www.ccnsa-nccah.ca/docs/determinants/FS-AboriginalExperiencesRacismImpacts-Loppie-Reading-deLeeuw-EN.pdf.

43 See *Radek*, above note 4.

44 See Paul Eid, "The Québec Human Rights Commission and the Construction of the Concept of Social Profiling" in Shelagh Day, Lucie Lamarche & Ken Norman, eds, *14 Arguments In Favour Of Human Rights Institutions* (Toronto: Irwin Law 2014); see also Marie-Eve Sylvestre & Céline Bellot, "Challenging Discriminatory and Punitive Responses to Homelessness in Canada" in Martha Jackman & Bruce Porter, eds, *Advancing Social Rights in Canada* (Toronto: Irwin Law, 2014) 30.

45 See Francis Dupuis-Déri, "Printemps érable ou Printemps de la matraque? Profilage politique et répression sélective pendant la grève étudiante de 2012" in *À qui la rue? : répression policière et mouvements sociaux* (Montréal: Les Éditions Écosociété, 2013). See, generally, École de service social, Université de Montréal, Observatoire sur les profilages, "Observatoire sur les profilages" (OSP), online: https://profilages.info/osp.

46 *Nassiah*, above note 1 at para 212.

47 On class actions, see also Center for Constitutional Rights, "Class-Action Lawsuit Challenges Stop-and-Frisk Policy" *CCR* (16 May 2012), online: https://ccrjustice.org/home/press-center/press-releases/class-action-lawsuit-challenges-stop-and-frisk-policy; San Grewal, "Peel Police Face $125 Million Class-Action Lawsuit" *Toronto Star* (26 November 2013), online: www.thestar.com/news/city_hall/2013/11/26/peel_police_face_125_million_classaction_lawsuit.html. See also Charelle Evelyn, "'Canadian-Style Systemic Racism': Black Public Servants File Suit Against Federal Government" *Hill Times* (3 December 2020), online: www.hilltimes.com/

2020/12/03/canadian-style-systemic-racism-black-public-servants-file-suit-against-federal-government/274648.

48　In cases where racial profiling results in criminal charges against individuals, the major remedy is that the criminal charges are dropped or, in some cases, the associated evidence not admitted into the trial. Section 24(2) of the *Canadian Charter of Rights and Freedoms* provides that where "a court concludes that evidence was obtained in a manner that infringed or denied any rights or freedoms guaranteed by this Charter, the evidence shall be excluded if it is established that, having regard to all the circumstances, the admission of it in the proceedings would bring the administration of justice into disrepute."

49　*Johnson*, above note 2.

50　*Ibid* at 35.

51　*Ibid* at 39.

52　*Ibid* at 41.

53　*Ibid* at 43. On restorative justice, see Saskatchewan Human Rights Commission, "A Restorative Approach" (Saskatoon, SK: SHRC, 2015), online: https://saskatchewanhumanrights.ca/wp-content/uploads/2020/03/RestorativeJustice.pdf.

54　*Johnson*, above note 2 at 44.

two | **When Rules Exclude: On Bowling and Equality**

1　*McLeod v Youth Bowling Council of Ontario* (18 July 1988), Ontario BOI 88-015 (Ontario Board of Inquiry).

2　*Ibid*. The details outlined in the following section about the case are based on the review of the facts included in the decision of the Board of Inquiry.

3　*Ibid* at 7.

4　*Ibid* at 8.

5　*Ibid* at 11.

6　*Ibid* at 12.

7　*Ibid* at 10.

8　*Ibid*.

9　*Ibid* at 12.

10　*Ibid* at 13.

11　*Ibid* at 14.

12　*Ibid* at 16.

13　*Youth Bowling Council of Ontario v McLeod*, [1990] OJ No 2047, 74 DLR (4th) 625 (Ont Div Ct).

14　*Ibid* at para 24.

15　*Ibid* at para 27.

16　*Ibid* at para 29.

17　*Ibid* at para 35.

18　*Youth Bowling Council of Ontario v McLeod* (1994), 20 OR (3d) 658.

19　Tammy McLeod's athlete profile can be found on Paralympics Canada's website. See Paralympics Canada, "Tammy McLeod," online: https://paralympic.ca/team-canada/tammy-mcleod.

20　Gerard Goggin, "Normality and Disability: Intersections Among Norms, Law, and Culture" (2017) 31:3 *Continuum* 337 at 338. This is an example of how "law produces cultural meanings, norms, representations, artefacts and expressions of disability, abnormality and normality, as well as how law responds to and is constituted by cultures of disability, abnormality and normality circulating in society more broadly."

21 The Supreme Court of Canada first recognized "adverse effect discrimination" in *Ontario Human Rights Commission v Simpsons-Sears Ltd*, [1985] 2 SCR 536 [*O'Malley*]. Indirect discrimination is the term that is often used at the international level (see General Comment No 20 (2009) — Non-discrimination in economic, social and cultural rights (art 2, para 2) of the *International Covenant on Economic, Social and Cultural Rights*, E/C.12/GC/20). In the United States, the term "disparate impact discrimination" is used (see discussion below).

22 *O'Malley*, above note 21.

23 *British Columbia (Public Service Employee Relations Commission) v BCGSEU*, [1999] 3 SCR 3 [*Meiorin*]. In making this determination, courts and tribunals must conclude that the gender differences in the test results are statistically significant and show group-based inequities.

24 *Griggs v Duke Power Co*, 401 US 424 (1971). In 1964, Black employees of a generating plant in the United States challenged their employer's standardized tests and high school diploma requirements for hiring and promotions. The US Supreme Court found that while the motivation may not have been discriminatory, the effects discriminated against Black Americans who had not had the opportunity to attend high school or receive any formal education due to racism. In contrast, see *Kahkewistahaw First Nation v Taypotat*, 2015 SCC 30, where the Supreme Court of Canada concluded that there was insufficient evidence to conclude that a high school diploma requirement resulted in discrimination.

25 *Fraser v Canada (Attorney General)*, 2020 SCC 28.

26 *Ibid* at para 53 [citation omitted].

27 *Ibid* at para 67.

28 *Robichaud v Canada (Treasury Board)*, [1987] 2 SCR 84 at para 10. This case concerns a sexual harassment complaint filed with the Canadian Human Rights Commission by Bonnie Robichaud, who claimed that she had been sexually harassed, discriminated against, and intimidated by her direct supervisor in her place of employment — the Department of National Defence. Her supervisor was found to have engaged in this conduct, but the key question before the Court was whether the Department of National Defence was also liable for the discriminatory conduct of its employee. The Supreme Court found that the department was liable, as the *Canadian Human Rights Act* — a statute that focuses on the effects rather than the causes of discrimination, with the goal of eliminating it from Canadian society — imposes liability on employers for all of their employees' conduct during their course of employment.

29 *Andrews v Law Society of British Columbia*, [1989] 1 SCR 143 at 169.

30 Craig Froehle, "The Evolution of an Accidental Meme: How One Little Graphic Became Shared and Adapted by Millions" (14 April 2016), online: https://medium.com/@CRA1G/the-evolution-of-an-accidental-meme-ddc4e139e0e4.

31 *Lepofsky v TTC*, 2007 HRTO 41. David Lepofsky, a blind lawyer in Toronto, had used the Toronto Transit system for almost thirty years, throughout which time he regularly advocated for himself and similarly disabled patrons regarding the inaccessibility of Toronto's public transportation. His objective was to have audible bus and subway station stop announcements that would allow visually impaired patrons to navigate the public transportation without assistance.

32   *Convention on the Rights of Persons with Disabilities*, 24 January 2007, A/RES/61/106, UNGAOR, 61st Sess, Supp no 49, art 2.

33   *Ibid.*

34   *Ibid.*

35   See David Lepofsky, "The Duty to Accommodate: A Purposive Approach" (1992) 1:1 *Canadian Labour Law Journal* 1.

36   *Meiorin*, above note 23 at paras 62–63.

37   Interestingly, bowling plays a powerful role in our imagination of community and inclusion. Robert Putnam's well-known book, *Bowling Alone: The Collapse and Revival of American Community* (New York: Simon & Schuster, 2000) documents the decline of social bonds and community in society using the bowling league as a central metaphor.

three | Excluded, Harassed, and Undervalued: The Struggle to Break Systemic Barriers

1   *CN v Canada (Canadian Human Rights Commission)*, [1987] 1 SCR 1114 at 1123 [*Action travail des femmes*].

2   See Patricia F Hewlin, "Wearing the Cloak: Antecedents and Consequences of Creating Facades of Conformity" (2009) 94:3 *Journal of Applied Psychology* 727; Patricia F Hewlin, "And the Award for Best Actor Goes to ... Facades of Conformity in Organizational Settings" (2003) 28:4 *Academy of Management Review* 633.

3   Royal Commission on Equality in Employment, *Equality in Employment: A Royal Commission Report* by Judge Rosalie Silberman Abella (Ottawa: Supply and Services Canada, 1984), online: www.bakerlaw.ca/wp-content/uploads/Rosie-Abella-1984-Equality-in-Employment.pdf at 9.

4   *Ibid.*

5   *Action travail des femmes*, above note 1. See also *Action Travail des Femmes v Canadian National Railway*, 1984 CanLII 9 (CHRT) [*Action Travail* CHRT]; *Re CNR Co and Canadian Human Rights Commission*, 1985 CanLII 3179 (FCA).

6   *Action travail des femmes* is an autonomous non-profit organization working to support socio-economically disadvantaged women of all ages and origins in their struggle to access decent work, particularly in non-traditional areas of work: "Qui Sommes-Nous?" *Action travail des femmes*, online: www.atf.typepad.fr/atf/mission.html.

7   See, for example, *Association of Ontario Midwives v Ontario (Health and Long-Term Care)*, 2014 HRTO 1370. See also *Commission des droits de la personne et des droits de la jeunesse c Gaz métropolitain inc*, 2008 QCTDP 24; *Gaz métropolitain inc c Commission des droits de la personne et des droits de la jeunesse*, 2011 QCCA 1201; *National Capital Alliance on Race Relations v Canada (Department of Health & Welfare)*, [1997] CHRD No 3 (CHRT).

8   *Action travail des femmes*, above note 1 at 1115.

9   *Ibid* at 1123.

10   Cited in the Canadian Human Rights Tribunal decision, *Action Travail* CHRT, above note 5.

11   *Ibid* at 1120.

12   *Ibid* at 1121.

13   *Ibid* at 1123.

14   See discussion of adverse effects discrimination in Chapter 2.

15   *Action travail des femmes*, above note 1 at 1126.

16   *Ibid* at 1126–27. Note that 13 percent was chosen as the goal since women across
     Canada generally constituted 13 percent of those employed in traditionally male
     jobs. Of course, even with the special quotas, three out of every four new hires
     could still be male.

17   *Ibid* at 1139 [emphasis added].

18   *Ibid* at 1145.

19   See Catherine Lu, *Justice and Reconciliation in World Politics* (Cambridge, UK:
     Cambridge University Press, 2017) at 33–36, where she distinguishes interactional
     from structural injustice. Lu draws on the work of philosopher Iris Marion Young,
     who outlines a theory of structural injustices: see Iris Marion Young, *Responsibility
     for Justice* (Oxford: Oxford University Press, 2011), ch 2.

20   Young, *ibid*.

21   Colleen Sheppard, *Inclusive Equality: The Relational Dimensions of Systemic Dis-
     crimination in Canada* (Montreal: McGill-Queen's University Press, 2010) at 6.

22   Ontario Human Rights Commission, *Count Me In!: Collecting Human Rights-Based
     Data* (Toronto: Queen's Printer for Ontario, 2009), online: www.ohrc.on.ca/en/
     count-me-collecting-human-rights-based-data.

23   See, for example, Tristin K Green, "Work Culture and Discrimination" (2005) 93:3
     California Law Review 623.

24   *McKinnon v Ontario (Correctional Services)*, 2011 HRTO 263.

25   Colleen Sheppard, "Systemic Inequality and Workplace Culture: Challenging the
     Institutionalization of Sexual Harassment" (1994–95) 3:1 *Canadian Labour &
     Employment Law Journal* 249 at 281.

26   *OPT v Presteve Foods Ltd*, 2015 HRTO 675.

27   *Ibid* at para 25. Janet McLaughlin, "Honouring Dr Kerry Preibisch" *Policy Note*
     (2 February 2016), online: www.policynote.ca/honouring-dr-kerry-preibisch.

28   See Marie Carpentier with Carole Fiset, *Systemic Discrimination Towards Migrant
     Workers*, Cat 2120-7.29.2, (Québec: Commission des droits de la personne et des
     droits de la jeunesse, 2011) at 25.

29   *AB v Joe Singer Shoes Limited*, 2018 HRTO 107. In this case, the sexual abuse and
     harassment occurred between 1990 and 2008, at which time AB filed a com-
     plaint with the police (at para 17). She further testified (at para 22) that the abuse
     included "forcing her to perform oral sex on him about twice a month for years.
     She testified most of the attacks in which he forced her to perform oral sex on
     him or forced her to have sexual intercourse with him happened in his office after
     hours after everyone else had gone home."

30   *Ibid* at para 143.

31   Beyond the workplace, as illustrated in Chapter 1 on racial profiling, the institu-
     tional power of police officers has significant consequences in the lives of individ-
     ual citizens. See *Nassiah v Peel (Regional Municipality) Services Board*, 2007 HRTO
     14; "Quand la police est une menace pour les femmes autochtones de Val-d'Or"
     ICI Radio Canada (22 October 2015), online: https://ici.radio-canada.ca/tele/
     enquete/2015-2016/episodes/360817/femmes-autochtones-surete-du-quebec-sq.

32   See *Ontario Human Rights Commission v Simpsons-Sears Ltd (sub nom Ont Human
     Rights Commission v Simpsons-Sears)*, [1985] 2 SCR 536. For a discussion of
     adverse impact discrimination, see Chapter 2.

33   See *British Columbia (Public Service Employee Relations Commission) v BCGSEU*, [1999] 3 SCR 3 [*Meiorin*].

34   This blurring of the line between direct and adverse effect discrimination is discussed in the Supreme Court of Canada decision in *Meiorin, ibid* at paras 27–29.

35   *Robichaud v Canada (Treasury Board)*, [1987] 2 SCR 84 at para 15.

36   *Ibid.*

37   See discussion in Colleen Sheppard, "Of Forest Fires and Systemic Discrimination: A Review of British Columbia (Public Service Employee Relations Commission) v. B.C.G.S.E.U." (2001) 46 *McGill Law Journal* 533 at 546. See also Dianne Pothier, "M'aider, Mayday: Section 15 of the Charter in Distress" (1996) 6 *National Journal of Constitutional Law* 295 at 317.

38   See cases cited in footnote 7. See also *First Nations Child and Family Caring Society of Canada et al v Attorney General of Canada (for the Minister of Indian and Northern Affairs Canada)*, 2016 CHRT 2; Cindy Blackstock, "The Complainant: The Canadian Human Rights Case on First Nations Child Welfare" (2016) 62:2 *McGill Law Journal* 285.

39   See *Moore v British Columbia (Education)*, [2012] 3 SCR 360; *Tessier v Nova Scotia (Human Rights Commission)* 2014 NSSC 65.

40   See chapters 5 and 8 for examples.

41   See, for example, Truth and Reconciliation Commission of Canada, *Honouring the Truth, Reconciling for the Future: Summary of the Final Report of the Truth and Reconciliation Commission of Canada* (2015), online: http://nctr.ca/assets/reports/Final%20Reports/Executive_Summary_English_Web.pdf; Commission d'enquête sur les relations entre les Autochtones et certains services publics au Québec, *Public Inquiry Commission on Relations Between Indigenous Peoples and Certain Public Services in Québec: Listening, Reconciliation and Progress — Final Report* (2019), online: www.cerp.gouv.qc.ca/fileadmin/Fichiers_clients/Rapport/Final_report.pdf.

four | **Taking Positive Steps: Equity Initiatives**

1   Royal Commission on Equality in Employment, *Equality in Employment: A Royal Commission Report* by Justice Rosalie Silberman Abella (Ottawa: Supply and Services Canada, 1984), online: www.bakerlaw.ca/wp-content/uploads/Rosie-Abella-1984-Equality-in-Employment.pdf [Abella Report].

2   See, for example, Peter Neary, *The Origins and Evolution of Veterans Benefits in Canada 1914–2004*, Canadian Forces Advisory Council (Ottawa: Veterans Affairs Canada, 15 March 2004) at 3, which documents the then-unique character of the veterans' benefits provided after World War I. Note, however, that returning Indigenous veterans were excluded from some of these land grant and bank loan programs. See also Standing Committee on Veterans Affairs, Indigenous Veterans: From Memories of Injustice to Lasting Recognition, by Neil R Ellis (Committee Chair), Catalogue No XC78-1/1-421-11E-PDF (Ottawa: House of Commons, February 2019) at 9–10. In the aftermath of World War II, there were also failures to include Indigenous veterans in benefit programs: see R Scott Sheffield, "Canadian Aboriginal Veterans and the Veterans Charter after the Second World War" in Christopher Mele & Teresa A Miller, eds, *Aboriginal Peoples and Military Participation: Canadian and International Perspectives* (Kingston, ON: Canadian Defence Academy Press, 2007) 77 at 84–86; National Round Table on First Nations

Veterans' Issues, *A Search for Equity: A Study of the Treatment Accorded to First Nations Veterans and Dependents of the Second World War and the Korean Conflict*, by R Scott Sheffield (Ottawa: The Assembly of First Nations, May 2001). See also *Report of the Royal Commission on Aboriginal Peoples: Looking Forward, Looking Back, vol 1* (Ottawa: Supply and Services Canada, 1996) at 529–31 and 555.

3   Hiring preferences for veterans continue to exist in the present day for public sector jobs, as codified in the *Public Service Employment Act*, SC 2003, c 22, ss 12, 13, and 39.1. Other forms of preferential hiring for veterans also exist; see, for example, Canada, Treasury Board Internal Audit and Evaluation Bureau Evaluation Report, *Evaluation of the Right of First Refusal for Guard Services* (Ottawa: Treasury Board of Canada Secretariat, 2014).

4   Some veterans with disabilities were given work in sheltered workshops, where they were paid less than the minimum wage: see Teuila Fuatai, "From Exploitation to Unemployment: Undoing Canada's Sheltered Workshop System" *Community Living Parry Sound* (15 April 2016), online: www.clps.ca/2016/04/from-exploitation-to-employment-undoing-canadas-sheltered-workshop-system; see also Dustin Galer, "A Place to Work Like Any Other? Sheltered Workshops in Canada, 1970–1985" (2014) 3:2 *Canadian Journal of Disability Studies* 1.

5   Canada, Royal Commission on Government Organization, *Management of the Public Service*, vol 1, Part 3 (Ottawa: Privy Council Office, 1962) (Chair: J Grant Glassco) at 267.

6   Canada, *Report of the Royal Commission on Bilingualism and Biculturalism, Book 3, The World of Work* by A Davidson Dunton & André Laurendeau (Commissioners) (Ottawa: Supply and Services Canada, October 1967) at para 763.

7   Public Service Commission of Canada, *Annual Report, 1971*, by John Carson (Ottawa: Information Canada, 1972) at 1. See discussion in Public Service Commission of Canada, *History of Employment Equity in the Public Service and in the Public Service Commission of Canada*, prepared by the Equity and Diversity Directorate, Cat No SC3-159/2011E-PDF (Ottawa, Public Service Commission of Canada: 2011), online: http://publications.gc.ca/collections/collection_2012/cfp-psc/SC3-159-2011-eng.pdf [*PSC Employment Equity Report*].

8   See the Abella Report, above note 1 at 199, where it is noted that, by 1982, pro-active hiring policies had succeeded in attaining a level of francophone representation in the federal public service that matched the proportion of Francophones in the general population of the country.

9   Canada, Office of the Commissioner of Foreign Languages, *Annual Report 2008–2009: Two Official Languages, One Common Space: 40th Anniversary of the Official Languages Act*, by Graham Fraser (Commissioner of Official Languages) (Ottawa: Minister of Public Works and Government Services Canada, 2009), online: www.clo-ocol.gc.ca/sites/default/files/ar_ra_e.pdf.

10   See Canada, Privy Council Office, *Report of the Royal Commission on the Status of Women* (Ottawa: Information Canada, 1970) at ch 2, "Women in the Canadian Economy" and at "List of Recommendations," Recommendations 26, 36, 37, and 41. In many ways, this continued the passive policies of the federal government towards the advancement of women's employment in the public service in this era. For a discussion of these previous policies, see, for example, Public Service Commission of Canada, *Sex and the Public Service*, by Kathleen Archibald, Catalogue No SC3-3670 (Ottawa: Queen's Printer for Canada, 1970) at 129ff [*PSC Employment Equity Report*].

11   Luc Juillet & Ken Rasmussen, *Defending a Contested Ideal: Merit and the PSC of Canada 1908–2008* (Ottawa: Governance Series, University of Ottawa Press, 2008) at 104.

12   Abella Report, above note 1 at 195.

13   See, for example, *PSC Employment Equity Report*, above note 7 at 12.

14   See the Abella Report, above note 1 for some commentary on the program. The Native Law Program at the University of Saskatchewan still exists in the present day.

15   Juillet & Rasmussen, above note 11 at 104.

16   See, for example, the Abella Report, above note 1 at 197, and also the *PSC Employment Equity Report*, above note 7 at 12–13.

17   Abella Report, above note 1 at 197. As discussed below, more recently, the Indigenous Blacks & Mi'kmaq Initiative (IB&M) at the Schulich School of Law at Dalhousie University has increased representation of Black and Mi'kmaq students.

18   For a discussion about internment camps for Japanese Canadians during World War II, see Ann Gomer Sunahara, *The Politics of Racism: The Uprooting of Japanese Canadians During the Second World War* (Toronto: Lorimer & Co, 1981). For a discussion about the head tax on Chinese Canadians, see David Dyzenhaus & Mayo Moran, *Calling Power to Account: Law, Reparations and the Chinese Canadian Head Tax Case* (Toronto: University of Toronto Press, 2000). For a discussion of antisemitism and discrimination against Jewish students and professionals, which was never subject to remedial initiatives, see, for example, Gerald Tulchinsky, *Canada's Jews: A People's Journey* (Toronto: University of Toronto Press, 2008) at 318–20. Also of note is the history of overt discrimination against gays and lesbians in federal public service, the RCMP, and the military in the mid-twentieth century: many gay and lesbian Canadians were fired or demoted out of their jobs, often ostensibly for security reasons. See, for example, Gary Kinsman, "Character Weakness and Fruit Machines: Towards an Analysis of the Anti-Homosexual Security Campaign in the Canadian Civil Service" (1995) 35 *Labour/Le Travail* 133 at 137–41. See also CBC News, "Trudeau Is Apologizing to LGBT Civil Servants: Here's Why" *CBC News* (28 November 2017), online: www.cbc.ca/news/politics/ trudeau-apology-lgbt-civil-servants-military-fired-discrimination-1.4421601.

19   While the racial focus of affirmative action in the United States is critical, as in Canada, the United States first introduced veteran preference programs after World War I.

20   See Jackie Mansky, "The Origins of the Term 'Affirmative Action'" *Smithsonian Magazine* (22 June 2016), online: www.smithsonianmag.com/history/learn-origins-term-affirmative-action-180959531, where she notes the first use of the term affirmative action in the *National Labor Relations Act*, 1935, as a remedy to an unfair labour practice.

21   Cited in Mansky, *ibid*.

22   *Ibid*.

23   Exec Order No 10925, 26 FR 1977 (1961).

24   Exec Order No 11246, As Amended, 30 FR 12319 (1965).

25   Mansky, above note 20.

26   Exec Order No 13672, 79 FR 72985 (2014). See also David Hudson, "President Obama Signs a New Executive Order to Protect LGBT Workers" *Obama White House* (21 July 2014), online: https://obamawhitehouse.archives.gov/blog/2014/ 07/21/president-obama-signs-a-new-executive-order-to-protect-lgbt-workers.

27 Abella Report, above note 1 at ii (Terms of Reference).

28 *Ibid* at 255.

29 *Ibid* at 226.

30 *Ibid* at 7. However, it is noteworthy that, as discussed in Chapter 3, the Supreme Court of Canada has upheld quotas to remedy systemic discrimination.

31 *Ibid* at 9.

32 For the most recent version of the *Act*, see *Employment Equity Act*, SC 1995, c 44. For an overview of the Federal Contractors Program, see Canada, Employment and Social Development Canada, "Federal Contractors Program" (7 May 2013), online: www.labour.gc.ca/eng/standards_equity/eq/emp/fcp/index.shtml ["Federal Contractors Program"]. Note that in 2013, the Federal Contractors Program limit was raised from $200,000 in annual federal grants or contracts to $1 million. For an assessment of the impact of employment equity, see Carol Agócs, ed, *Employment Equity in Canada: The Legacy of the Abella Report* (Toronto: University of Toronto Press, 2014).

33 See, for example, in Quebec, *Act respecting equal access to employment in public bodies*, CQLR c A-2.01. See also Abigail Bakan & Audrey Kobayashi, *Employment Equity Policy in Canada: An Interprovincial Comparison/Politique d'équité en matière d'emploi au Canada: une comparaison interprovinciale* (Ottawa: Status of Women Canada, 2000).

34 *Employment Equity Act*, above note 32, ss 2 and 5

35 For an assessment of the strengths and weaknesses of the federal legislation, see Agócs, ed, above note 32. In July 2021, the federal government set up a Task Force to modernize the Employment Equity Act. See www.canada.ca/en/employment-social-development/corporate/portfolio/labour/programs/employment-equity/task-force.html.

36 "Federal Contractors Program," above note 32.

37 *Ibid*.

38 See *Pay Equity Act*, CQLR c E-12.001 [Québec *Pay Equity Act*]; *Pay Equity Act*, RSO 1990, c P.7 [Ontario *Pay Equity Act*]; *The Pay Equity Act*, CCSM c P13 [Manitoba *Pay Equity Act*]; *Pay Equity Act*, SNB 2009, c P-5.05 [New Brunswick *Pay Equity Act*]; *Pay Equity Act*, RSNS 1989, c 337 [Nova Scotia *Pay Equity Act*]; *Pay Equity Act*, RSPEI 1988, c P-2 [Prince Edward Island *Pay Equity Act*]. Of note is the absence of proactive pay equity legislation at the federal level: see Andrée Côté & Julie Lassonde, *Status Report on Pay Equity in Canada* (2007) National Association of Women and the Law, Final Report of the Workshop on Pay Equity (Ottawa); House of Commons, Special Committee on Pay Equity, *It's Time to Act* (June 2016) (Chair: Anita Vandenbeld).

39 For a recent Supreme Court of Canada discussion of some of the complexities of pay equity, see *Quebec (Attorney General) v Alliance du personnel professionnel et technique de la santé et des services sociaux*, 2018 SCC 17 [*Alliance*]; *Centrale des syndicats du Québec v Quebec (Attorney General)*, 2018 SCC 18.

40 Québec *Pay Equity Act*, above note 38; Ontario *Pay Equity Act*, above note 38; Manitoba *Pay Equity Act*, above note 38; New Brunswick *Pay Equity Act*, above note 38; Nova Scotia *Pay Equity Act*, above note 38; Prince Edward Island *Pay Equity Act*, above note 38.

41 *Pay Equity Act*, SC 2018, c 27, s 416.

42 See Hilal Kuspinar, *Affirmative Action and Education Equity in Higher Education in the United States and Canada* (LLM Thesis, McGill University Faculty of Law, 2016), online: https://escholarship.mcgill.ca/concern/theses/xw42nb48x.

43 Michelle Williams-Lorde, "The IB&M Initiative: Reflections on 20 Years" in *Reflections: 20 Years After the Marshall Inquiry* (2009) 27:4 *Society Record* (published by the Nova Scotia Barristers' Society), online: http://archives.nsbs.org/societyrecord/81092.pdf 33 at 35.

44 Nova Scotia, *Royal Commission on the Donald Marshall, Jr., Prosecution: Digest of Findings and Recommendations* by T Alexander Hickman, Lawrence A Poitras & Gregory T Evans (Commissioners) (Halifax: McCurdy's Printing and Typesetting Limited, December 1989), online: www.novascotia.ca/just/marshall_inquiry/_docs/Royal%20Commission%20on%20the%20Donald%20Marshall%20Jr%20Prosecution_findings.pdf.

45 *Ibid* at 26, Recommendation 11.

46 See Terry H Anderson, *The Pursuit of Fairness: A History of Affirmative Action* (Oxford: Oxford University Press, 2004).

47 Carl Cohen & James Sterba, *Affirmative Action and Racial Preference: A Debate* (New York: Oxford University Press, 2003) at 194.

48 *Regents of the University of California v Bakke*, 438 US 265 (US Supreme Court) [*Bakke*].

49 For more recent examples, see *Fisher v University of Texas at Austin*, 133 US 2411 (2013); *Grutter v Bollinger*, 539 US 306 (2003); *Gratz v Bollinger*, 539 US 244 (2003); and *Schuette v Coalition to Defend Affirmative Action*, 572 US 291 (2014). For insightful commentary on the *Fisher* case, see Richard Thompson Ford, "Did the Supreme Court Just Admit Affirmative Action Is About Racial Justice?" *Stanford Law School Blogs* (21 July 2016), online: https://law.stanford.edu/2016/07/21/did-the-supreme-court-just-admit-affirmative-action-is-about-racial-justice.

50 Schulich School of Law, "Indigenous Blacks and Mi'kmaq Initiative" (Dalhousie University), online: www.dal.ca/faculty/law/indigenous-blacks-mi-kmaq-initiative.html.

51 For an example of an affirmative action initiative that included both the revision of rules and policies for everyone, as well as quotas, see *CN v Canada (Canadian Human Rights Commission)*, [1987] 1 SCR 1114 [*Action travail des femmes*], discussed in Chapter 3 in this book.

52 Tarunabh Khaitan, *A Theory of Discrimination Law* (Oxford: Oxford University Press, 2015) at 232.

53 *Action travail des femmes*, above note 51.

54 *Bakke*, above note 48 at 407.

55 See *Canadian Charter of Rights and Freedoms*, Part I of the *Constitution Act, 1982*, being Schedule B to the *Canada Act 1982* (UK), 1982, c 11, s 15(2) [*Charter*]; *Employment Equity Act*, above note 32; or Québec *Pay Equity Act*, above note 38.

56 Abella Report, above note 1 at 10.

57 *R v Kapp*, [2008] 2 SCR 483 at para 33 [*Kapp*].

58 *Alliance*, above note 39 at para 31, citing both *Alberta (Aboriginal Affairs and Northern Development) v Cunningham*, 2011 SCC 37 at para 41, and *Kapp*, *ibid*.

59 *Action travail des femmes*, above note 51 at 1143–44.

60 As French poet and novelist Anatole France put it, "The law, in its majestic equality, forbids the rich as well as the poor to sleep under bridges, to beg in the streets, and to steal bread" (cited in the Abella Report, above note 1 at 1.)

61 See John Porter, *The Vertical Mosaic: An Analysis of Social Class and Power in Canada*, 50th Anniversary Edition (Toronto: University of Toronto Press, 2015).

62 Bernard Boxill, *Blacks and Social Justice*, revised ed (Lanham, MD: Rowman & Littlefield Publishers, 1992).

63 *Ibid*. See also discussion in Thomas Hill Jr, "The Message of Affirmative Action" (1991) 8:2 *Social Philosophy & Policy* 108 at 118.

64 See Mari Matsuda, "Looking to the Bottom: Critical Legal Studies and Reparations" (1987) 22 *Harvard Civil Rights-Civil Liberties Law Review* 323 at 380–85 and 398.

65 See *Griggs v Duke Power Co*, 401 US 424 (1971).

66 Carol Aylward, "Adding Colour — A Critique of: An Essay on Institutional Responsibility: The Indigenous Blacks and Micmac Programme at Dalhousie Law School" (1995) 8 *Canadian Journal of Women & the Law* 470 at 481.

67 See Matthew McRae, "The Story of Slavery in Canadian History" Canadian Museum for Human Rights, online: https://humanrights.ca/story/the-story-of-slavery-in-canadian-history.

68 See, for example, McGill University Office of the Provost and Vice-Principal (Academic), "McGill University Action Plan to Address Anti-Black Racism 2020–2025" (September 2020), online: www.mcgill.ca/provost/files/provost/action_plan_to_address_anti-black_racism.pdf.

69 Mary P Rowe, "Barriers to Equality: The Power of Subtle Discrimination to Maintain Unequal Opportunity" (1990) 3:2 *Employee Responsibilities & Rights Journal* 153; Insight Education Systems, "Micro-inequities: Managing Unconscious Bias" online: https://insighteducationsystems.com/microinequities-the-power-of-small; Mary P Rowe & Anna Giraldo-Kerr, "Gender Microinequities" in Kevin L Nadal, ed, *SAGE Encyclopedia of Psychology and Gender: Gender Microinequities* (Thousand Oaks, CA: SAGE Publications, 2017), online: http://mitsloan.mit.edu/shared/ods/documents/?DocumentID=4275.

70 *Bakke*, above note 48.

71 For a review of the evidence in the United States on the importance of racial and sex representation in police forces, see, for example, National Research Council, Division of Behavioural and Social Sciences, and Education, *Fairness and Effectiveness in Policing: The Evidence* (Wesley Skogan & Kathleen Frydl, eds) (Washington, DC: The National Academies Press, 2004) at 147–52.

72 *Royal Commission on the Donald Marshall, Jr., Prosecution: Digest of Findings and Recommendations*, above note 44 at 10–12. In recent years, press reports have suggested that of all the cities in Canada, only Halifax has a police force that is broadly representative of the community that it serves: see, for example, Jacques Marcoux, Katie Nicholson & Vera-Lynn Kubinec, "Police Diversity Fails to Keep Pace with Canadian Populations" *CBC News* (14 July 2016), online: www.cbc.ca/news/canada/police-diversity-canada-1.3677952.

73 For an early expression of this idea, see J Donald Kingsley, *Representative Bureaucracy: An Interpretation of the British Civil Service* (Yellow Springs, OH: The Antioch Press, 1944). Some economic research appears to support the hypothesis that representation according to gender and race significantly impacts policy choices: see, for example, Raghabendra Chattopadhyay & Esther Duflo, "Women as Policy Makers: Evidence from a Randomized Policy Experiment in India" (2004) 72:5 *Econometrica* 1409; Rohini Pande, "Can Mandated Political Representation Increase Policy Influence for Disadvantaged Minorities? Theory and Evidence from India" (2003) 93:4 *American Economic Review* 1132.

74 See, for example, Christina S Haynes & Ray Block, "Role-Model-In-Chief: Under-standing a Michelle Obama Effect" (2019) *Politics & Gender* 1. See also Adelle Blackett, "Mentoring the Other: Cultural Pluralist Approaches to Access to Justice" (2001) 8:3 *International Journal of the Legal Profession* 275; Anita L Allen, "On Being a Role Model" (1990) 6:1 *Berkeley Women's Law Journal* 22.

75 Blackett, above note 74 at 276, referencing Lani Guinier, "Of Gentlemen and Role Models" (1990) 6:1 *Berkeley Women's Law Journal* 93. Blackett's work on mentoring is an important addition to an exclusive focus on role models.

76 Colleen Sheppard, "Challenging Systemic Racism in Canada" in Elaine Kennedy-Dubourdieu, ed, *Race and Inequality: World Perspectives on Affirmative Action* (London: Routledge, 2006) 43.

77 Iris Marion Young, "Political Responsibility and Structural Injustice" (Lindley Lecture, delivered at the University of Kansas, 5 May 2003) (Lawrence, KS: Department of Philosophy, University of Kansas, 2003) at 3–6.

five | Equitable Freedom and Dancing Shoes

1 Ayla Lefkowitz, "Dresses, Drinks, and Misogyny" *McGill Daily* (2 February 2012), online: www.mcgilldaily.com/2012/02/dresses-drinks-and-misogyny.

2 Alanna Vagianos, "Grad Students Says Princeton Prof Who Sexually Harassed Her Was Given Slap on the Wrist" *Huffpost* (15 November 2017), online: www.huffingtonpost.com/entry/princeton-professor-sexual-harassment- not-punished_us_5a01d203e4b0368a4e872655.

3 Quoted in Robyn Doolittle, "Why Police Dismiss 1 in 5 Sexual Assault Claims as Baseless" *Globe and Mail* (3 February 2017), online: www.theglobeandmail.com/news/investigations/unfounded-sexual-assault-canada-main/article33891309.

4 Adrienne Rich, "Taking Women Students Seriously" (March 1978) 11 *The Radical Teacher* 40, online: www.jstor.org/stable/20709173?seq=1.

5 Sexual violence includes sexual assault and harassment. See specific definitions in the recent Ontario and Quebec legislation, discussed in the conclusion below. In the recent Quebec law, *An Act to prevent and fight sexual violence in higher education*, CQLR c P-22.1, online: www.assnat.qc.ca/en/travaux-parlementaires/projets-loi/projet-loi-151-41-1.html, sexual violence is defined (at art 1) as "any form of violence committed through sexual practices or by targeting sexuality, including sexual assault. It also refers to any other misconduct, including that relating to sexual and gender diversity, in such forms as unwanted direct or indirect gestures, comments, behaviours or attitudes with sexual connotations, including by a technological means."

6 Nancy J Hirschmann, *The Subject of Liberty: Toward a Feminist Theory of Freedom* (Princeton, NJ: Princeton University Press, 2003).

7 *Ibid* at 7.

8 See Jennifer Nedelsky, "Reconceiving Autonomy: Sources, Thoughts and Possibilities" (1989) 1:1 *Yale Journal of Law & Feminism* 7.

9 M Bergeron et al, "Violence sexuelles en milieu universitaire au Québec: Rapport de recherché enquête ESSIMU" (2016) *Université de Québec à Montréal* at 34.

10 *R v Ewanchuk*, [1999] 1 SCR 330 at para 69.

11 *Janzen v Platy Enterprises Ltd*, [1989] 1 SCR 1252 at 1284 [*Janzen*].

12 Ontario Human Rights Commission (OHRC), "Sexual Harassment and Sex Discrimination at Work," online: www.ohrc.on.ca/en/ohrc-policy-position-gender-specific-dress-codes/sexual-harassment-sex-discrimination-work [OHRC].

13 *Declaration on the Elimination of Violence against Women*, GA Res 48/104, UNGAOR, 48th Sess, Supp No 49 (vol 1) UN Doc A/48/659 (1993), art 2.

14 See OHRC, above note 12, citing *Cugliari v Telefficiency Corporation*, 2006 HRTO 7 at para 189, where Dr Sandy Welsh, a professor in the Department of Sociology at the University of Toronto, testified that "there is often an escalation in behaviour from initially grey behaviour into more directed comments and physical or sexual touching."

15 Brian Rubineau & Nazampal Jaswal, "Response is Not Prevention: Management Insights for Reducing Campus Sexual Assault" (2017) 27:1 *Education Law Journal* 19 at 31–33.

16 See Bergeron et al, above note 9 at 31, and see Carrie Bourassa et al, "Campus Violence, Indigenous Women, and the Policy Void" in Elizabeth Quinlan et al, eds, *Sexual Violence at Canadian Universities: Activism, Institutional Responses, and Strategies for Change* (Waterloo: Wilfrid Laurier University Press, 2017) 45 at 55–56.

17 See Sherene Razack, "Gendered Racial Violence and Spatialized Justice: The Murder of Pamela George" (2000) 15:2 *Canadian Journal of Law & Society* 91 (on the murder of Pamela George by two university student athletes); see also Indigenous Foundations, "Marginalization of Aboriginal Women in Canada," online: https://indigenousfoundations.arts.ubc.ca/marginalization_of_aboriginal_women.

18 Research reveals that gender identity minorities, including non-binary and transgender individuals are at higher risk: see Bergeron at al, above note 9 at 31.

19 *Janzen*, above note 11 at 1288.

20 See Chapter 2 for an detailed discussion of adverse impact discrimination.

21 Royal Commission on Equality in Employment, *Equality in Employment: A Royal Commission Report* by Justice Rosalie Silberman Abella (Ottawa: Supply and Services Canada, 1984), online: www.bakerlaw.ca/wp-content/uploads/Rosie-Abella-1984-Equality-in-Employment.pdf at 9.

22 Carly Parnitzke Smith & Jennifer J Freyd, "Institutional Betrayal" (2014) 69:6 *American Psychologist* 575 at 576.

23 Ava Williams, quoted in Doolittle, above note 3.

24 *Ibid*.

25 See Alana Prochuk, *We Are Here: Women's Experiences of the Barriers to Reporting Sexual Assault* (Vancouver: West Coast Leaf, 2018) at 12–13.

26 Natasha Novac, "Against Unfounding: Sexual Assault Investigation & A Proposed Class Action Against Police" *theCourt.ca* (17 November 2017), online: www.thecourt.ca/against-unfounding-sexual-assault-investigation-a-proposed-class-action-against-police; see also Statement of Claim, Ava Williams (31 March 2017), online: www.oaith.ca/Legal%20Counsel%20Media%20Release.pdf.

27 See Karen Busby & Joanna Birenbaum, *Achieving Fairness: A Guide to Campus Sexual Violence Complaints* (Toronto: Thomson Reuters, 2020). For a discussion of the importance of effective, accessible, and equitable investigative processes in the context of the Canadian military, see Government of Canada, National Defence, *External Review into Sexual Misconduct and Sexual Harassment in the Canadian Armed Forces* by Marie Deschamps (27 March 2015), online: www.canada.ca/en/department-national-defence/corporate/reports-publications/sexual-misbehaviour/external-review-2015.html.

28 METRAC, Andrea Gunraj et al, "Sexual Assault Policies on Campus: A Discussion Paper" (30 October 2014), online: www.metrac.org/wp-content/uploads/2014/11/final.formatted.campus.discussion.paper_.26sept14.pdf at 9. See also the requirement in Quebec legislation for a stand-alone policy.

29 *Ibid* at 10.

30   *Ibid*, citing MD Schwartz & WS Dekerseredy *Sexual Assault on the College Campus: The Role of Male Support* (Thousand Oaks, CA: SAGE, 1997) at 158.

31   *Ibid* at 14.

32   *Ibid* at 10–11.

33   *Ibid* at 12.

34   For an early discussion of the perpetrator perspective, see Alan Freeman, "Legitimizing Racial Discrimination Through Anti-Discrimination Law" (1978) 62 *Minnesota Law Review* 1049.

35   *O'Malley v Simpsons-Sears Ltd* (sub nom *Ont Human Rights Comm v Simpsons-Sears*), [1985] 2 SCR 536 at 547. Cited with approval in *Robichaud v Canada (Treasury Board)*, [1987] 2 SCR 84 at para 9.

36   Anne Forrest & Charlene Senn, "Theory Becomes Practice: The Bystander Initiative at the University of Windsor" in Elizabeth Quinlan et al, *Sexual Violence at Canadian Universities: Activism, Institutional Responses and Strategies for Change* (Waterloo: Wilfred Laurier Press, 2017) ch 9 at 177.

37   York U & METRAC, York University Safety Audit Report (METRAC, 2010), online: https://web.archive.org/web/20171025070328/http://safety.yorku.ca/files/2013/01/METRAC-Audit-Report.pdf at 8.31 at 8.

38   *Ibid* at 38–56.

39   *Report of the Task Force on Respect and Equality: Ending Sexual Violence at the University of Ottawa* (2014), online: www.uottawa.ca/president/sites/www.uottawa.ca.president/files/report-of-the-task-force-on-respect-and-equality.pdf at 9. See also Tracy Peter & Don Steward, *The University of Manitoba Campus Climate Survey on Sexual Violence: A Final Report* (January 2019), online: https://umanitoba.ca/sites/default/files/2019-09/UM%20Campus%20Climate%20Survey%20on%20Sexual%20Violence%202019.pdf.

40   The Bystander Initiative: A UWindsor Initiative to End Sexual Violence, "Research," online: www.bystanderinitiative.ca/research; see also Forrest & Senn, above note 36. See University of New Hampshire, "Prevention Innovations Research Centre: Bringing in the Bystander," online: www.cola.unh.edu/prevention-innovations-research-center/bringing-bystander; the University of Windsor website also cites VL Banyard et al, "Sexual Violence Prevention Through Bystander Education: An Experimental Evaluation" (2007) 35:4 *Journal of Community Psychology* 463.

41   Charlene Y Senn, "An Imperfect Feminist Journey: Reflections on the Process to Develop an Effective Sexual Assault Resistance Programme for University Women" (2011) 21:1 *Feminism & Psychology* 121 at 125.

42   *Ibid* at 130.

43   Yale University, "Yale Policy on Teacher-Student Consensual Relations" online: http://catalog.yale.edu/dus/university-policy-statements/teacher-student-consensual-relations. See also McGill Policy on Sexual Violence, s 8.1 (2016), online: www.mcgill.ca/secretariat/files/secretariat/policy_against_sexual_violence.pdf.

44   Yale University, above note 43.

45   *Ibid*.

46   Office of the Dean of the Faculty of Princeton University, "Consensual Relations with Students Policy," online: https://dof.princeton.edu/policies-procedure/policies/consensual-relations-students.

47   See Columbia University Mailman School of Public Health, "SHIFT: The Sexual Health Initiative to Foster Transformation," online: www.mailman.columbia.edu/research/sexual-health-initiative-foster-transformation/news-0.

48 Jennifer S Hirsch et al, "Social Dimensions of Sexual Consent Among Cisgender Heterosexual College Students: Insights from Ethnographic Research" (2018) 64:1 *Journal of Adolescent Health* 26 at 33.

49 *Ibid.*

50 *Ibid.*

51 Rubineau & Jazwal, above note 15 at 32–33.

52 K Osatuke et al, "Civility, Respect, Engagement in the Workforce (CREW) Nationwide Organization Development Intervention at Veterans Health Administration" (2009) 45:3 *Journal of Applied Behavioural Science* 384. See also Colleaga, "Civility, Respect, and Engagement in the Worplace (CREW)," online: www.colleaga.org/case-study/civility-respect-and-engagement-workplace-crew.

53 Susan Sturm, "Second Generation Employment Discrimination: A Structural Approach" (2001) 101:3 *Columbia Law Review* 458.

54 *Ibid* at 468.

55 See the Everyday Discrimination Scale in DR Williams, "Racial Differences in Physical and Mental Health: Socioeconomic Status, Stress, and Discrimination" (1997) 2:3 *Journal of Health Psychology* 335.

56 Task Force on Misogyny, Sexism and Homophobia, *Report of the Task Force on Misogyny, Sexism and Homophobia in Dalhousie University Faculty of Dentistry* (26 June 2015), online: https://cdn.dal.ca/content/dam/dalhousie/pdf/cultureofrespect/DalhousieDentistry-TaskForceReport-June2015.pdf.

57 *Ibid* at 29.

58 *Ibid* at 34.

59 See Simona Chiose, "Justice on Campus" *Globe and Mail* (1 April 2016), online: www.theglobeandmail.com/news/national/education/canadian-universities-under-pressure-to-formalize-harassment-assaultpolicies/article29499302.

60 SO, 2016, c 2, online: www.ola.org/en/legislative-business/bills/parliament-41/session-1/bill-132.

61 *Ibid.* See also Ontario Human Rights Commission, "Policy on Preventing Sexual and Gender-Based Harassment" (May 2013), online: www.ohrc.on.ca/en/policy-preventing-sexual-and-gender-based-harassment-0.

62 Bill 151, *An Act to prevent and fight sexual violence in higher education institutions*, above note 5.

63 *Ibid*, art 1.

64 *Ibid.*

65 *Ibid*, art 3.

six | Caring about Equality in Indigenous Communities

1 Canada, Truth and Reconciliation Commission of Canada, *They Came for the Children: Canada, Aboriginal Peoples and Residential Schools* (Ottawa: Truth and Reconciliation Commission of Canada, 2012), online: www.publications.gc.ca/site/eng/9.695530/publication.html [*They Came for the Children*].

2 Patricia Monture, "Ka-Nin-Geh-Heh-Gah-E-Sa-Nnh-Yah-Gah" (1986) 2 *Canadian Journal of Women & the Law* 159 at 159, where she writes that "only when we understand caring will we understand equality." See also Colleen Sheppard, "Chapter 5: Caring and Relations of Equality" in *Inclusive Equality: The Relational Dimensions of Systemic Discrimination in Canada* (McGill-Queens University Press, 2010) at 103.

3   *Pictou Landing Band Council v Canada (Attorney General)*, 2013 FC 342 [*Pictou Landing*]. Sadly, Maurina Beadle died in the fall of 2019. See "Remembering Maurina Beadle, the Mi'kmaw Woman Who Fought Canada on Jordan's Principle and Won" *APTN National News* (15 November 2019), online: www.aptnnews.ca/ national-news/remembering-maurina-beadle-the-mikmaw-woman-who-fought-canada-on-jordans-principle-and-won.

4   Reserves are lands set aside for First Nations communities: see *Indian Act*, RSC, 1985, c I-5, s 18. For a compelling critique of the *Indian Act*, including the reserve system, see, for example, John Milloy, *Indian Act Colonialism — A Century of Dishonour, 1869–1969* (Research Paper for the National Centre for First Nations Governance, May 2008), online: http://fngovernance.org/ncfng_research/milloy.pdf (accessed 3 June 2020).

5   *First Nations Child and Family Caring Society of Canada et al v Attorney General of Canada (for the Minister of Indian and Northern Affairs Canada)*, 2016 CHRT 2 [*First Nations Caring Society* January 2016]. See also Cindy Blackstock, "The Complainant: the Canadian Human Rights Case on First Nations Child Welfare" (2016) 62:2 *McGill Law Journal* 285.

6   *Pictou Landing*, above note 3 at para 6.

7   At the time, the federal government department responsible for providing healthcare services on reserves was called the Department of Aboriginal Affairs and Northern Development Canada (AANDC). It was subsequently called Indigenous and Northern Affairs Canada (INAC) and in 2017 it was replaced by two new departments — Crown-Indigenous Relations and Northern Affairs Canada (CIRNAC) and Indigenous Services Canada (ISC). See Government of Canada, "Indigenous and Northern Affairs Canada" (October 2018), online: www.aadnc-aandc.gc.ca/eng/1100100010002/1100100010021.

8   For a discussion of federal and provincial jurisdiction, see Martha Jackman, "Constitutional Jurisdiction over Health in Canada" (2008) 8 *Health Law Journal* 95 at 106–9.

9   See Government of Canada, Health Care Services for First Nations and Inuit, "Honouring Jordan River Anderson," online: www.sac-isc.gc.ca/eng/1583703111205/ 1583703134432.

10   Private Members' Motion M-296, *House of Commons Debates*, 39-1 (18 May 2007) at 1339 (Tabled by NDP MP Jean Crowder, unanimously passed 12 December 2007).

11   *Pictou Landing*, above note 3

12   *Ibid* at para 97.

13   *Ibid*.

14   *Ibid* at para 110. Justice Mandamin noted (at para 10) that Jeremy's mother "takes him on the pow-wow trail, travelling to communities where pow-wows are held. She says Jeremy is happiest when he is dancing with other First Nations people and singing to traditional music."

15   *Ibid* at paras 23–26 and 100–5.

16   See Federation of Saskatchewan Indian Nations (FSIN), "Homecare on Reserve: A Framework" (Saskatoon: FSIN, 1990); see also Pat Armstrong & Hugh Armstrong, "Thinking it Through: Women, Work and Caring in the New Millennium" in Karen R Grant et al, eds, *Caring For/Caring About: Women, Home Care, and Unpaid Caregiving* (Aurora, ON: Garamond Press Ltd, 2004) 5 at 24 and 26ff.

17 Shelly Thomas Prokop et al, "Aboriginal Women and Home Care" in Karen R Grant et al, eds, *Caring for/Caring About: Women, Home Care, and Unpaid Caregiving* (Aurora, ON: Garamond Press Ltd, 2004) 147 at 147.

18 *Ibid* at 148.

19 *Ibid*.

20 *Pictou Landing*, above note 3 at para 10.

21 *First Nations Caring Society* January 2016, above note 5.

22 *Ibid* at para 459.

23 *Ibid* at para 120.

24 *Ibid* at para 349. See also Hadley Friedland, "Tragic Choices and the Division of Sorrow: Speaking About Race, Culture and Community Traumatisation in the Lives of Children" (2009) 25 *Canadian Journal of Family Law* 223.

25 *First Nations Caring Society* January 2016, above note 5 at para 404.

26 *Ibid* at para 464.

27 *Ibid* at para 481.

28 For a full listing of CHRT remedial orders since the 2016 decision, see Canadian Human Rights Tribunal, "Search Decisions," online: https://decisions.chrt-tcdp.gc.ca/chrt-tcdp/en/nav.do.

29 See *They Came for the Children*, above note 1; John S Milloy, *A National Crime: The Canadian Government and the Residential School System, 1879 to 1986* (Winnipeg: University of Manitoba Press, 1999).

30 Marlene Brant Castellano, Linda Archibald & Mike DeGagné, *From Truth to Reconciliation: Transforming the Legacy of Residential Schools* (Ottawa: Aboriginal Healing Foundation, 2008), online: www.ahf.ca/downloads/from-truth-to-reconciliation-transforming-the-legacy-of-residential-schools.pdf. See also Rosalie Chappell, *Social Welfare in Canadian Society, Fourth Edition* (Toronto: Nelson Education, 2010) at 312.

31 Canada, National Inquiry into Missing and Murdered Indigenous Women and Girls, *Reclaiming Power and Peace: The Final Report of the National Inquiry into Missing and Murdered Indigenous Women and Girls*, vol 1a, online: www.mmiwg-ffada.ca/wp-content/uploads/2019/06/Final_Report_Vol_1a.pdf at 339.

32 Cindy Blackstock, "First Nations Child and Family Services: Restoring Peace and Harmony in First Nations Communities" in Kathleen Kufeldt & Brad McKenzie, eds, *Child Welfare: Connecting Research, Policy, and Practice* (Waterloo, ON: Wilfred Laurier University Press, 2003) 331 at 331. See also National Council of Welfare Reports, *First Nations, Métis and Inuit Children and Youth: Time to Act* (Ottawa: National Council of Welfare, 2007), online: http://publications.gc.ca/collections/collection_2007/hrsdc-rhdsc/HS54-1-2007E.pdf at 85.

33 Indigenous Services Canada News Release, "Bill C-92: An Act respecting First Nations, Inuit and Métis children, youth and families receives Royal Assent" (21 June 2019), online: www.canada.ca/en/indigenous-services-canada/news/2019/06/an-act-respecting-first-nations-inuit-and-metis-children-youth-and-families-receives-royal-assent.html.

34 For a critical review, see Marlee Kline, "Child Welfare Law, 'Best Interests of the Child' Ideology, and First Nations" (1992) 30:2 *Osgoode Hall Law Journal* 375 online: https://digitalcommons.osgoode.yorku.ca/cgi/viewcontent.cgi?article=1726&context=ohlj.

35 See Indigenous Services Canada, "Jordan's Principle: Substantive Equality Principles" (Government of Canada), online: www.sac-isc.gc.ca/eng/1583698429175/

1583698455266 (accessed 4 June 2020). See also Vandna Sinha, Colleen Sheppard, Kathryn Chadwick, Maya Gunnarsson & Gabriella Jamieson, "Substantive Equality and Jordan's Principle: Challenges and Complexities" (2021) 35 *Journal of Law and Social Policy* 21, online: https://digitalcommons.osgoode.yorku.ca/jlsp/vol35/iss1/2.

36   *Pictou Landing*, above note 3 at para 26 (affirming full funding for long-term institutional care), paras 62 and 104 (community services estimate of $350 per day for institutional care), and para 11 (regarding cost estimate of home care). Also of note in this case is the hidden value of home care done by family members over a period of many years. See also Armstrong & Armstrong, above note 16.

37   Justice Leonard S Mandamin, who delivered the *Pictou Landing* decision, is one of Canada's leading Indigenous justices. Justice Mandamin has remarked that Indigenous perspectives are "crucial in family law cases" and that "[t]here's a need to have an appreciation, or a willingness to look into, the family circumstances and context of indigenous families." See Cristin Schmitz, "Nation 'Woefully' Short of Judges with Indigenous Roots at Top Levels" *The Lawyer's Daily* (5 May 2016), online: www.thelawyersdaily.ca/articles/2099/nation-woefully-short-of-judges-with-indigenous-roots-at-top-levels; see also Nic Meloney, "Supreme Court Ruling Shows Need for More Indigenous Parliamentarians and Judges, Says Lawyer" *CBC News* (17 October 2018), online: www.cbc.ca/news/indigenous/supreme-court-mikisew-ruling-parliament-senators-mps-judges-1.4863942.

38   Lorne Sossin, "An Intimate Approach to Fairness, Impartiality and Reasonableness in Administrative Law" (2002) 27:2 *Queen's Law Journal* 809 at 809 and 843.

39   *Ibid* at 854.

40   *Ibid* at 841.

41   *Ibid*.

42   See Colleen Sheppard, "Jordan's Principle: Reconciliation and the First Nations Child" (2018) 26:4 *Constitutional Forum constitutionnel* 3.

43   For a discussion of the self-governance dimensions of Jordan's Principle, see National Collaborating Centre for Aboriginal Health, "Child Welfare Services in Canada: Aboriginal and Mainstream" (January 2009), online: www.ccnsa-nccah.ca/docs/health/FS-ChildWelfareServices-EN.pdf; and see, for example, Nancy Stevens, Rachel Charles & Lorena Snyder, "Giidosendiwag (We Walk Together): Creating Culturally Based Supports for Urban Indigenous Youth in Care" (2018) 28 *Journal of Law & Social Policy* 101.

44   SC 2019, c 24, s 8(a).

45   *Ibid* at s 9(3), 11(d).

46   The legislation has been criticized, however, for failing to provide for adequate funding for child welfare and family services — a critical barrier to ensuring the equitable treatment of First Nations children: see Naiomi Walqwan Metallic, Hadley Friedland & Sarah Morales, *The Promise and Pitfalls of C-92: An Act respecting First Nations, Inuit, and Métis Children, Youth and Families* (Toronto: Yellowhead Institute, 2019).

47   See Chapter 3 in this book.

48   For example, in one of the follow-up rulings in the *First Nations Caring Society* case, two twelve-year-old girls, Jolynn Winter and Chantel Fox, from the Wapapeka First Nation in Ontario, died by suicide in 2017, after the community was repeatedly denied adequate funding for suicide prevention programs: *First Nations Child &*

Family Caring Society of Canada et al v Attorney General of Canada (representing the Minister of Indigenous and Northern Affairs Canada), 2017 CHRT 7.

49   Nancy Fraser, "From Redistribution to Recognition? Dilemmas of Justice in a 'Post-Socialist' Age" (1995) 1:212 *New Left Review* 68 at 82.

seven | **Seeking Justice and Belonging: The Complexity of Identity**

1   For an overview of Canadian anti-discrimination law, see Colleen Sheppard, "Anti-discrimination Law in Canada and the Challenge of Effective Enforcement" in Marie Mercat-Bruns, David B Oppenheimer & Cady Sartorius, eds, *Comparative Perspectives on the Enforcement and Effectiveness of Antidiscrimination Law: Challenges and Innovative Tools* (New York: Springer International Publishing, 2018) 83. See also Colleen Sheppard, "The Principles of Equality and Non-discrimination: A Comparative Analysis — Canada" (European Parliamentary Research Service: 2020), online: www.europarl.europa.eu/RegData/etudes/STUD/2020/659362/ EPRS_STU(2020)659362_EN.pdf.

2   See the Québec *Charter of Human Rights and Freedoms*, CQLR c C-12, art 10; Ontario *Human Rights Code*, RSO 1990 c H 19, s 2(1) & (2).

3   See Library of Parliament, *Bill C-16: An Act to amend the Canadian Human Rights Act and Criminal Code* by Julian Walker (Legislative Summary) (Ottawa: Library of Parliament, October 2016), and Ontario, Legislative Assembly of Ontario, Bill 30, *An Act to amend the Human Rights Code with respect to genetic characteristics*, 2nd Sess, 41st Parl, 2016.

4   Kimberlé Crenshaw, "Demarginalizing the Intersection of Race and Sex: A Black Feminist Critique of Antidiscrimination Doctrine, Feminist Theory and Antiracist Politics" (1989) *University of Chicago Legal Forum* 139 at 140; Kimberlé Williams Crenshaw, "Race, Reform, and Retrenchment: Transformation and Legitimation in Antidiscrimination Law" (1988) 101:7 *Harvard Law Review* 1331 at 1341.

5   International Labour Organization, *Time for Equality at Work: Global Report Under the Follow-Up to the ILO Declaration on Fundamental Principles and Rights at Work* (Report I (B) delivered at the International Labour Conference 91st Session, Geneva, 2003), online: www.ilo.org/wcmsp5/groups/public/---dgreports/---dcomm/ ---publ/documents/publication/wcms_publ_9221128717_en.pdf at 37.

6   Black Lives Matter, "About Black Lives Matter," online: https://blacklivesmatter.com/ about.

7   See Mitu Gulati & Devon W Carbado, "The Fifth Black Woman" (2001) 11 *Journal of Contemporary Legal Issues* 701; Kenji Yoshino, *Covering: the Hidden Assault on Our Civil Rights* (New York: Random House, 2007) [Yoshino, "Covering"].

8   Gulati & Carbado, above note 7 at 701ff.

9   See Martha Minow, *Making All the Difference: Inclusion, Exclusion, and American Law* (Ithaca, NY: Cornell University Press, 2016) at 20–23, on the "dilemma of difference."

10   Srilata Ravi, "Métis, Métissse and Métissage: Representations and Self-Representations" in Srilata Ravi, Mario Rutten & Beng-Lan Goh, eds, *Asia in Europe, Europe in Asia* (Singapore: ISEAS-Yussof Ishak Institute, 2015) at 299.

11   *Canada (Attorney General) v Mossop*, [1993] 1 SCR 554, 149 NR 1.

12   *Turner v Canada Border Services Agency*, 2015 CHRT 10 [*Turner* CHRT 2015].

13   The Canadian Human Rights Tribunal released its first decision regarding Levan
      Turner's case in June 2010. See *Turner v Canada Border Services Agency*, 2010
      CHRT 15 at para 147 [*Turner CHRT 2010*]. Judicial review of this decision in the
      Federal Court and Federal Court of Appeal resulted in a new hearing at the CHRT:
      see *Turner v Canada (Attorney General)*, 2011 FC 767; *Turner v Canada (Attor-
      ney General)*, 2012 FCA 159 [*Turner FCA 2012*]; *Turner v Canada Border Services
      Agency*, 2014 CHRT 10 [*Turner CHRT 2014*]; *Turner CHRT 2015*, *ibid*. The second
      CHRT decision found in favour of Turner: see *Canada (Attorney General) v Turner*,
      2015 FC 1209. This decision was then reviewed: see *Turner v Canada (Attorney
      General)*, 2017 FCA 2; and *Turner v Canada Border Services Agency*, 2018 CHRT 1.
      For the decision during which a new hearing was ordered, see *Turner v Canada
      Border Services Agency*, 2017 CHRT 15.

14   *Turner CHRT 2010*, above note 13 at para 147.

15   *Turner FCA 2012*, above note 13 at para 33.

16   *Ibid* at para 49.

17   *Ibid* at para 48.

18   *Turner CHRT 2014*, above note 13 at paras 22–26.

19   *Ibid* at para 24, quoting from *Maillet v Canada (Attorney General)*, 2005 CHRT 48
      at para 6 [emphasis added], which in turn was based on the decision in *Basi v
      Canadian National Railway Company*, [1988] CHRD No 2, where the "subtle scent
      of discrimination" phrase was first used. For an extended discussion of eviden-
      tiary issues, see Colleen Sheppard & Mary Louise Chabot, "Obstacles to Crossing
      the Discrimination Threshold: Connecting Individual Exclusion to Group-Based
      Inequalities" (2018) 96:1 *Canadian Bar Review* 1.

20   *Turner CHRT 2014*, above note 13 at para 29. The Supreme Court of Canada deci-
      sion in *Quebec (Commission des droits de la personne et des droits de la jeunesse) v
      Montréal (City); Quebec (Commission des droits de la personne et des droits de la
      jeunesse) v Boisbriand (City)*, 2000 SCC 27 is cited as authority.

21   *Turner CHRT 2014*, above note 13 at para 31, citing *Radek v Henderson Development
      (Canada) and Securiguard Services (No 3)*, 2005 BCHRT 302 at para 464.

22   *Turner CHRT 2014*, above note 13 at para 262.

23   For additional examples of intersectional cases, see Sirma Bilge & Olivier Roy, "La
      discrimination intersectionnelle : la naissance et le développement d'un concept
      et les paradoxes de sa mise en application en droit antidiscriminatoire" (2010)
      25:1 *Canadian Journal of Law and Society* 51; and Ontario Human Rights Commis-
      sion, "An Intersectional Approach to Discrimination: Addressing Multiple Grounds
      in Human Rights Claims: Discussion Paper" (Toronto: Policy and Edication Branch,
      2001), online: www.ohrc.on.ca/en/intersectional-approach-discrimination-
      addressing-multiple-grounds-human-rights-claims.

24   See Colleen Sheppard, Multiple Discrimination in the World of Work, International
      Labour Organization, Working Paper # 66 (Geneva: December, 2011), online:
      www.ilo.org/wcmsp5/groups/public/---ed_norm/---declaration/documents/
      publication/wcms_170015.pdf at 5–10; see also Sarah Hannett, "Equality at the
      Intersections: The Legislative and Judicial Failure to Tackle Multiple Discrimination"
      (2003) 23:1 *Oxford Journal of Legal Studies* 65; Kathryn Abrams, "Title VII and the
      Complex Female Subject" (1993) 92 *Michigan Law Review* 2479.

25   Hannett, above note 24 at 71.

26   Gulati & Carbado, above note 7.

27   *Ibid* at 717–18.

28   *Ibid* at 719.

29   Kimberly A Yuracko, "Trait Discrimination as Race Discrimination: An Argument about Assimilation" (2006) 74:3 *George Washington Law Review* 365.

30   Yoshino, "Covering," above note 7 at ix.

31   Patricia F Hewlin, "And the Award for Best Actor Goes to . . . : Facades of Conformity in Organizational Settings" (2001) 28:4 *Academy of Management Review* 633 at 639.

32   Sandra E Cha et al, "Being Your True Self at Work: Integrating the Fragmented Research on Authenticity in Organizations" (2019) 13:2 *Academy of Management Annals* 633. See also Patricia F Hewlin, "Authenticity on One's Own Terms" in Laura Morgan Roberts, Lynn Perry Wooten & Martin N Davidson, eds, *Positive Organizing in a Global Society — Understanding and Engaging Differences for Capacity Building and Inclusion* (New York: Routledge, 2015).

33   Yoshino, "Covering," above note 7 at 18. See also Kenji Yoshino, "The New Equal Protection" (2011) 124 *Harvard Law Review* 747.

34   Minow, above note 9 at 20.

35   On the idea of partial agency, see Kathryn Abrams, "Sex Wars Redux: Agency and Coercion in Feminist Legal Theory" (1995) 95:2 *Columbia Law Review* 304 at 346–50.

36   Amin Maalouf, *Les identités meurtrières* (Paris : Éditions Grasset: 1988) at 33: "I do not have several identities. I have only one, made up of all of the elements that have shaped it" [author's translation].

37   *Ibid.*

38   Megan Gannon, "Race Is a Social Construct, Scientists Argue: Racial Categories Are Weak Proxies for Genetic Diversity and Need to be Phased Out" *Scientific American* (5 February 2017), online: www.scientificamerican.com/article/race-is-a-social-construct-scientists-argue.

39   For a complex case involving a custody dispute of a biracial child, see *Van de Perre v Edwards*, 2001 SCC 60. See also the discussion of the case in Lawrence Hill, *Black Berry, Sweet Juice — On Being Black and White in Canada* (Toronto: Harper Collins, 2001) at 150–70.

40   See online: www.ohrc.on.ca/en/teaching-human-rights-ontario-guide-ontario-schools/appendix-1-glossary-human-rights-terms. See also, Karim Murji & John Solomos, eds, *Racialization: Studies in Theory and Practice* (Oxford: Oxford University Press, 2005); City for all Women Initiative, "Racialized People: Equality & Inclusion Lens Snapshot" (City of Ottawa, 2016) at 3, online: https://documents.ottawa.ca/sites/documents/files/racializd_ss_en.pdf.

41   See, for example, *Plessy v Ferguson*, 163 US 537 (1896), a classic race discrimination case where the constitutional doctrine of separate but equal was accepted by the US Supreme Court. In addition to contesting segregation, Plessy had argued that he was "seven-eighths Caucasian and one-eighth African blood; that the mixture of colored blood was not discernible in him, and that he was entitled to every right, privilege and immunity secured to citizens of the United States of the white race" (Brown J at 541).

42   See House of Commons, Standing Committee on Canadian Heritage, *Taking Action Against Systemic Racism and Religious Discrimination including Islamophobia* (February 2018) (Chair: Hon Hedy Fry), online: www.ourcommons.ca/Content/Committee/421/CHPC/Reports/RP9315686/chpcrp10/chpcrp10-e.pdf.

43   See Murji & Solomos, eds, above note 41.

44   *Chap 18: An Act to amend and consolidate the laws respecting Indians*, Statutes of Canada, s 3, as it appeared on April 12, 1876.

45 For a historical overview, see John Milloy, "Indian Act Colonialism: A Century of Dishonour, 1869–1969" (2008) National Centre for First Nations Governance Research Paper, online: www.fngovernance.org/ncfng_research/milloy.pdf.

46 See Sharon McIvor, "Aboriginal Women's Rights as 'Existing Rights'" (1995) 15:2 & 3 *Canadian Women's Studies* 34. Sharon McIvor took her case against the Canadian government to the United Nations Human Rights Committee under the *Optional Protocol of the International Covenant on Civil and Political Rights*. In their January 2019 decision, the Committee concluded that the *Indian Act* continues to discriminate against Indigenous women, their children, and their grandchildren: see United Nations Human Rights Committee, *Views adopted by the Committee under article 5(4) of the Optional Protocol, concerning communication No 2020/2010*, CCPR/C/124/D/2020/2010, ICCPR.

47 James Tully, *Strange Multiplicity: Constitutionalism in an Age of Diversity (The Seeley Lectures)* (Cambridge, UK: Cambridge University Press, 1995) at 11.

48 Recognition of the human rights dimensions of these issues is reflected in the historic US Supreme Court ruling finding that employment discrimination against LGBTQ2S+ individuals is provided under the rubric of sex discrimination: see *Bostock v Clayton Country*, 590 US ___ (2020).

49 Ivan Coyote, *Tomboy Survival Guide* (Vancouver: Arsenal Pulp Press, 2016) at 218.

50 *Cunningham and others v BC (Ministry of Health) (No 2)*, 2017 BCHRT 92.

51 *Ibid* at para 13.

52 *Ibid*.

53 *Ibid* at para 29.

54 *Ibid* at para 30.

55 Sumi Cho, Kimberlé Williams Crenshaw & Leslie McCall, "Toward a Field of Intersectionality Studies: Theory, Applications, and Praxis" (2013) 38:4 *Journal of Women in Culture & Society* 785 at 795.

eight | **When Speech Hurts: Conflicting Freedoms**

1 Robert Fulghum, *All I Need To Know I Learned in Kindergarten* (New York: Villard Books, 1988).

2 For James Komar's comments to the media, see CBC News, "Top Court Upholds Key Part of Sask Anti-Hate Law" *CBC News* (27 February 2013), online: www.cbc.ca/news/politics/top-court-upholds-key-part-of-sask-anti-hate-law-1.1068276. While I was writing this chapter in June 2019, a lesbian couple in London, England, was physically attacked on a public bus by a group of young men. Following the attack, they were subjected to hate speech on social media. See BBC News "London Bus Attack: Arrests after Gay Couple Who Refused to Kiss Beaten" *BBC News* (7 June 2019), online: www.bbc.com/news/uk-england-london-48563393.

3 *The Saskatchewan Human Rights Code, 2018*, SS 2018, c S-24.2, s 14(1).

4 See *Wallace v Whatcott*, 2005 CanLII 80912 (SK HRT) [*Whatcott* SK HRT]. Note that the Saskatchewan Human Rights Tribunal was abolished in 2010. This case was appealed to the Supreme Court of Canada, which upheld the findings against Whatcott: see *Saskatchewan (Human Rights Commission) v Whatcott*, 2013 SCC 11 [*Whatcott* SCC].

5 See the discussion of equitable freedom in Chapter 5. This case also concerned freedom of religion. However, that is not the focus of this chapter. See Ontario

Human Rights Commission, "Policy on Competing Human Rights" (2012), online: www.ohrc.on.ca/sites/default/files/policy%20on%20competing%20human%20 rights_accessible_2.pdf.

6　*R v Keegstra*, [1990] 3 SCR 697 at 745–48, 117 NR 1 [*Keegstra*].

7　*Ibid* at 748.

8　Dangerous Speech Project, "About the DSP" *Dangerous Speech Project* (2019), online: http://dangerousspeech.org/about-the-dsp.

9　The DSP prefers not to use the term "hate speech" because hate speech is often "hard to define clearly and consistently": Susan Benesch et al, "Dangerous Speech: A Practical Guide" *Dangerous Speech Project* (9 January 2020), online: http:// dangerousspeech.org/guide. See also Susan Benesch, "Dangerous Speech: A Proposal to Prevent Group Violence" *World Policy Proposal* (12 January 2012), online: www.worldpolicy.org/wp-content/uploads/2016/01/Dangerous-Speech-Guidelines-Benesch-January-2012.pdf.

10　The Dangerous Speech Project does not recommend censorship. See Benesch et al, above note 9.

11　*Keegstra*, above note 6 at 746.

12　*Ibid*.

13　*Whatcott SK HRT*, above note 4 at 26.

14　Mari Matsuda, "Public Response to Racist Speech: Considering the Victim's Story" (1989) 87:8 *Michigan Law Review* 2320 at 2336.

15　*Commission des droits de la personne et des droits de la jeunesse (Gabriel et autres) c Ward*, 2016 QCTDP 18 at paras 25–27. Note that this case involved allegations of discriminatory harmful speech rather than hate speech.

16　*Ibid*.

17　*Ibid* at para 97. The decision of the Quebec Human Rights Tribunal was affirmed by the Quebec Court of Appeal, although there was a dissenting opinion: see *Ward c Commission des droits de la personne et des droits de la jeunesse (Gabriel et autres)*, 2019 QCCA 2042, http://canlii.ca/t/j3p58. It was then appealed to the Supreme Court of Canada. As this book was going to press, the Supreme Court of Canada rendered its decision in *Ward*, rejecting Jérémy Gabriel's discrimination claims and upholding the freedom of expression of the comedian, Mike Ward: see *Ward v Quebec (Commission des droits de la personne et des droits de la jeunesse)*, 2021 SCC 43. The majority, drawing on the *Whatcott* decision, took the position that in a case such as this, the Quebec Charter only prohibits severe hateful speech that vilifies or conveys detest for the humanity of an individual based on a prohibited ground — being ridiculed based on one's disability is not enough. The majority also appeared to be of the view that a defamation action would have been more appropriate in the circumstances. In a powerful dissenting judgment, Justice Abella wrote (at para 116):

> This country has spent generations working towards creating a society that values human rights and protects individuals from harm caused by their differences of race, religion, disability, colour, or sexual orientation, among other grounds. We would never tolerate *humiliating or dehumanizing conduct* towards children with disabilities; *there is no principled basis for tolerating words that have the same abusive effect*. Wrapping such discriminatory conduct in the protective cloak of speech does not make it any less intolerable when that speech amounts to wilful emotional abuse of a disabled child [emphasis added].

18   *Keegstra*, above note 6 at 746.

19   *Ibid.*

20   *Whatcott* SCC, above note 4 at para 75.

21   See Justice Bertha Wilson's concurring opinion in *Edmonton Journal v Alberta (Attorney General)*, [1989] 2 SCR 1326 at 1351ff, 102 NR 321. See also Reema Khawja, "The Shadow of the Law: Surveying the Case Law Dealing with Competing Rights Claims" (Toronto: Ontario Human Rights Commission, 2012), online: www.ohrc.on.ca/en/shadow-law-surveying-case-law-dealing-competing-rights-claims at 2.

22   See *R v McCrea*, 2004 BCCA 229, for a case regarding verbal abuse by the police against the accused.

23   Catharine A MacKinnon, *Only Words* (Cambridge, MA: Harvard University Press, 1993) ch 3 at 71.

24   *Ibid* at 72.

25   *Harper v Canada (Attorney General)*, 2004 SCC 33 at para 92.

26   See Shaheen Shariff, *Confronting Cyber-Bullying: What Schools Need to Know to Control Misconduct and Avoid Legal Consequences* (New York: Cambridge University Press, 2009); see also Darcy Hango, *Cyberbullying and Cyberstalking Among Internet Users aged 15 to 29 in Canada* (Statistics Canada: 2014), online: www150.statcan.gc.ca/n1/en/catalogue/75-006-X201600114693.

27   Matsuda, above note 14 at 2369. Matsuda discusses the example of a teacher in Arkansas, who resigned after using a racial slur. The teacher expressed sincere regret and was soon reinstated with the help of her students.

28   See *Keegstra*, above note 6 at 763–64.

29   *International Covenant on Civil and Political Rights*, 19 December 1966, 999 UNTS 171 art 20 (entered into force 23 March 1976, accession by Canada 19 May 1976).

30   *International Convention on the Elimination of All Forms of Racial Discrimination*, 21 December 1965, 660 UNTS 195 art 4(a) (entered into force 4 January 1969). For an overview of international and comparative prohibitions on hate speech, see Oxford Pro Bono Publico, "Comparative Hate Speech Law: Annexure" *Law Faculty of the University of Oxford* (2012), online: www.law.ox.ac.uk/sites/files/oxlaw/1a._comparative_hate_speech_annex.pdf.

31   For a review of legal prohibitions on hate speech, see Julian Walker, "Hate Speech and Freedom of Expression: Legal Boundaries in Canada" (2018) Legal and Social Affairs Division, Library of Parliament Background Paper, online: https://lop.parl.ca/staticfiles/PublicWebsite/Home/ResearchPublications/BackgroundPapers/PDF/2018-25-E.pdf. See also *Criminal Code*, RSC 1985, c C-46, ss 319(1), (2), and 318(4), enumerating the identifiable groups. Section 318 prohibits "advocating or promoting genocide," which is defined in section 318(2) as the "killing of members of identifiable groups" or "deliberately inflicting on the group conditions of life calculated to bring about its physical destruction."

32   See *Keegstra*, above note 6; *R v Zundel*, [1992] 2 SCR 731 [*Zundel*].

33   *Criminal Code*, above note 31 at ss 319(1)(a) and (2)(a).

34   *Ibid* [emphasis added].

35   Section 1 provides that "the *Canadian Charter of Rights and Freedoms* guarantees the rights and freedoms set out in it subject only to such reasonable limits prescribed by law as can be demonstrably justified in a free and democratic society." See *Canadian Charter of Rights and Freedoms*, s 1, Part I of the *Constitution Act, 1982*, being Schedule B to the *Canada Act 1982* (UK), 1982, c 11.

36 *Saskatchewan Human Rights Code*, above note 3, s 14(1)(b).

37 *Canadian Human Rights Act*, RSC, 1985, c H-6, s 12. Interestingly, section 13, which prohibited exposing a person or persons to hatred based on prohibited grounds by way of online telecommunication, was repealed in order to ensure "there is no infringement on freedom of expression guaranteed by the *Canadian Charter of Rights and Freedoms*." See Bill C-304, *An Act to amend the Canadian Human Rights Act (protecting freedom)*, 1st Sess, 41st Parl, 2013, Summary (assented to 26 June 2013, SC 2013, c 37). See also Canadian Human Rights Commission, *Report to the Canadian Human Rights Commission Concerning Section 13 of the Canadian Human. Rights Act and the Regulation of Hate Speech on the Internet*, by Richard Moon (Ottawa: Canadian Human Rights Commission, 2008).

38 *Quebec Charter of Human Rights and Freedoms*, c 12 at art 11.

39 See Ontario Human Rights Commission, "Landmark Human Rights Case Settled" (27 August 2011) OHRC News Centre, online: www.ohrc.on.ca/en/news_centre/landmark-human-rights-case-settled.

40 *Michael McKinnon v Ministry of Correctional Services*, (April 1998) BOI 98-010 (Board of Inquiry), online: https://archive.org/details/boi98_010_0/mode/2up.

41 *Calego International inc c Commission des droits de la personne et des droits de la jeunesse*, 2013 QCCA 924. The President of Calego had stated the following (at para 11): "This is Canada, not China. We take shower and shampoo every day, wash hands with soap, flush the toilet after use. Don't piss on the floor.... This is my kitchen, not yours. My kitchen, I want it clean. You Chinese eat like pigs." The evidence further revealed that the lack of cleanliness in kitchen was not the fault of the Chinese workers. There had been a large influx of employees using the kitchen and no measures had been taken by the company to clean it properly. For further clarification on protection against discriminatory speech in the Quebec Charter, see the Supreme Court of Canada decision in *Ward*, above note 17.

42 *Ibid* at para 52 (unofficial translation). The original French text reads: « Les Plaignants sont arrivés depuis peu au Canada avec l'espoir d'y vivre une vie meilleure, sinon eux-mêmes du moins leurs enfants. Disposant de peu de ressources, connaissant plus ou moins la langue, ce sont des personnes vulnérables. Âgées de 35 à 45 ans, détentrices de diplômes universitaires, elles doivent tout de même recommencer au bas de l'échelle, payées au salaire minimum, dans cet entrepôt. »

43 See Philip H Osborne, *The Law of Torts*, 5th ed (Toronto: Irwin Law, 2015) at ch 7, "Defamation." In some cases, the line between individual and group-based harms is very difficult to draw, creating complex and contested caselaw: see, for example, *Bou Malhab v Diffusion Métromédia CMR inc*, 2011 SCC 9, [2011] 1 SCR 214.

44 This was a major concern of Justice McLachlin in her dissenting opinion in *Keegstra*, above note 6, and her majority reasons in *Zundel*, above note 32.

45 Iris Marion Young, *Democracy and Inclusion* (Oxford: Oxford University Press, 2002) at 21–25. See also Donna Greschner, "Abortion and Democracy for Women: A Critique of *Tremblay v Daigle*" (1990) 35:3 *McGill Law Journal* 634.

46 *Native Women's Assn of Canada v Canada*, [1994] 3 SCR 627 at para 92.

47 Mary Eberts, Sharon McIvor & Teressa Nahanee, "The Woman's Court of Canada: Native Women's Association of Canada v Canada" *The Court* (15 August 2008), online: www.thecourt.ca/the-womens-court-of-canada-native-womens-association-of-canada-v-canada at para 85.

48 *Ibid* at para 114.

49 See, for example, Employment and Social Development Canada, *ESDC Code of Conduct* (Ottawa: Treasury Board of Canada Secretariat, 2016), which applies to public sector workers in Canada; and McGill University, *Code of Student Conduct and Disciplinary Procedures* (Montréal: McGill University, 2019), which applies to students and on-campus activities at McGill.

50 On Professor Jordan Peterson's refusal to use students' chosen pronouns, see Patty Winsa, "He Says Freedom, They Say Hate. The Pronoun Fight Is Back" *Toronto Star* (15 January 2017), online: www.thestar.com/news/insight/2017/01/15/he-says-freedom-they-say-hate-the-pronoun-fight-is-back.html.

51 Canadian Association of University Teachers, "The Politics of Free Speech" (December 2018), online: www.caut.ca/bulletin/2018/12/politics-free-speech.

52 See Brian Rubineau & Nazampal Jaswal, "Response is Not Prevention: Management Insights for Reducing Campus Sexual Assault" (2017) 27:1 *Education Law Journal* 19. See Chapter 5 in this book.

53 See Susan Sturm, "Second Generation Employment Discrimination: A Structural Approach" (2001) 101:3 *Columbia Law Review* 458.

54 Press and Information Team to the Delegation of the USA, "Countering Illegal Hate Speech Online — EU Code of Conduct Ensures Swift Response" *Delegation of the European Union to the United States* (4 February 2019), online: https://eeas.europa.eu/delegations/united-states-america/57617/countering-illegal-hate-speech-online-%E2%80%93-eu-code-conduct-ensures-swift-response_en; Andre Obler, "How Technology Can Be Used to Combat Online Hate Speech" *World Economic Forum* (13 March 2018), online: www.weforum.org/agenda/2018/03/technology-and-regulation-must-work-in-concert-to-combat-hate-speech-online.

55 Michèle Finck, "Artificial Intelligence and Online Hate Speech" (Centre on Regulation in Europe (CERRE), 2019) Issue Paper, online: www.cerre.eu/sites/cerre/files/CERRE_Hate%20Speech%20and%20AI_IssuePaper.pdf.

56 See Canadian Anti-Hate Network, "Canadian Anti-Hate Network to Publish Names of 250 Neo-Nazi Party Members in Canada" *Canadian Anti-Hate Network* (10 June 2019), online: https://www.antihate.ca/canadian_anti_hate_network_to_publish_names_of_250_neo_nazi_party_members_in_canada.

57 Aidan White, "Ethical Challenges for Journalists in Dealing with Hate Speech" UN Office for the High Commissioner for Human Rights (no date), online: www.ohchr.org/Documents/Issues/Expression/ICCPR/Vienna/CRP8White.pdf; and Poni Alice JameKolok, "5 Ways to Counter Hate Speech in the Media Through Ethics and Self-Regulation" UNESCO, online: https://en.unesco.org/5-ways-to-counter-hate-speech.

58 *Someone* — Social Media Education Every Day, Project Someone, online: https://projectsomeone.ca [Project Someone].

59 *Ibid*, "Projects," online: https://projectsomeone.ca/projects.

60 *Ibid*, "About," online: https://projectsomeone.ca/about. Renée Dunk, "Global Affairs Canada awards $1M in Funding to Concordia-Created Anti-Terrorism Initiatives in the Middle East" *Concordia News* (9 November 2018), online: www.concordia.ca/news/stories/2018/11/09/global-affairs-canada-awards-1-m-in-funding-to-concordia-created.html.

61 Charles H Jones, "Regulating Campus Hate Speech: Is It Constitutional?" *National Council on Crime and Delinquency: Focus* (June 1992), online: www.nccdglobal.org/sites/default/files/publication_pdf/campus-hate-speech.pdf.

62 Elizabeth Anderson, *Praise Song for the Day*: A Poem for Barack Obama's Presidential Inauguration (Minneapolis, MN: Graywolf Press, 2009).

63 Project Someone, above note 58.

64 Dangerous Speech Project, above note 8.

65 "Majority of Residents Say Sask. Is Becoming More Welcoming To LGBTQ Community: Poll" *CBC News* (19 June 2019), online: www.cbc.ca/news/canada/saskatchewan/saskatchewan-lgbt-pride-welcoming-1.5180209.

66 *Ibid.*

conclusion | **With Glowing Hearts**

1 *National Anthem Act*, RSC 1985, c N-2.

2 Vancouverite1989, "Vancouver 2010: With Glowing Hearts (4-minute version)" (11 February 2010) at 00h:00m:17s, online: *YouTube* www.youtube.com/watch?v=oAo3hJxNA90. The phrase "with glowing hearts" was also used as a slogan for the 2010 Vancouver Olympics.

3 See "In All of Us Command: Story of an Anthem: French-Canadian Origins" (nd), online: https://exhibits.library.utoronto.ca/exhibits/show/ocanada/french-canadian-origins; see also Helmut Kallmann, Gilles Potvin & Andrew Mcintosh, "'O Canada'" in *The Canadian Encyclopedia* (7 February 2018), online: www.thecanadianencyclopedia.ca/en/article/o-canada.

4 Brian Thompson, *Anthems and Minstrel Shows: The Life and Times of Calixa Lavallée, 1842–1891* (Kingston, Ontario: McGill-Queen's University Press, 2015) at 21–22.

5 *Ibid* at 22.

6 *Ibid* at xxv.

7 Laila El Mugammar, "The Hidden Racist History of 'O Canada'" *Maclean's* (30 June 2020), online: www.macleans.ca/opinion/the-hidden-racist-history-of-o-canada.

8 *Ibid.*

9 Philip SS Howard, "A Laugh for the National Project: Contemporary Canadian Blackface Humour and its Constitution Through Canadian Anti-Blackness" (2018) 18(6) *Ethnicities* 843 at 844.

10 *Ibid.*

11 *Ibid* at 849.

12 *Ibid* at 847.

13 Philip SS Howard, "On the Back of Blackness: Contemporary Canadian Blackface and the Consumptive Production of Post-Racialist, White Canadian Subjects" (2018) 24:1 *Journal for the Study of Race, Nation and Culture* 87 at 87. For a list of more recent blackface incidents, see Adina Bresge, "From Minstrel Shows to Campus Firestorms, Canada's Long History of Blackface" *National Post* (19 September 2019), online: https://nationalpost.com/pmn/news-pmn/canada-news-pmn/from-minstrel-shows-to-campus-firestorms-canadas-long-history-of-blackface.

14 Peter Zimonjic, "Trudeau Says He Is 'Deeply Sorry' He Appeared in Brownface at School Gala in 2001" *CBC News* (18 September 2019), online: www.cbc.ca/news/politics/trudeau-brownface-arabian-nights-1.5289165.

15 *Ibid.*

16 El Mugammar, above note 7.

17 See "In All of Us Command: Story of an Anthem: French-Canadian Origins," above note 3; Kallman, Potvin & Mcintosh, above note 3.

18   Government of Canada, "Origin of the Names of Canada and its Provinces and Territories" (12 November 2016), online: www.nrcan.gc.ca/earth-sciences/geography/origins-canadas-geographical-names/origin-names-canada-and-its-provinces-and-territories/9224. As noted on the federal government website: "The name 'Canada' likely comes from the Huron-Iroquois word 'kanata,' meaning village or settlement."

19   Kallmann, Potvin & Mcintosh, above note 3. See also, Suzanne Thomas, "St-Jean Baptiste Celebrations" *The Canadian Encyclopedia* (16 December 2013), online: www.thecanadianencyclopedia.ca/en/article/st-jean-baptiste-celebrations-emc.

20   See "In All of Us Command: Story of an Anthem: The Search for English Lyrics," above note 3.

21   *National Anthem Act*, above note 1.

22   Kallmann, Potvin & Mcintosh, above note 3.

23   Veterans Affairs Canada, "Timeline: Women Have Been a Part of Canada's Military for over 100 Years. Here's a Look at Their History" (14 February 2019), online: www.veterans.gc.ca/eng/remembrance/those-who-served/women-and-war/timeline. According to Veterans' Affairs historical website, over forty women nurses lost their lives during World War I, with twenty to thirty being killed by enemy action.

24   *Ibid.*

25   Canadian Museum of History, "Making Medicare: The History of Health Care in Canada, 1914–2007" (21 April 2010), online: www.historymuseum.ca/cmc/exhibitions/hist/medicare/medic-1c05e.html. Sometimes I think about all the women who have lost their lives in childbirth. It was not until the 1950s that maternal mortality rates began to decline significantly.

26   It is often important, as well as a very effective strategy, to change how one lives or conducts oneself as a pathway to changing society more broadly. See "National Anthem Act," 2nd reading, *Senate Debates*, 37-1 vol 139 (21 February 2002) at 1430 (comments by Senator Vivienne Poy).

27   Kallmann, Potvin & Mcintosh, above note 3. The City Council also wanted to change "Our home and native land" to "Our home and cherished land": see discussion below.

28   *Ibid*; Bill S-39, *An Act to amend the National Anthem Act to include all Canadians*, 1st Sess, 37th Parl, 2001–2002 (first reading 19 February 2002) [Bill S-39].

29   *Ibid.*

30   *Ibid.*

31   Bill C-210, *An Act to Amend the National Anthem Act (gender)*, RS c N-21. Bélanger introduced the Bill using voice generator technology, given the effects of his illness on his speech; he had been diagnosed with amyotrophic lateral sclerosis (ALS).

32   *Ibid.*

33   Alex Marshall, "The Women Who Fought To Make Canada's National Anthem Gender-Neutral" *BBC News* (9 February 2018), online: www.bbc.com/news/stories-42977303; CBC Archives, "True Patriot Love: The Evolving Words Of Canada's National Anthem" *CBC News* (1 July 2019), online: www.cbc.ca/archives/true-patriot-love-the-evolving-words-of-canada-s-national-anthem-1.5183755.

34   See Bill C-210, Schedule 1, above note 31, for the official music and lyrics.

35   Nuu-Chah-Nulth Tribal Council, "Governance Structure" (nd), online: https://nuuchahnulth.org/governance-structure.

36   Judith Sayers, "O Canada, Your Home's on Native Land" *First Nations in BC Know-ledge Network* (29 June 2016), online: https://fnbc.info/blogs/judith-sayers/ o-canada-your-homes-native-land.

37   After reading through all of the various versions of the anthem, I came up with my own version in English — a slightly revised combination of Stanley Weir's and Mercy E Powell McCulloch's lyrics.

> O Canada!
> Where pines and maples grow. Great prairies spread and mighty rivers flow.
> With glowing hearts we see thee rise, From East to Western Sea,
> A land of hope for all to share The True North, strong and free!
> O Canada! Glorious and free;
> From echoing hills our anthems proudly ring.
> O Canada in praise of thee we sing.

No religion, no military, no appropriation of the land, no gendered lyrics. There is still nationalism, which may need to be reassessed, but that is the topic of another book.

38   Erin Macleod, "Inside the Small, Significant Change Just Made to Canada's National Anthem" *National Public Radio* (9 February 2018), online: www.npr.org/ sections/therecord/2018/02/09/584613825/inside-the-small-significant-change-just-made-to-canadas-national-anthem.

39   See discussion of Jérémy Gabriel's case in Chapter 8 of this book.

Selected Additional Readings

Agócs, Carol, ed. *Employment Equity in Canada: The Legacy of the Abella Report* (Toronto: University of Toronto Press, 2014)

Aylward, Carol A. *Canadian Critical Race Theory: Racism and the Law* (Halifax, NS: Fernwood, 1999)

Backhouse, Constance. *Colour-Coded: A Legal History of Racism in Canada, 1900–1950* (Toronto: University of Toronto Press, 1999)

Busby, Karen & Joanne Birenbaum. *Achieving Fairness: A Guide to Campus Sexual Violence Complaints* (Toronto: Thomson Reuters, 2020)

Crépeau, François & Colleen Sheppard, eds. *Human Rights and Diverse Societies: Challenges and Possibilities* (Cambridge: Cambridge Scholars, 2013)

Shelagh Day, Lucie Lamarche & Ken Norman, eds. *14 Arguments in Favour of Human Rights Institutions* (Toronto: Irwin Law, 2014)

Eliadis, Pearl. *Speaking out on Human Rights: Debating Canada's Human Rights System* (Montreal: McGill-Queen's University Press, 2014)

Faraday, Fay, Margaret Denike & M. Kate Stephenson, eds. *Making Equality Rights Real: Securing Substantive Equality under the Charter* (Toronto: Irwin Law, 2009)

Hill, Lawrence. *Black Berry, Sweet Juice: On Being Black and White in Canada* (Toronto: HarperFlamingo, 2001)

Jackman, Martha & Bruce Porter, eds. *Advancing Social Rights in Canada* (Toronto: Irwin Law, 2014)

Mercat-Bruns, Marie, David Oppenheimer & Cady Sartorious, eds, *Enforcement and Effectiveness of Discrimination Law in a Global World* (Switzlerland: Springer Press, 2018)

Milloy, John S. *A National Crime: The Canadian Government and the Residential School System, 1879 to 1986* (Winnipeg: University of Manitoba Press, 1999)

Minow, Martha. *Making All the Difference: Inclusion, Exclusion, and American Law* (New York: Cornell University Press, 1990)

Monture-Angus, Patricia. *Thunder in My Soul: A Mohawk Woman Speaks* (Halifax, NS: Fernwood Press, 1995)

Moreau, Sophia. *Faces of Inequality — A Theory of Wrongful Discrimination* (Toronto: Oxford University Press, 2020)

Pothier, Dianne & Richard Devlin, eds. *Critical Disability Theory: Essays in Philosophy, Politics, and Law* (Vancouver: UBC Press, 2006)

Rodgers, Sandra & Sheila McIntyre, eds. *Diminishing Returns: Inequality and the Canadian Charter of Rights and Freedoms* (Markham: LexisNexis Butterworths, 2006)

Royal Commission on Equality in Employment, *Equality in Employment: A Royal Commission Report*, by Judge Rosalie Silberman Abella (Ottawa: Supply and Services Canada, 1984), online: www.bakerlaw.ca/wp-content/uploads/Rosie-Abella-1984-Equality-in-Employment.pdf

Satzewich, Vic. *Racism in Canada* (Toronto: Oxford University Press, 2011)

Sheppard, Colleen. *Inclusive Equality: The Relational Dimensions of Systemic Discrimination in Canada* (Montreal: McGill-Queen's University Press, 2010)

————. *The Principles of Equality and Non-Discrimination: A Comparative Analysis — Canada* (European Parliamentary Research Service: 2020), online: www.europarl.europa.eu/RegData/etudes/STUD/2020/659362/EPRS_STU(2020)659362_EN.pdf

Tanovich, David M. *The Colour of Justice: Policing Race in Canada* (Toronto: Irwin Law, 2006)

Truth and Reconciliation Commission of Canada Reports (2015), online: https://nctr.ca/records/reports

Index

F after a page number indicates a figure.

About the Author

COLLEEN SHEPPARD is a professor at the Faculty of Law, McGill University, a member of the McGill Centre for Human Rights and Legal Pluralism, and a fellow of the Royal Society of Canada. Her teaching and research focus on equality rights, systemic discrimination, and Canadian constitutional law. She has published widely on these issues both nationally and internationally.